존경하고 사랑하는 당신에게 1982. 12. 15

사랑하는 홍빈 지연모 지연 정화에게

사랑하는 홍범에게

사랑하는 홍권에게

주님의 성탄을 진심으로 축하하며 언제나 주님과 같이 있기를 빕니다
주님의 풍성한 은혜로서 더욱 건강하고 영적으로나 도덕적으로나 지적으로나
큰 발전있기를 축원합니다

K.O.J

그리고 여의 제수 홍훈 혜경 홍준 혜영에게
대현 제수 형우 홍민 연우 연학에게
[illegible] 기타 모든 일가친척들에게
모든 벗들과 염려해주신 [illegible] 집에 동거하는 여러분에게도
성탄을 축하하고 새해 만복을 빌면서 그간의 은혜를 감사드립니다.

K.O.J

주님께 드리는 기도문

사랑하는 예수 그리스도 우리의 주님! 오늘은 주님의 성탄의 날입니다. 하느님께서 주님을 참하느님이자 참인간으로 이세상에 보내신 날입니다 주님의 탄생으로 이세상은 성화되었으며 하느님의 복음속에 전혀 새로운 시대로 접어들게 되었습니다 [illegible]

[illegible]

prison writings

KIM DAE JUNG

Translated by
Choi Sung-il and
David R. McCann

Foreword by
David R. McCann

University of California Press
Berkeley • Los Angeles • London

University of California Press
Berkeley and Los Angeles, California
University of California Press, Ltd.
London, England

Printed in the United States of America

1 2 3 4 5 6 7 8 9

Library of Congress Cataloging in Publication Data

Kim, Dae-jung, 1925–
Prison writings.

Translation of: Kim Dae-jung okchung sŏgan.
1. Kim, Dae-jung, 1925– —Correspondence.
2. Yi, Hŭi-ho—Correspondence. 3. Politicians—Korea (South)—Correspondence. 4. Political prisoners—Korea (South)—Correspondence. I. Title.
DS922.42.K57A4 1986 951.9'5043'0924 [B] 86–19365
ISBN 0–520–05482–2 (alk. paper)

Contents

Foreword

On September 17, 1980, a South Korean court-martial found Kim Dae Jung guilty of plotting rebellion and attempting to create an organization to put himself in power. The trial was a farce, but the sentence of death was not. International uproar followed the announcement of the sentence, and similar to what had happened in 1973 when Japan, the United States, and other foreign powers learned that Kim had been kidnapped from his hotel in Japan by South Korean CIA agents, international attention and protest stayed the government's hand. For the second time in less than a decade, the South Korean government's clear intent to execute the leader of the political opposition was frustrated.

During the period of Kim Dae Jung's imprisonment—five months in solitary confinement under sentence of death and then, from January 24, 1981, until his release on December 23, 1982, under an indeterminate sentence—he was allowed to communicate only with his family and only through one aerogramme a month. Each "letter" in this series of twenty-nine, then, was written on a single sheet submitted to the scrutiny of prison officials, and then sent to his home. These letters from prison are a remarkable testament to an individual's surpassing strength of will in confrontation with a state that has done all it can to destroy him and to a stubborn, human hope that lives on in the most extreme and inhuman circumstances.

In their quiet expression of faith in Christ and of a

prolonged refusal to succumb, these letters are like the gardens Kim Dae Jung remembers or describes in several of his letters. In the fourteenth letter, for example, he writes:

> I have learned that the climbing roses, the Rose of Sharon, and the other flowers in the yard have all blossomed. Their images are vivid, and I have the most urgent wish to see them. . . .
>
> On the exercise ground here, there is an elongated flower bed. These days, after their full bloom, the cockscombs and China asters are withering. Because I tended them with the greatest care during my exercise time, the flowers in my area were in fuller bloom than those elsewhere. This was the happiest part of my daily routine. My greatest anticipation these days is to see the chrysanthemums bloom.

Within a prison, within a brutally oppressive society, and confined to a space too small, one would think, for any significant life to grow—these letters bloom.

Chronology

The conditions of Kim Dae Jung's imprisonment, trials, house arrest, banishment from politics, death sentence, exile, return to South Korea, and continuing confinement are representative of Korean politics in the long, historical perspective. In the Korean War, the Japanese occupation from 1910 to 1945, the debate and rebellion of the Enlightenment Period, 1880–1905, and the factional disputes that plagued the Yi dynasty, Korea has been a land divided against itself.

The following chronology puts Kim Dae Jung's case in the context of key events in South Korean politics during the last twenty-five years.[1] The historian, in

1. For further information, see *Human Rights in Korea* (New York: Asia Watch Committee, 1986) and *Democracy in South Korea: A Promise Unfulfilled* (New York: International League for Human Rights and International Human Rights Law Group, 1985).

turn, might ascribe those events to earlier conditions. In the chronology can be seen, indirectly, the argument that Kim Dae Jung's predicament reflects the questionable legitimacy of the only two individuals to have held political power for any significant period of time in the last quarter-century: Generals Park Chung Hee and Chun Doo Hwan.

April 1960: Student protests at election fraud perpetrated by Syngman Rhee grow into massive demonstrations. Army troops called on to fire at demonstrators refuse to do so. Syngman Rhee is ousted.

August 15, 1960: Democratic government is established.

May 16, 1961: Military coup, engineered by Kim Chong Pil, who went on to design and direct the South Korean CIA (KCIA), and Park Chung Hee, who subsequently became president.

1963: Under increasing pressure within South Korea and from abroad, Park resigns from the military and establishes a civilian government, the Third Republic.

1967: Park wins reelection to the presidency.

1971: Park narrowly defeats Kim Dae Jung, a member of the National Assembly from Mokpo, even with extensive vote buying and enormous election fraud. Adding insult to injuries, Kim Dae Jung is later indicted with violating election law: the indictment is allowed to lapse in 1986.

1973: Kim Dae Jung is abducted from his hotel in Tokyo by KCIA agents and removed by boat to the Sea of Japan, where the agents prepare to kill him by weighting him and throwing him overboard. American aircraft spot the KCIA boat and keep it under surveillance, preventing the assassination. Strong protests from the Japanese and U.S. governments and continued surveillance of the boat force the South Koreans to abandon their plan. They return to South Korea, where Kim Dae Jung is released and then placed under house arrest.

1979: Increasing dissatisfaction with the Yushin Constitution and the antidemocratic policies of the South Korean government lead to widespread popular demonstrations. Apprehensive about an uprising similar to those in 1960 which led to Syngman Rhee's downfall, Park and his circle take increasingly severe measures to control the demonstrations. On October 26, Park and his bodyguard are assassinated by the head of the KCIA. Choi Kyu Ha, prime minister under Park, is named interim president. There is widespread enthusiasm for democratic reforms and elections. On December 12, Chun Doo Hwan leads a military putsch; rival generals and others are arrested or killed.

Spring 1980: Demonstrations for a return to a democratic government. On April 16, Chun Doo Hwan is named acting head of the KCIA. On May 17, Chun arrests democratic leaders including Kim Dae Jung, stops the democratization process, and consolidates his power. On May 18, he sends paratroopers against demonstrators in the city of Kwangju. In subsequent repeated attacks against the citizens of Kwangju, South Korean troops massacre between one thousand and two thousand people: students, the old, the young, men and women.

August 14, 1980: Kim Dae Jung and twenty-three of his associates are put on trial, accused of involvement in the Kwangju demonstrations and of other acts termed "far-fetched" by an American observer.

August 27, 1980: Chun Doo Hwan becomes temporary president.

September 17, 1980: Kim Dae Jung is court-martialed

and given the death sentence. The United States and Japan protest, though with some caution as the South Korean government could decide to ease the pressure of opinion by carrying out the sentence immediately.

January 1981: Kim Dae Jung's sentence is commuted to one of indeterminate duration. Chun Doo Hwan becomes the first head of state to visit Ronald Reagan after his inauguration as president.

February 25, 1981: Chun Doo Hwan is elected president of South Korea.

December 23, 1981: Kim Dae Jung is released from prison and sent to the United States for health reasons.

February 8, 1985: Kim Dae Jung returns to South Korea. Mindful of the assassination of Benigno Aquino just eighteen months before, a large entourage of American government, press, and other observers accompanies him.

1985–1986: Kim Dae Jung continues to live under the South Korean government's close scrutiny. During this time, house arrest is imposed twenty nine times between his return and by the end of July, 1986. Because he is still under a suspended sentence, the government can return him to prison at any time.

Acknowledgments

I wish to express my appreciation to the following people who have financially cooperated in the publication.

Ch'oe Pyŏnggu
Ch'oe Changhak
Chŏng Pyŏngdak
Chŏng Kijin
Hwang Chaesŏn
Chong Hyŏnggi
Kang Taein
Kang Taeyang
Kim Kyŏngjae
Kim Yŏngjŏl
Yi Tonman
Yi Chŏngin
Yi Chongwŏn
Song Sŏn'gŭn
Yu Ilyong

Impending Death and Faith in the Resurrection of Jesus

November 21, 1980

To my beloved wife:

The continuing trials and troubles that our family has had to endure since last May 17 are far worse than any we have yet confronted, and amid them all, the anguish you have had to bear is far worse than the rest of us have faced. Yet through your faith and self-discipline you have endured, and I am deeply grateful for your courage and religious spirit. I am also deeply thankful to the Lord for blessing you with such strength and faith. How could we have endured the last six months without your strength and love?

I am glad and thankful in all of this because you and I, our family, and our friends have been able to go on with even stronger faith. Through their imprisonment and torture our two sons have reached an even firmer faith, and I hear that Dae-hyun and other friends from the secretarial staff who are even now experiencing persecution have either taken up or sustained their religious beliefs. This has made me realize once again that one's faith does indeed grow stronger in adversity.

I had until now thought of myself as one who possessed considerable religious fiber, and yet, standing at the very edge of the precipice looking out on imminent death, I feel my religious faith, as it concerns my existence, grow weaker each day. Hope and despair, joy and fear, the anguished conflict over resolution and doubt—all of these assail me daily, and I am not able to free myself from their recurrence. It is painful for me to realize that my feelings and my knowledge are such as to make it difficult for me to accept the existence of the invisible God, His presence in me, His unreserved love for me, His granting me my present ordeal out of such love, His attending to all things for me, and, even at the present hour, His ceaseless endeavor to create good from all this. More than once I have felt angered and despondent at the inadequacy of my faith.

In the midst of numberless conflicts and irresolution, I have come to feel determined that faith is not to be founded on feelings or knowledge but on one's free will to decide. The decision must be a conscious and free act, and our joy, gratitude, and praise must come first from that conscious will. Only then can it be complemented by our emotions. In this behalf, I pray for the help of the Holy Spirit in setting my vision firmly on Jesus.

The basis of my will and resolve is the gospel of Jesus, the heart of which is the Resurrection. I have come to believe that when one can truly believe in the Resurrection, one can then believe in the Holy Presence, redemption, the holy guidance, the presence everywhere of God's love, and the hope for eternal happiness in paradise.

Although the Resurrection truly is a religious mystery, I believe that it has considerable objective basis as a historical event. Jesus' disciples, who abandoned Him in their concern for their own lives, returned after His tragic and helpless death to devote themselves to evangelism. They did this with renewed faith—in the face of all manner of adversities, even death. They could not have done this without experiencing His Resurrection.

Furthermore, I do not think it possible to explain the conversion of the Apostle Paul, his superhuman and self-sacrificing efforts at proselytization, and his eventual martyrdom without citing his experience of the resurrected Jesus. Paul had never been in Jesus' presence during His lifetime, after all; and yet, even after His death, he pursued his efforts to spread the Christian faith with a true passion and sense of mission.

Unfailing belief in the Resurrection provides me with the greatest strength to sustain my faith. I struggle with every ounce of my strength not to lose sight of Him and to keep hold of His love. Always, my prayer is:

> I believe the Lord loves me. Jesus has brought me to my present circumstances, and He would not have done so if it were not best for me. I cannot know what Jesus intends; I can only obey and praise Him, trusting in His love.
>
> No matter what my feelings, no matter how harsh my circumstances, and no matter what tomorrow may bring, I am determined to keep my hope that Jesus will always be with me, that He will never leave me.

Judged in the way of the world, I have not been a good husband or father. And I have caused so much sorrow for my brothers and relations. When I think of all the people who have been sacrificed or persecuted on my account, I feel as if I am suffocating. I can only pray and pray again that Jesus has given them all His blessing.

I feel glad and I have high hopes for the future of our family because I have such a wonderful wife in you and such decent and promising children in Hong-il[1] and his wife and in Hong-up[2] and Hong-gul[3] who are so understanding of me. I know full well that it is you who have been instrumental in leading our family to the path of faith and harmony.

From the bottom of my heart, I beseech you to for-

1. The author's eldest son.
2. The author's second son.
3. The author's third son.

give me for my countless failures in serving you as a good husband.

Please give my heartfelt regards to everyone in the family.

A Father's Guilt

November 24, 1980

To my dear son Hong-up:

I feel a heavy weight as I think of you—a feeling of guilt. Though you have passed the age of thirty, because of your father your hopes for marriage have twice been destroyed and you have not been able to find a job in the business world, where you have always wanted to work. It is not just that I have not been able to help you; I have repeatedly been an obstacle to your happiness and future. How could my heart not ache? And when I see how you persevere without any sign of resentment, I feel even more distressed. I pray to God for your future happiness. I can only hope that the bitter experiences you have undergone will become an asset to you in the future.

I have never chosen favorites among my children, but you are aware, I know, of my fondness and love for you. I can still recall the happiness and love I felt whenever you were riding beside me. Your bearing and graciousness are truly a blessing, a gift of God's love.

When we worked together recently, I was greatly impressed by your qualities of judgment, your ability to manage, and your prudence. I can tell you, therefore, that my hopes and expectations for you have grown considerably. While it is true that you still have more to learn and some way to go before you have developed fully your own perspective and expertise, these things can be attained through persistent effort. The most important attributes, however, are one's talents and heart, and in those respects I have the very highest expectations for you.

Our family, as I have said before, is fortunate in being united in having caring hearts, love, and faith in God. I am grateful that all of us—you, your mother, your brothers, and your sister-in-law—have been able to persevere despite the hardships.

Despite my imprisonment and precarious future, I still feel happy that I have so few worries about my family. I know that I can entrust you to God's care in everything.

Faith in God simply means love. Of the two kinds of love—love of oneself and love of God and one's neighbors—one is selfish, isolating, and demeaning, while the other, the love of the Creator above all things in the universe and the genuine love of one's neighbors, leads to happiness and eternal life.

Love of God does not mean we must love Him first. Rather, He loved us first, creating the world and leaving it in our care, sending His only son to us to spread the gospel, and, finally, opening the way for us to deliver ourselves from sin through the crucifixion of His innocent son, Jesus.

Through Jesus' resurrection, God gave us hope for eternal life. God is with you at this very moment. He loves you, and He creates the good for you from all the right and wrong in your life when you genuinely believe in and obey Him. It is only natural, therefore, that you love God; your love is but a small return for His unbounded love.

Love for our neighbors is no different. Our neighbors are all God's children, whether they are Christians or not. It is only natural that we love those who are our brothers before God. To love especially those of our neighbors who need our care and encouragement is one of the most important of God's commandments. And when we consider how much loving care we receive from others, in food, shelter, clothing, education, health, and other ways, loving them is only a fitting return for all the love they have given us.

What I mean by this is that one should never think one has been beneficent or faithful in loving one's neighbors or God. I have recently felt overwhelmed at the realization of how inadequate is the love we give—no matter how great it may be—in repaying, even in the smallest way, the love we have been given by our neighbors and by God.

Loving is difficult because one must forgive and embrace those whom one does not care to love or even hates. It may not be possible to love someone who is not emotionally acceptable. It is possible only, I believe, when we depend on God and seek His assistance.

There are several ways in which this might happen. First of all, there is the fact that I am a sinner. If all of my misconduct, or the evil thoughts I have harbored in my life, were flashed up on a screen, before God and all people, would I still be able to face others and say I cannot forgive them? Second, to be unforgiving or hateful toward others is to inflict pain on one's own heart through hatred and sin; it is masochistic behavior. Third, genuine peace and harmony cannot be established in human society if we reject forgiveness and love. We cannot be free of anxiousness, nor truly happy. That this is so is easily understood when we think of the example of nazism or communism. Last, only the truly magnanimous and strong are capable of forgiving and loving. Let us persevere, then, praying always that God will help us to have the strength to love and forgive our enemies. Let us together, in this way, become the loving victors.

Forgiving the Enemy

December 7, 1980

Dear Hong-gul:

Yesterday I received your letter of November 25. If only you could imagine how much happiness and comfort your letter brought me. When I think of all the hardships my family and relatives have had to endure on my account, I feel sick at heart. But the suffering you have experienced is extreme. While you were in grade school, you had to go through the ordeal of my abduction. In middle school, you saw my imprisonment. And during two years of high school, you have first had to suffer through my house arrest and now through this situation. When I try to imagine what a terrible shock this must have been to you in your childhood and adolescence, I feel guilty of having done this all to you, myself, even though unintentionally. And yet I cannot describe my feelings of joy and gratitude when I see how well you have come through it all, strengthened in great adversity by belief in God and by His help.

Dear Hong-gul, I believe that God loves me endlessly, that He is always by my side. I believe also that He has ordained that I stand where I am now because of His love for me. I am certain God has a complete plan for me and is working on my behalf all the time. I do not doubt that everything will be resolved according to His design and my life will be expended in furthering His glory and the happiness of our people.

Believing these things, even in my present circumstances, I have sought to praise and thank the Lord and to live a life that is built on an inner happiness. At first I did find it difficult to accommodate my feelings to this purpose, but as the days passed by, and with the aid of the Holy Spirit, I have regained my peace of mind, even hope and joy in my feelings today. I feel most grateful for this change. And when I learn how our family and brothers have been strengthened in their faith by this ordeal, I know again the strength of God's love.

My dear Hong-gul, your father neither blames anyone nor feels the need to hold a grudge against anyone. This change took place the last time I was in prison. During those three years, I read a great number of books on the divine teaching, and I spent a great deal of time meditating on the words and actions of Jesus. As I sought to bring their messages into my life, I came to realize fully that I could not truly be a disciple of Jesus if I did not purge myself of all recriminations and hatred. Also, I am more than ever aware of my own guilt, the mistakes I have made in my life, and the pernicious thoughts I have harbored. What if all these were to be enumerated one after the other, before Jesus? How could I ever judge any other person guilty? This realization has struck me to the quick. We are all sinners, and so we must forgive others, even our worst enemies. Only those who are strongest in the presence of God are capable of forgiving, and we should forgive gladly because it leads to peace and reconciliation.

We must not render futile Jesus' forgiveness of his executioners. Trying to understand others by seeking to imagine oneself in their place is the most effective way to become capable of forgiving. I know that if you try throughout your life to understand, to love, and to forgive others, then whatever your social standing, wealth, or status may be, you will always know a future that is full of peace and happiness.

I am mortified to have come to this realization so late in my life.

Dear Hong-gul, as I have said before, you possess qualities of character not usually found in people. I have never known you to lie. I have never heard you find fault with others or betray them. I have always been surprised at your remarkable tenacity—you stay at something for years once you have determined to do so. First, it was automobiles; then, weapons and the martial arts; then, athletics; and now, literature seems to be occupying your attention.

You do of course have shortcomings. One is a seeming lack of concern for neighbors, but I know that if you patiently cultivate the strengths I have mentioned, you are sure to find happiness and success. I hope that you proceed toward the goals in your life with humility before God and neighbors and with a mental attitude that remains positive.

During your last visit to the prison, you spoke of your intention to major in sociology or philosophy. I shall jot down a few of my thoughts on that, but understand that space does not permit me to be thorough, and, besides, there is no immediate urgency. Just keep this letter with you until you are ready to begin your studies in college, and then read it once more. You may find it useful.

To begin with, sociology is that discipline in the social sciences which considers the social, collective life of humankind, especially such human relations as social behavior, the actions of social groups, and problems in human societies generally. I believe it was the nineteenth-century French philosopher Comte who founded the discipline. In my own view, the focus of sociological inquiry should be on social relations and how they may effect a universal happiness for all individuals in society. True and complete human happiness requires far more than the political freedoms and the social and economic well-being that are provided for in the advanced nations of Europe and America. Human alienation, a phenomenon that is characteristic of modern society, must be replaced by active participation, and the moral decay of the human spirit must give way to a moral revival. I believe that sociology must be strongly mindful of the four prerequisite elements for human happiness: liberty, participation, morality, and sufficient food.

Regarding philosophy, as Windelbard (1848–1915), founder of the so-called southwestern German school, stated in his General Introduction, philosophical concepts seem to vary greatly with individual scholars and the times. In brief, philosophy can be characterized as the discipline which draws on the analysis and synthesis of all the sciences for its method; to discover the fundamental principle regarding existence and value, which represent the outer boundaries of philosophical inquiry, is its goal.

Philosophical inquiry is divided into phenomenology and the theory of consciousness. Phenomenology is, in turn, divided into theories of essence and of the universe. The former deals with the essential natures of the universe, God, and man, and the latter is concerned with the question of how they form and change.

Study of the nature of essence can follow any of three approaches: the qualitative, the quantitative, or that based on a general theory of being. In the historical perspective, the quantitative approach subsumes two radically opposing viewpoints: monism and pluralism. Similarly, two contrasting views, spiritualism and materialism, comprise the qualitative approach. The theory of being, meanwhile, rests on a deductive line of analysis, one that starts with the universe and then arrives at man. In contrast, existential theories, in their focus on the attempt to explain human existence, are inductive.

Considerations of the nature of the universe rest on a theory or axiom of causation that holds that the formation and change of things reflect the relationship between cause and effect. This view is in contrast to teleological arguments, which stress the ultimate end of an absolute being.

In theories of consciousness there seem to be three fields, also characterized by conflicting viewpoints. Rationalist and experiential theories oppose each other in their accounts of the focus and substance of consciousness. Realism and nominalism confront each other with regard to the subjectivity and objectivity of consciousness. In the contrast between realism and nominalism, meanwhile, regarding the issue of the truth or falsity of consciousness, there is the underlying conflict between absolutism and relativism.

Although I am only an amateur in the area of philosophy, based on the few books I have been able to read, I have come to the conclusion that the conflicting elements I have noted above could and indeed should be integrated to constitute a universal truth. The process of this integration cannot, however, be just a simple synthesis; instead, the theory of essence should resolve its inner contradictions through a creative approach to evolution and progress. What I mean to say is that the necessary unifying process cannot be static and mechanical; it should be dialectical, fostering harmonious, integrative development among all manner of contradictions and confrontations. As I see it, philosophy ought to move toward what I call, for lack of a better term, a philosophy of creative and dialectical synthesis.

I hope you will consult Teilhard de Chardin's thoughts on evolutionary theology, while keeping in mind the observations I have made.

As I write these words I try to imagine whether they will pass your review or be met with a condescending smile when you pursue your studies in philosophy. Let me suggest that diagramming my explanations will make them both simple and clear.

Parents always wish the very best for their children and hope they will far surpass them. I am certain that God will bless your future.

Father

The Way of a Wife

December 19, 1980

To Jee-young's mother:

I am writing this letter after your visit today. Because of the brief time allowed for visiting hours it was utterly impossible for me to convey these thoughts to you, so I am setting them down now, hoping that you will find them useful. I should say first of all that I am not writing as your father-in-law. Rather, I am composing this letter with the feeling that I am your own father and in the hope that you will know happiness throughout your life. I would be so pleased if you read it and share some of my feelings.

How can any of us express in words the ordeal we have had to endure for the past seven months? And yet, in spite of everything, your mother and the rest of the family have persevered admirably, and your perseverance has given me, Dae-hyun, and Hong-il immeasurable solace and encouragement. Although this is your first encounter with this sort of adversity, you have handled everything without losing any of your composure—all this with two small children. I simply do not know how to describe my gratitude. I am gratified by your inner sturdiness and outer resilience as well as your strength of character. What is most gratifying of all is how members of the immediate family and relatives as well have used this opportunity to renew or reinforce their love of God and faith in Christ. This has to be the greatest joy and blessing amid the current adversity. For the rest of your life, remember that the Lord Jesus always resides in you and that you should cultivate the practice of thinking, speaking, and behaving like Him.

A true Christian must love God and welcome Jesus

as the Savior, seek forgiveness of sin through the sacred blood of He who died on the cross, and reach salvation by believing in the certain discovery of the path to eternal life through the Resurrection.

It is equally important to love our neighbors and care for them as we would for ourselves, as Jesus taught. You should not neglect devotion to the goal of social salvation, in accordance with the love of Christ, for such devotion can help to bring about a society that can assure happiness to those who are suffering now and stand in need. Individual and social salvation are the two faces of Christian religion, inseparable one from the other. One cannot truly be said to be Christian if one lacks commitment and involvement with both.

Regarding Hong-il, I must tell you that I find him genuinely trustworthy, and I feel strongly about his future promise. He is a far better person, a better Christian, and a better family man than I managed to be at his age. His gifts are also remarkable in terms of his capacity of judgment, persuasiveness, trust and solidarity with friends, and ability to manage difficult situations. If he continues to develop his theoretical understanding and his capacity to work with others in a magnanimous way and if he perfects his command of foreign languages, I have no doubt that his future will be remarkable. We must remember, after all, that he already possesses the most important ingredient for success, his good health.

What I hope for you especially is that you will be able to remain just as solid and humble as you now are so that you can serve as a helpful partner in your husband's development.

Keeping these points in mind and also keeping the conviction to be always by your husband's side, you can maintain a special concern for what he is involved in and serve as his ablest and most trustworthy confidante. This is not an easy task. Because a woman's world is the home, she can easily stay uninformed about the affairs of the world. For that reason, she must make a conscious effort to consult newspapers or other materials and keep informed about public opinion on matters of relevance to her husband's endeavors. A woman must make it a constant practice to ask whether there are matters in which she can advise her husband. If a woman cannot provide consultation and useful advice to her husband in his work, she has failed to be a wife; she is no more than a housekeeper. Man and wife are one in body, thought, and emotion and should act accordingly.

When I suggest that you concern yourself with your husband's work and offer help, I am not suggesting that you interfere or attempt to be domineering. A wife who is cut off from her husband's thoughts and activities is unfortunate, but the greatest misfortune is when a wife dominates her husband. If a wife is uninvolved in what her husband does, they will become spiritually separated. But if she meddles in his business and bosses him around, she will cripple him and lose the happiness that she should derive from holding him in esteem and depending on his success. A most discriminating wife, therefore, will have thorough knowledge of her husband's work, to the point that she can consider possibilities and offer sound judgment. She will not impose these judgments on him, however; instead, she will offer suggestions and understated advice so that he can carry through on his own. She must at all times make sure that her husband is seen to be making the final decisions.

For lack of space, I shall set down a few other points briefly.

A wife should always be able to discover her husband's true merits and potential, and by informing him of these discoveries and encouraging him, help him to move ahead with a challenging spirit and renewed confidence.

If her husband does something unconscionable, immoral, or cowardly, a wife must be resolute in opposing him, even at the risk of losing him entirely. She who acts this way earns his respect.

A wife should always preserve the beauty that is appropriate to her age. To do this, she should never be remiss in filling her inner, spiritual life with the true, the good, and the beautiful, while taking care that her outward appearance is neat, not luxurious, and always in harmony with her personality. This is of utmost importance in keeping her husband by her in a happy frame of mind.

Keeping the home neat, organized, and beautiful, and preparing meals that are pleasing to the husband's taste will work wonders in promoting his attentiveness to the family. At the same time, this effort will provide important, experiential education for the children.

It is a mistake to avoid consulting husbands on family affairs in the belief that this is the way to take care of them. Important matters should always be discussed with husbands so as to draw their attention to the home.

As the children grow, a husband and wife should expand the areas of their mutual consultation. Regular family meetings are essential for promoting the harmony and togetherness of the family.

When Hong-il returns home, decide your future through discourse. Make sure that you discuss matters prudently and thoroughly; if necessary, consult your parents, siblings, and relatives. Once decided, adhere to a plan for the rest of your lives, no matter what happens. Your goals should be set high, but you should work at them one step at a time.

Do not overexert yourselves or be lackadaisical.

To thank God during hardship is not to rejoice at the adversity itself. Rather, it is to bear witness to His loving efforts even in the midst of difficulties. For those who believe in God and strive to live righteously according to His will, adversity represents a trying moment for growth but never a final disaster.

Throughout human history, there have invariably been two sides: good and evil. Something good can turn into a calamity, while something bad can be seen as a blessing in disguise. For example, a rich man's son might fall into debauchery because of money, but money might motivate the son of a poor family to try even more vigorously.

Religious and moral education in early childhood has a lifelong influence. We must exert ourselves, therefore, to make clear to our children that there is good that cannot be abandoned no matter what the sacrifices or losses and there is evil that must not be perpetrated no matter what the circumstances. Help them to realize that God is always with them.

Jee-young and Chung-hwa seem to have quite different personalities. I will not go into any details here because you know them far better than I. As their parents, I hope you will guide them well so that they will be able to develop their own, individual characters and live a life founded on faith in God and morality. I think about your children every day.

As you know, I have often talked about the following three rules of our family. First, always be faithful to God and conscience. Second, be a pioneer of your own destiny without relying on anyone but God. Third, do not crave wealth in excess of that needed for security in life. These three rules are interrelated.

Draw up your own plan for Hong-il's future. If he is released from prison in the near future, go over the plan with him; if not, help him study and reflect upon the direction you have outlined for his future.

Do not forget about those who are suffering on our account, and remember to console and encourage them, if only spiritually. I hope you will do this on my behalf.

Be particularly mindful of your health and the health of your children. Especially in times like these, everyone in the family should take good care of their health. God's love will not fail to protect our family and all of you.

Let us all march on with faith in Saint Paul's words: for those who keep faith, everything will be seen to produce good results.

Father

Even If the Whole World Should Refuse to Acknowledge Him

January 17, 1981

To you with my love and respect:

It was exactly eight months ago today that I left home. How great must the anguish have been for you and the relatives during all these months! For you, I have only words of gratitude.

Because of His tender care, our family and brothers have come to be united in His love and, through faith, have surmounted the difficulties. Isn't all this an enormous blessing? I know only too well that your faith has had much to do with all this. I am indeed fortunate to have a praiseworthy wife, children, daughters-in-law, and grandchildren. For my brothers also, I have only loving thoughts.

No matter what fate may befall me, I have entrusted everything to Christ, our Lord, and I pray every day that my fate will be resolved according to His wishes. Even if everyone in this world were to refuse to acknowledge Him, I will love Him. Even if every theologian were to contend that our Lord Jesus is not the Son of God, I will believe Him. Even if every scientist were to ridicule the idea of His resurrection, my faith will not be affected.

Our Lord Jesus personified the ideal love, which is not attainable in the realm of humanity. There is no doubt that His resurrection is not simply an object of religious faith but an event that changed the course of history. As I have said earlier, if one did not believe in the Resurrection, one would be hard pressed to explain the courage and self-sacrificing devotion of the previously timid disciples after Christ's death. And one could not explain the conversion and the passionate evangelism of Saint Paul, who had once been hostile to Jesus. Furthermore, a great number of the apostolic letters and the Gospels were based on the resurrection of Jesus. If it were not true, how could all these writings have been so remarkably consistent and internally coherent despite having been written by many different people at different times and places?

A genuine affirmation of the Christian faith depends on whether or not one accepts the resurrection of Jesus as historically valid. I am confiding this to you as my religious confession from the bottom of my heart.

The happiness we derive from becoming Christians consists of loving, not hating, our enemies and of offering to our troubled neighbors and others our loving hearts and service as the will of Christ. If we did not believe in Jesus, how could we ever extract ourselves from our misgivings at all the sins we have committed? Just think of how many people plunge themselves into the lamentable practice of trying, by drinking or debauchery, to forget or escape the punishment of conscience; and is it not because we believe in eternal life through the Resurrection that we find a reason and the courage to strive to live righteously, despite all the worldly troubles and persecutions? As I ponder these points, I have an opportunity to appreciate deeply our happiness as believers.

At this moment, I have such a strong feeling of satisfaction and gratitude for our three children and daughter-in-law. Considering their attitudes and behavior, I believe they all have bright futures and are firmly anchored in their resolve to live justly. I do not have the slightest doubt that all this is attributable to your love, patience, and persuasive influence. I am at a loss for words to describe how fortunate and grateful I feel.

I have given Hong-il a number of responsibilities, and, judging carefully from the way in which he has borne himself during the current adversity, he seems quite capable of sorting things out by himself and accomplishing what I have not been able to do. It goes without saying that his success will require great efforts on his part and your guidance and assistance as well. Fortunately, our daughter-in-law possesses greater inner strength, calmness, and wisdom than we could ever expect, which is a great boon for Hong-il.

As I already wrote him directly, Hong-up surprises me by his ability to take care of things and his balanced judgment. His humanness hardly requires any elaboration. I pray constantly that his choices in such important matters as marriage and occupation will be successful.

Although Hong-gul is too young for me to judge, my expectations for him are great, nonetheless. As you know well, his forthright conscience, unadulterated heart, and astounding ability to concentrate on a particular matter make me very hopeful of his future. Your responsibility is great in all this, just as is your contribution. As I always say, my heart aches whenever I think of my brothers and close colleagues and the great hardship and suffering I have caused them. I pray to Jesus for His blessing on them.

Dae Jung

Beginning of Another Journey into Tormented Life

January 29, 1981

My dear children Hong-il, Jee-young's mother, Hong-up, and Hong-gul:

I am reflecting now on God's endless love, which once more has saved my life. Especially when I consider that His blessing has delivered me from certain death four times, I can feel only unbounded rejoicing and gratitude.

Every time I think of the days you have all spent in anguish and suffering, particularly when I think about Hong-il, who is still being held in prison, pain and anguish fill my heart. My love for all of you is strong. I have determined to be a good father, the father of a blissful family. And yet I have caused you great pain and torment. In deep remorse, I can only pray to Jesus every day that your trials will in the end lead to some good.

Your father has decided to entrust to Jesus each day of this ordeal that promises to continue longer still. I shall use it as an opportunity to further my spiritual depth and increase my knowledge. I shall also try hard to maintain my health so as to prepare myself better for the time when I will be able to serve Jesus according to His wishes.

According to Jesus, those who want to follow Him must be prepared to leave behind even their parents and brothers and walk behind Him, carrying the cross on their backs. If we mean to pursue truth in a society seething with sin and irrationality and recast it in love and justice as God would want, we must be ready to sacrifice everything in our possession. This is the sine qua non. We do not accept Jesus' stern demand because of our overflowing emotions or our deference to the absolute authority, nor do we submit ourselves to it simply because He is the Son of God. We do so because

He showed us the way by setting an example of self-sacrifice. No matter how great the pain, humiliation, and solitude I experience, they can never be severer than the suffering Jesus endured in the course of His persecution. To know this provides me with immeasurable solace and permits me to regard my current predicament as a way to share with Him the ordeal He had to undergo.

Our faith cannot be perfected overnight. Throughout our lives, we hesitate between faith and doubt, hope and despair, answers and questions. Yet there is no need for us to feel despondent or defeated at such moments. As long as we maintain our love and faith in God and cling to Jesus by His sleeves, God will deliver us, despite all our mistakes, sins, and doubts, just as He granted forgiveness and salvation to the prodigal son or to Paul in his failing.

In the Old Testament, God was presented not only as God of love but as God of jealousy, recrimination, and judgment; but Jesus showed us instead that the true image of God is one of forgiveness and love.

We have to realize that Jesus asks us to take Him as our caring friend and confide in Him all our joys and troubles and hopes and worries. Jesus hopes we will treat Him as our affectionate teacher, one who would not hesitate to forgive us, time and again, so long as we confess and seek his forgiveness when we err.

I believe our lives will be most meaningful if we spend them by participating with Him in the task whose aim is to bring about the days when God's will is done in this world as in heaven. For this end, as children of God, we must dedicate ourselves to the two-fold purpose of individual and social salvation; that is, we must help our neighbors and devote ourselves to the betterment of our society. We must synchronize and harmonize these two enterprises just like the two wheels of an ox-cart.

I am putting down the following thoughts for your reference just as they come to my mind.

Whatever you do, make sure that you consult your mother and consider all the options with her. I hope you will also engage in religious discussion with her. More than anything else, I am pleased and grateful that you are maintaining a warm and understanding relationship with your mother through mutual care and trust.

Do not forget to thank and console those who are suffering on our account. This goes for their families as well. On behalf of your father, please carry this out with utmost sincerity.

When each of you makes a decision on your future, stay with that decision for ten years without losing your concentration. I can tell you from my own experience that one can surely lay down a foundation for success if one puts one's mind as well as all of one's efforts to a task for just this much time. When the pinnacle of the chosen profession is reached, one can then use this as a launching pad to achieve even greater heights in other directions. For example, if one were to attain the status of a consummate businessman, this could serve as a base for moving into politics, social work, education, or the arts. The greatest failing comes from imprudently changing course before reaching the top.

The goal of life should be set in terms of living meaningfully rather than of what to become. Depending on circumstances, it simply may not be possible to reach the pinnacle in one's endeavors. Nonetheless, if one has always sought to live in a meaningful way, that person's life cannot be considered a failure even though its objective was not reached. It might even be said to have been a worthwhile and happy life.

An individual may sometimes encounter difficulty or bad luck that is beyond control. In such situations, one should never lose one's poise or become hasty. One should wait for the storm of trial to pass. This should not, however, mean failing to prepare for the time when opportunities will open again.

My experience suggests the following requisites of health. First, avoid overeating, overdrinking, and overexertion. Second, if something is causing anguish, it should be analyzed in a concentrated manner for a relatively short time. Reach a firm decision, and then do not let the problem continue to cause pain. Third, always get sufficient sleep. And fourth, it is necessary to maintain a spiritually dignified and balanced posture.

Once you have started a family, mutual respect between man and wife should be valued as much as love. This requires, in turn, that both work hard to discover each other's merits and provide encouragement. Further, in all matters of importance, whether these are found within or outside the family, man and wife should be each other's closest and most valuable counselors as well as partners.

Sundays should be used as occasions for the family to spend time together to promote understanding through discussions and participation in common events. I do not believe love within the family is something that should be explained; it is to be felt.

I beseech all of you to be as loving and caring to your cousins as you are to your own siblings.

Father

*The Beginning of a Solitary Period**

February 21, 1981

To my beloved and respected wife and my beloved children:

I am pleased and gratified to learn from the letters you and the children sent that there is love and mutual

*This is the author's first letter to his family after being transferred to Chungju Prison on January 31, 1981.

support in our family. When I think about the pain and bitterness you and the children have had to endure during the last ten months, my heart aches and guilt overcomes me. As you have mentioned in your letter, Hong-gul's situation, in particular, is a matter of tearful reflection. Imagine the psychological conflict and burden he must have undergone every day in school. I am only thankful he has persevered so steadfastly. I did not expect Hong-il and Jee-young's mother to be able to stand up to this first tribulation in their lives as well as they have. I am thanking the Lord because I believe this experience will turn out to be a useful lesson and will help them in their joint efforts to build a successful future. Judging from Hong-up's recent letters, I feel that his faith is becoming deeper and stronger. When I think of all the hardships I have caused him, I am ashamed to call myself his father. Nevertheless, I am happy and grateful that he has survived the situation marvelously and still genuinely loves and respects me.

Our brothers and their families also have stood together with strong and renewed faith during the current crisis. I thank them, and I thank God Who made it all possible. I am proud and deeply indebted to you, as I am aware of the vital role your faith and love have played in all this. Situations can cause us pain but can never make us unhappy.

It is only twenty days since I was transferred here and ten days since the family came to visit, but it seems as if all this happened half a year ago. This latest episode has made me realize for the first time in my life how boring the passage of time is and how devastating solitude is. Relying on faith, I try to bolster my weakening spirit and strive to endure this spiritual test by engaging in a dialogue with Jesus or by reading.

You cannot imagine how it hurt me to see the tears in your eyes during your last visit. In fact, because I had worried about how my tears might affect you, I prayed to God every day that I would not let my tears show during family visits. Under the present circumstances, however, how can we help but feel the weight of the most sorrowful and tangled emotions? But faith has kept us from despair and fatalism; it has given us comfort and the hope that through our Father's love and compassion, which were shown in Jesus, we may be delivered.

I became aware of all this on my first day here. Even though it was not a new experience for me, I felt wretched when my head was shaved and I had to change my clothes immediately on arrival. When I was led to my assigned cell, I thanked Jesus for the present adversities, which I see as His expression of love in allowing me to share with Him such tribulation, humiliation, and the loneliness of the crucifix.

The cell was icy cold. I hurried through my dinner and rushed under the blankets, but my body kept shivering with cold. Under the blankets I began to weep, and I kept calling out, "My Father!" Tears streamed down my cheeks. After a while, fatigue overcame me and I fell asleep. In my sleep I could hear people outside the cell, working on something. When I pulled down the blanket to look, I saw they were installing the electric stove I had brought with me from Seoul. I had asked that it be installed but was taken by surprise, for I did not dream the work would be done on the same day I made the request. The workers and the guards who were standing there looked like angels to me. In all my life I had never felt so strongly God's presence and His tender care for me. This is how God took care of the chronic condition that makes me so susceptible to cold.

As you said, I certainly am a person with enormous cause to feel grateful. Think how much pain and inconvenience I am inflicting on my children, brothers, relatives, friends, and colleagues. Although it was unintentional, the damage has been great and of long duration. When I remember that these friends and relations have not uttered a word of complaint but instead have been praying for us, how can I express my humility and gratitude? I can only pray to Jesus day and night that He will grant them His blessing.

For the past ten months, I have thought about why God has put me and all of us through this endless trial and why He has inflicted this terrible predicament on us. I think I have found answers to some parts of the question, but I am still groping for an adequate understanding of others. Nevertheless, I firmly believe God loves us boundlessly and is always with us. He watches over all our affairs, and I believe He will bring all things together for good in this world. Believing this, I try to sustain hope patiently and tenaciously. I am glad that in this adversity my lifelong convictions and loyalty to the people have been strengthened further as part of my faith in God.

When sometimes I tell you and our children my views on religion, it is not because I consider myself in any way more advanced than you. I simply hope you will help me work out the ideas I have been thinking about but have not been able to finish. In a recent letter, Hong-il wrote that he finds it "awkward these days even to pray, because faith seems to be coming apart at the seams." This is an honest confession, characteristic of Hong-il. Even I am constantly asking myself whether my basic attitude has not changed now that I have hurdled the threat of death. It is only human that this sort of thing should happen. After all, isn't it inevitable that not everyone can become towering figures in religion or be just at all times? Even though we keep believing and then doubting, sinning and then repenting, so long as we stay by God's side to the end, He will not abandon us. Jesus does not save us because of our justness or beneficence. Instead, He blesses us as our Savior because He sees the faith that does not let us turn from Him even though we sin and because He bears witness to our beneficent efforts that are our joyous response to God's grace.

During the course of normal social life, it will often be difficult to have time enough to pray together. I want to suggest to Hong-up and Jee-young's mother that they make it a daily practice to pray since it can be done almost any time during the day. (This goes for Hong-gul as well.) For example, consider the following:

1. While riding a bus, one could pray for the safety and happiness of one's fellow passengers.

2. When crossing a street, one could pray for the safety of those at the intersection.

3. When dealing with people who work in restaurants or teahouses, one could pray for their human relations to be troublefree.

4. When one gets together with friends at school or on dates, one could pray for their health and happiness.

If one could exercise one's creativity in this fashion, praying could become a daily routine. Naturally, this is easier said than done. But if one forgets, all one has to do is get back to it on a daily basis; if one becomes lackadaisical, one should apologize to God and start over again. To try to become a religious leader or to be known as infallibly just is rather dangerous. A person attempting such a thing often breaks the faith when it brings pain instead of joy, or becomes a hypocrite. This particular point should be firmly grasped if one wants to lead a religious life.

One of the most important things religion offers in the modern era is that it can make us genuinely free individuals: a Christian is free from the agony of trying to find a meaning for existence in this world, as the whole reason for existence is to love God and participate in His plan for human salvation; a Christian believer, by virtue of faith in God, is freed from the despair that stems from death, sickness, and hardship; a Christian attains freedom from the cares of life by entrusting his or her life to God; a Christian is blessed and free because of faith and the love of God and neighbors; and, a Christian is free to love and forgive enemies according to the will of God. We should thank God for having given us all this freedom, and we should be eternally grateful for and cherish our privileged status as Christians, which endows us with such freedom.

Please give my regards to our two in-law families. I am constantly praying. Please also send my regards to our relatives at Pil-dong and elsewhere as well as to our friends who live with us. And please find for me the following titles:

1. Kant, *The Critique of Practical Reason*
2. Galbraith, *The Age of Uncertainty*
3. Galbraith, *Economics and Public Purpose*
4. Solzhenitzyn, *The Gulag Archipelago* (and the English edition, which is at home)
5. Other religious literature that deals with life experiences, especially in the Communist sphere

As I pray to God for the news of spring we both await, I bid farewell again, picturing in my mind your face and the faces of our family.

Let Us Overcome the World of Evil!

March 19, 1981

My dear and respected wife and my beloved children:

My greatest happiness is waiting every day for the letters from home and reading them. I cannot describe what great comfort and strength I gain from hearing the affectionate news from my beloved family. Your recent letters tell me that you are worried too much about my situation and your inability to do anything about it. I beg you to stop. I am fully aware that my present circumstances are the cause of your concern. Since your last visit on the 9th, I have been able to arrange things much better, so please do not worry too much. I have honestly set aside my own apprehensions and have been trying and praying to overcome this situation.

Sorrowful tears are only natural when we think of the appalling and unjustified adversity that has afflicted our family since last May. All the wailing and supplication in the world is not enough to help us forget the memory of the last ten months. We have our God, however, to Whom we can plead our case by revealing all that is in our minds when we are sad. God wipes away our tears and gives us true solace, courage, and hope. Jesus Christ overcame this world with boundless love, complete obedience to God, and unassailable faith in God's trustworthiness. The affliction, degradation, and solitude He suffered reassure us. The glory He attained and the promise He made to us are the source of courage and hope that enables us to dry our tears and rise up. In your letters, I have come across the frequent use of the phrase "Overcome this world as Jesus did." I believe the way to accomplish this is to forgive our enemies, to love and make peace with them, just as Christ did.

In all the countless troubles we have gone through since last May, I can count more than ten instances in which Christ has blessed us. We know well, for example, that my life was saved, that our family has been firmly united in our belief in Jesus, that we are all healthy, that we all care for and love one another, and that we are tenderly looked after by our many friends. It is rare indeed for someone to survive imminent death four times in a lifetime, which makes me wonder with joy and gratitude what has led God to love me so much.

Under the present circumstances, I think it is important for us always to turn to Jesus with the belief that He has infallible plans for us. It is equally important for us to believe that, in spite of our present problems, our mental attitude will eventually decide whether we will receive our Lord's grace, because it is His purpose to bring all things together for good. We often have doubts or complaints, wondering why God does not prevent the evil in this world and the victimization of innocent people. Here is my conclusion to this question.

First, if God roots out all the evil humans are capable of, He would be taking away His greatest gift to mankind, that is, freedom—freedom not only to perpetrate evil at times but also to confront Him. This would reduce humans to an animallike existence, with their actions conditioned only by instincts and reflexes. Then we would not be able to act justly to master this world together with God.

Second, God can, at any time, put a stop to the evil done by humans and reverse its consequences. God also has the power to bestow glory on the victims of evil by rewarding them later in history or in His kingdom. In the end, God does not take any pleasure from the evils that occur in this world, nor does He encourage them. Rather, He wants us to have faith in His justice, to repudiate evil, to defend this world from evil, and to share actively in bringing progress and perfection to this world. God expects us to dedicate ourselves to these endeavors so that we may realize as soon as possible the day when the world will be filled with peace and love, the day of judgment and fulfillment. A Christian way of life dedicated to making progress toward the ultimate, the Second Coming, is a most worthwhile life. I believe we should understand all our troubles and problems in this light.

Jesus Christ is the Son of God, but in terms of His true essence, He is God and the only human without sin. God announces His presence before us through

Christ, and it is also through Christ that He offers salvation and keeps all His promises to us. It is Christ's life, His death on the cross, and His resurrection that enable us to recognize Him as the Son of God, the Lamb of our redemption, and our Savior. Of all these, the resurrection of Jesus is the crucial point. Belief in the Resurrection determines whether we regard Christ simply as a sage or as our Savior. I am not going to repeat what I believe are some of the fundamentals of our faith in the Resurrection because I touched on these in my earlier letter from Seoul. I will only say that when we believe in the resurrected Jesus, our faith finally finds a secure foundation. The conscience is the innermost chamber of the mind, in which we have a private audience with God. This is the value of conscience. It forewarns us against sinning and makes us repent for the sins we have already committed, but it cannot pardon us for our sins. Even though it is often said that all one has to do is live without shaming one's conscience, I do not consider this the way to a full life.

Now let me write down a few things about our family affairs. More than anything else, I thank the Lord that you, Hong-up, and Mr. Lee escaped that automobile accident, though it was a narrow escape, and I am grateful that our brother's wife suffered only a minor injury. Please let us not get into any more trouble than we already have. It rains more often in spring, so I want you to make sure to rely on public buses. I know well I have been a most inadequate husband from the very first day of our marriage, but you must know that throughout the ten-year period of our suffering, I have always approached you with great care and deep affection. I cannot describe how much I cherish you and love our children. I hope you will understand how important you are and take good care of your health, remembering that you are also doing this for me.

Letters from Yun-soo and Yun-hak[1] arrived the other

1. The daughters of the author's second youngest brother, Dae-hyun.

day. I was much comforted and pleased by their affectionate words. Please write to me often about our family and what is happening. Did Hong-gul's schoolwork improve a little last semester? I wonder whether everyone in the family is well. What about our dogs, Smarty and Captain?

Let me tell you about a dream I had recently. I almost wrote about it in my last letter but decided against it because I felt embarrassed. It was, nonetheless, a happy and glorious dream for me which I have finally decided to share with my family. It was on the night of February 4, only five days after I arrived here. In the dream I was put on a huge freight cart and taken by workers to a suburban area. On the right-hand side of the wide road, there was a broad field stretching beyond the horizon where I was to be left to die. Suddenly, there was a change in the plan. I was dumped by the roadside and then put back on the cart. It was a very wintry day, and I did not have any clothing. I knew I would certainly freeze to death, even if they were going to wheel me back to town. Suddenly, there was a ray of light sent by God. When I looked up, there were two red beams of light coming down, but I could not see beyond because their source was hidden by clouds. These rays of light blanketed me in a zigzag pattern and warmed my whole body. Even the men pulling the cart seemed to enjoy the warmth they provided. The cart returned to town without incident, and the dream ended when the cart stopped in front of a Korean-style tile-roofed house, one that looked like a public assembly hall. Although only a dream, it left me with a happy, positive feeling. I am sure both you and the children will be pleased by it.

Please send me the books I have listed at the end.

To Jee-young's mother:

I have been receiving your letters without any problems. You cannot imagine the comfort and joy I find in the news about Jee-young and Chung-hwa. I certainly agree with you that Jee-young is smart and Chung-hwa is generous. They must be so anxious to see their father. At the beginning of March, I was hoping for the release of those in Taejon Prison. I was greatly disappointed because I could not see Hong-il's face during the March family visit. If my frustration was that great, yours must have been beyond words. When I think about you, your mother-in-law, and the other family members outside, who have suffered pain and sorrow to a much greater degree than those of us inside, I do not quite know how to express my apology and my appreciation for the way you have persevered. I take great pride in Hong-il and expect a lot from him. It is remarkable the way you and your husband have been helping each other to weather the present adversity. Frequent visits will become more difficult now that the sentence has been confirmed, so you should consult with him about his reading list while he is in prison. And do not call Chung-hwa by the nickname she dislikes so much. My experience suggests this is not a wise thing to do in bringing up children.

To Hong-up:

I felt very reassured when I read in your letter that you were not terribly concerned about your future because you would leave it in the hands of God. Your future will undoubtedly be bright if you continue to be as generous with your thoughts as you are now and if you maintain your complete faith in God. As I have told you before, I know from experience that you possess sound judgment and the ability to handle things. Now concentrate your efforts on preparing for the future. I also know from experience that one's mental attitude determines whether one can make good use of whatever situation arises. The engine of progress and development is nothing more than persistent effort.

I find it most regrettable now that I failed to become

proficient in English when I was under house arrest in 1979. Based on my experience, I believe that whether we are talking about religious living, studying, or acting generously, it is important and productive to be persistent without becoming impatient. There will certainly be frustrations, doubts, and boredom, and excuses can always be found for discontinuing our efforts. It is important at such times to convince oneself to start once again with fresh enthusiasm. In one sense, life is a process of self-debate, self-persuasion, and self-determination, and there are many fresh starts.

I learned from your mother's letter about your homecoming. I think it is good that you have returned home. Among the books I have read recently, *The Third Wave*, *The New Industrial State*, *One Faith*, and *The Uncertain Age* were very helpful. Try them.

To Hong-gul:

I am wondering how your nasal examination turned out. Please let me know. Whenever I think about the subject of the two poems you entered in the poetry contest, they remind me again of the heartbreak you must have suffered in the last year. Tears fill my eyes every time I think about it. For a young man, you have withstood it all very well. God will surely bless you.

This year will be most important in deciding the course of your future. As you said, your best efforts will get you into the college of your choice. The examinations are a project that will require careful planning and preparation. It will be helpful to draw up a monthly plan of academic reviews and tables containing the substance of each review. Follow through, checking your progress as you go along. I hope your diligence will bring success. I am sure it will be helpful for you to discuss your plans for the year with your mother and brothers and to have a family meeting to draw them up together and share your thoughts.

I wish you a healthy and lively day, every day.

1. Walter Nigg, *Friedrich Nietzsche* (Pundo Publishing Co.).
2. Walter Nigg, *Dostoevsky* (Pundo Publishing Co.).
3. Walter Nigg, *The Christian Saints* (Pundo Publishing Co.).
4. Friedrich Nietzsche, *Thus Spake Zarathustra* (Munye Publishing Co.).
5. Bertrand Russell, *A History of Western Philosophy* (Munye Publishing Co.).
6. Maruyama, *Nippon no gendai shisho* (The Modern Thoughts in Japan) (Chongno Publishing Co.).
7. John Hick, *Philosophy of Religion* (Chongno Publishing Co.).
8. Plato, *Dialogues* (translated by Ch'ŏe Myŏnggwan) (Chongno Publishing Co.).
9. *Science and Christianity* (Chongno Publishing Co.).
10. W. Lipmann, *The Fall and Resurgence of Democracy* (Taehan Christian Publishing Co.).
11. Chindan Hakhoe, *Han'guksa* (A History of Korea), 7 vols (Ŭlyu Munhwa-sa).
12. *Ilbon munhwaŭi wŏllyu rosŏŭi pigyo Han'guk munhwa* (A Comparative Study of Korean Culture as the Origin of Japanese Culture) (Samsŏng).
13. Berkeley, *Saint Paul, a Man and His Life* (Christian Academy).
14. James Robinson, *Honestly to God* (Taehan Christian Publishing Co.).
15. Abraham Cohen, *Everyman's Talmud* (Taehan Christian Publishing Co.).
16. Norman Jacobs, *Culture and Arts in a Mass Society* (Taehan Christian Publishing Co.).
17. Raymond Vernon, *The Economic and Political Consequences of Multinational Enterprise* (Hyŏnam-sa).
18. Pyŏn Hyŏngyun, *Han'guk kyŏngjeŭi chindan kwa pansŏng* (The Diagnosis of and Reflection on Korean Economy) (Chisik Sanŏp).

19. Im Chongch'ŏl, *Kukje kyŏngjeron* (A Theory of International Economics) (Ilsin-sa).

20. Arnold Toynbee, *A Study of History* (translated by Kang Kich'ŏl).

21. *Sinjŏllyak sasangsa* (A New History of Thoughts in Military Strategy) (Kirin-wŏn).

22. Elia Kazan, *America, America.*

Literary Works

1. Fedor M. Dostoevsky, *The Idiot, The Possessed, The Adolescent.*

2. Leo Tolstoy, *Resurrection.*

3. Nikolai V. Gogol, *Dead Souls.*

4. Albert Camus, *The Stranger* (Shinmun Publishing Co.).

5. Charles Dickens, *Mr. Scrooge* (Shinmun Publishing Co.).

6. Somerset Maugham, *Of Human Bondage* (Shinmun Publishing Co.).

7. Boris Pasternak, *Dr. Zhivago* (Shinmun Publishing Co.).

8. Albert Camus, *The Myth of Sisyphus* (Wangmun-sa).

9. Friedrich Nietzsche, *Human, All Too Human* (Inmun Publishing Co.).

10. Shima Ryotaro, *Tokugawa Ieyasu* (vols. 1, 2) (Inmun Publishing Co.).

A Letter from the Eldest Son from Taejon Prison

April 22, 1981

With my love and respect to you and my beloved children:

Yesterday was a very happy day for me. In the afternoon I received letters from you and Hong-up and a totally unexpected one from Hong-il. For several hours I could not read them. I was quite overwhelmed with excitement and tears blurred my vision. I was finally able to read them when I went to bed.

The letter [from Hong-il] contained the following passages: "My Father, whom I strive to meet, if only in dreams"; "gratitude to Lord Jesus for saving my father's life"; "It still gives me chills to think how cramped our hearts were during those hours"; "God's care was needed in order to endure that trial"; "I remember my father's love at such times, like the time when Hong-up and I climbed the Octagonal Shrine at Namsan mountain, each of us holding your hand and had our picture taken"; "I am concerned to hear that you are not all that well. Please be strong and stay healthy"; "I am praying from the bottom of my heart to Lord Jesus"; "I have been able to stay calm and collected thanks to the pride I feel in my wonderful parents and also to my wife's thoughtful care for our household"; "I am writing often to Hong-up and Hong-gul and I keep reminding myself to spend time meaningfully and to solidify our fraternal love"; "I have recently received letters of encouragement, books, and gifts from various sources—all of which are a great help"; "I am determined to make life here worthwhile by gaining something from it. Otherwise, all this will have been nothing but a cause for regret"; "As a child of the Creator, I will become flax so that I can burn myself to brighten the world and salt so that I can melt myself to prevent the corrosion of the world. I will strive to live a true life"; "The Supreme Court decision is due today, but I have no expectations whatsoever"; "The 20th is Jee-young's birthday. . . . I have been told that Jee-young told people, 'If you know where my dad is, please take me to him. I have money to pay you. I want to see him!' They say that my two children pray before they eat and when they go to bed they pray 'Please help our grandfather and father stay healthy and to return home soon' "; "Final court ruling on my case is imminent and I will write you as often as possible." You cannot imagine how deeply moved I was, how happy and proud. When I saw that the letter was dated the 14th, I gave thanks, seeing it as a great Easter gift from Christ.

In the wake of Easter Sunday, I felt even more strongly than ever that God is the epitome of love. The essence of God is said to be love; His essence is such that His existence is not conceivable without love for mankind. This is why He Himself came to mankind, but instead of showing gratitude, men betrayed, and ran away from, Him. The history of mankind is a continuing drama of God's endless love and mankind's repeated betrayal. Finally, God sent His beloved Son to the cross as the sacrificial lamb and, by causing His resurrection, demonstrated His unbounded love for, and confidence in, mankind. Von Hoeffer has said, "What is God? . . . God is the encounter with Jesus Christ. In this encounter with Jesus Christ, Christ exists only for others." He further argued that in realizing this we will experience genuine repentance for our [sinful] human existence, which is the way for us to know God. The touching analogy of the prodigal son best describes God's love and His relationship to us:

> When His small child tried to leave home, God knew that it was a mistake but did not interfere with his freedom;
>
> When he returned home genuinely repentant, God

accepted him with great joy. There were no conditions attached, no reprimands or questions;

We have to note that the repentance of the prodigal son was shown in his constant self-effacement; and

It is naturally human for the eldest son to grumble and to cite his own accomplishments and justness. But we should be wary of the smug self-righteousness into which people who profess to believe are prone to fall.

At Easter, I was deeply touched when I read the last three sections of the gospel—those dealing with the Last Supper, the arrest of Christ, the Crucifixion, and the Resurrection. The most moving of all was the scene of Christ's protesting prayers, which included these words: "my mind is greatly vexed that I am on the verge of dying. . . . Father . . . please take this cup from my lips. But do so only according to your will and not mine. My mind is willing but the flesh is weak. . . . [I am] burdened with worries and anxieties."

In my present situation, the image of Christ uttering these words made my heart pound and my eyes fill with tears. Although He is God Himself, our Lord Jesus is at the same time just like us, a human being in whose very human vexations and weaknesses I recognize myself. These reflections made me weep and gave me much relief. Yet our Lord Jesus overcame His weaknesses and obeyed God. This made me realize once again that in my current anguish and troubles, as long as I do not turn my sight away from God or withdraw my love and obedience from God, I will not be in hell—no matter how great my suffering and vexation.

I was grateful beyond words that the authors of the gospel recorded so candidly these moments of Christ's weakness. It is not humanly possible for us to become religious leaders by seeming to be immune to anguish and fear. We must be honest and humble before God, and Christians must be honest before men as well. A great number of the clergy and laity are afraid of revealing their human weaknesses or religious doubts. They behave as if obsessed with the need to appear to be the most impeccably devout persons. Yet when they are by themselves, they are beset with a sense of the emptiness and meaninglessness of their lives, and they may even regret having become Christians. We have to reflect on why they do so.

We become Christians not because we are perfect; it is because of our imperfection that we come to depend on God. Becoming Christian does not make one perfect; it only signals a first step toward perfection under God's love and direction. Therefore, as believers we should be able to show one another our shortcomings, anguish, and doubts. Further, we should be able to admit candidly that as Christians we are by no means perfect. Otherwise, we will find ourselves shackled by hypocrisy, strapped in a straitjacket of double standards and strife. These thoughts occurred to me on Easter week as I reflected on Christ's human weaknesses.

Next May 10 is our wedding anniversary.[1] When our marriage was barely ten days old, I was implicated in an antirevolutionary incident led by the Democratic party and sent to prison for one month by the military government. Our marriage thus began in hardship. Subsequently, there have been three imprisonments, three brushes with death, three elections to the National Assembly, the 1971 presidential election, and, above all, the birth of Hong-gul. By virtue of your marvelous support, I have been able to maintain a way of life that has been faithful to my conscience and God. I do not know how to express my grateful feelings that your bond with Hong-up and Hong-il is founded on love even greater than the love between myself and them and that you are embracing with love our first daughter-in-law and Jee-young and Chung-hwa. I can

1. The author was married to Lee Hee-ho on May 10, 1962. His first wife, the mother of Hong-il and Hong-up, died in 1959.

hardly find words to describe my gratitude and happiness. Please accept my respect, love, and appreciation now, in advance of May 10th.

From a religious standpoint, when we married ours was a somewhat awkward union between a Catholic and a Protestant. Thinking about it today, however, our marriage can serve as an example of an ecumenical movement. The World Council of Churches, formed after World War II, and the Second Vatican Assembly, held in the mid-1960s, are monumental events in the history of Christianity that represent great strides toward the unification of the Catholic and Protestant churches under the condition of pluralism. The long-standing feud between the two churches since Martin Luther's Reformation of 1517 has yielded to conciliation: the Catholic church claims the contentions of the Protestant church comprise its original message, and the Protestant church now admits the Catholic church's claims should not be ignored.

Furthermore, such issues as marriage, the worship of Mary, the authority of the pope, and the responsibilities of the church, which have been the focal points of such intense controversies, are said to be giving way to mutual understanding. What is most important today is the categorical refutation of Christianity by communism, the increasing circulation of scientific atheism, and the prevalence of religious indifference and neglect. Dedication to social progress is most urgently needed if we are to build a heavenly kingdom in this world according to the will of our Lord Jesus and refine and complete the kingdom to hasten the Second Coming. Such is the mission of Christianity, which makes dialogue and cooperation between the Catholic and Protestant churches a natural development. As I reflect on our churches today, one persistent question makes me feel fretful and impatient—as Christians, are we fulfilling our mission to serve as the light and the salt of this world by inspiring men to look up to and love our

Lord Jesus, or are we making mankind look at the Lord with sarcasm and indifference?

In letters from you and Hong-up, I read about the planting of a rose tree and the greening of the grass in the yard. I can visualize the scene and understand your care as you tend the yard, thinking of me. When I go outdoors for exercise here, I find the azaleas in full bloom. As I watch each of the buds grow closer every day to blossoming, I can fully appreciate how much tender effort must be spent to accomplish anything at all. There used to be a bunch of forsythia on the far side of the wall, and each day I watched their charming blossoms with great delight. But several days ago, they all disappeared overnight. I thought their ending was strangely clear-cut and beautiful as well.

My health is the same as when you last visited. It is not getting any worse, but I am a bit more sensitive these days because of my ear. I have not been rubbing it, as you suggested, because I am not sure it would do any good. In addition to reading the Bible and praying, I devote myself every day to my studies. Since my arrival here, I have read books on theology, philosophy, history, and economics, and I have learned a great deal. While reading the 13th volume of Toynbee's *Study of History*, I thought it might be a good idea to set a daily target of thirty pages, and I have been keeping to it.

I was happy to hear that my younger brother's wife has fully recovered. I am delighted that Hong-jun[2] is growing up. I am also happy to hear about Hye-kyung's[3] graduation and faith. Let me congratulate, if belatedly, Hyung-joo[4] and Yun-soo[5] for their successful entrance into schools, and please tell Hyung-joo,[6]

2. The eldest son of the author's brother Dae-ui.
3. Dae-ui's first daughter.
4. Dae-ui's second son.
5. The first daughter of the author's brother Dae-hyun.
6. Dae-hyun's eldest son.

Hong-min,[7] and Yun-hak[8] to do well in school. The same goes for Hwe-young.[9] Send my regards to Messrs. Lee and Cho, auntie, and Hwe-sook,[10] all of whom are staying with our family. And convey my regards and apologies to your sisters and brothers.

I do not know how to express my thanks that Jee-young's mother has stood up so well to everything and has been bringing up the children with such care. Once Hong-il's sentence becomes final, she will feel emptier than before and suffer great psychological pain. I hope, however, that she will continue to overcome these difficulties through faith and belief in her wonderful husband's future. I send my belated congratulations on Jee-young's birthday, and I am delighted to see Chung-hwa growing into an innocent, pretty girl.

It is extremely lucky Hong-up is staying home. I pray every day that his present predicament will be a great source of strength in the future.

I told Hong-gul during his last visit that because only eight months remain before his college entrance examination, he should concentrate exclusively on preparing for it so that he can enter Korea University—the university he is so fond of. I pray every day for his success. Please tell him to write to me every week about how things are going.

I wonder how Hong-jun's father is doing with his leg. And how about my sister-in-law?

I am very grateful to Hyung-joo's father for his magnanimous attitude. All this is due to our Lord Jesus. For the others in Taejon, I can only be thankful and apologetic.[11] I pray for them every night.

I pray for your health and peace of mind.

7. Dae-hyun's second son.
8. Dae-hyun's second daughter.
9. Dae-ui's second daughter.
10. A domestic at the author's home.
11. This refers to the author's aides who are being held in Taejon Prison.

1. Karl Jaspers, *The Great Philosophers.*

2. Ruth Benedict, *Patterns of Culture.*

3. Kim Chunsŏp, *Siljon ch'ŏlhak* (Existentialism).

4. *Karl Jaspers* (Korea University Press).

5. J. Kenneth Galbraith, *Money, Whence It Came, Where It Went.*

6. Gunnar Myrdal, *Asian Drama: An Inquiry into the Poverty of Nations* (I have it at home).

7. Gunnar Myrdal, *Against the Stream: Critical Essays on Economics.*

8. *Tonghak hyŏngmyŏng kwa Chŏn Bong-chun* (I have it at home).

9. Henri Charrière, *Papillon* (A novel).

10. Other records of the Christian experience.

P.S. Be sure to classify the books (philosophy, history, fiction, etc.) you send and also to list their authors in your letter.

Joyous Reunion

May 22, 1981

To you with love and respect and to my beloved children:

The visit on the 12th was indeed a joyous occasion.[1] You cannot imagine how restless I was until I came face-to-face with all of you because I was not sure you would come. It is really a blessing that both Dae-hyun and Hong-il seem healthy. About the others still in

1. The author's youngest brother, Dae-hyun, and eldest son, Hong-il, were released from prison through an order of executive clemency.

prison, my heart is as tormented as yours. I pray for them every day. It is gratifying to note that the present adversity has helped them in their faith and their growth as men. From letters from the three of you, Jee-young's mother, and Yun-soo, I can picture the children of the two families rejoicing, which fills my heart with delight. Since your last visit I have found, to my good fortune, a great deal of solace and emotional stability.

I spent all of May 17th with my emotions in a turmoil. Trying to fathom your state of mind and that of the other family members, I felt as if ten thousand different feelings were pressing on my heart. It has been an appalling year, an unreal year. How can we express our shock, sorrow, and torment? How full of anguish you and the family must have been, shuddering with nightmarish imaginings. Whenever I picture these things in my mind, tears fill my eyes. My life has been a thorny path, but what I have gone through the past year far exceeds all the adversities and pain I experienced before this.

We cannot deny, however, that even in the midst of such adversities we were richly blessed by Lord Jesus. How many people have been rescued from certain death four times? I am overcome by emotion when I ask myself why I deserve such great love from God. That is not all. Through this whole terrible interlude, not a single life has been lost, and everyone has been healthy. Now two of us have been returned home. The greatest blessing is that He is watching over our entire family as an unconquerable fortress of belief.

God has given comfort and strength through faith to our family, brothers, and even our friends. I offer my limitless gratitude to God when I think about all the kindness extended to us by so many people. On Sunday, the 17th, I gave profound thanks to the Lord Jesus for the abundant grace during the past year and also prayed that in the coming year He would bless us with joy and freedom and that He would safeguard our family and friends.

One prominent psychologist has said that man is the lord of creation because of his freedom of choice but is also no more than a beetlelike creature because of his inability to see an inch ahead. This statement rings true when I think back on the last year. It also makes the same point as my favorite phrase, "What is important is not so much what you become as how you live." In reality, no matter what one wants to become, one has no power to control it. Our freedom of choice is limited to how we live. When we realize this, we can attain genuine serenity as well as complete reliance on God. In Nietzsche's lexicon, even the superman, though fully armed with power, must rely on the Almighty for the outcome once he has made the best possible choice.

Remember, when you visited me in Seoul after the commutation of my sentence, I said, "In the future I will strive for the growth of my spiritual faith, the enhancement of my knowledge, and the maintenance of health. I want the family to share these objectives with me so that we do not spend our time idly." Please convey these words to Dae-hyun and Hong-il.

One of the books I read recently deeply impressed me with these recommendations to the Korean Christian church:

1. Do not treat Christianity as a metaphysical abstraction. Christ actually lived in this world as a human being like us, which makes him a concrete phenomenon.

2. Do not be obsessed with self-centered, individual salvation. Christ lived only for others.

3. Do not be preoccupied with heaven in the other world. Resurrection means living in this world once again, as a new being.

4. Do not seek out God only under dire conditions or when faced with the reality of sin or death. We have to meet Christ amid a happy life of health and hope.

5. Do not pursue immortality in the name of greatness. We have to seek salvation in everyday life.

Actually, Christ Himself epitomizes a normal life on earth. His birth signifies the secularization of God, and He lived a completely secular life. His death was intended for the salvation of the secular world, and His resurrection became a reality through His reappearance in it.

Today, all mankind shares the same goals: freedom, justice, and peace without discrimination on the basis of race, religion, or national origin. This is also the heart of Christian theology. Freedom is the thrust of Christ's salvation, and peace is the basis of the teachings of the gospel. Christ came to this world to save, not to prove or define truth, and to serve, not to be served. Also, Christ came to this world not merely to bring joyous messages from the kingdom of God; He was sent in order that God's purpose would be accomplished on earth as in heaven. All of us, therefore, are invited to join in the making of history and to speed the coming of Christ so the progress and completion of this world may be accomplished through the creation of a heavenly kingdom on earth. This is a society in which the individual and the community are one, a society based on the guarantee of freedom and human rights and love for all. This is also a society in which individual salvation is collective salvation and vice versa and in which the belief of an ordinary person is the same as that of a prophet.

It would be false to say one can love an invisible God when one cannot even love one's neighbors, God's children, who are, after all, quite visible. We cannot say we are taking part in Christ's mission of salvation when we do not get actively involved in the creation of a new world, the paradise on earth, which is God's first purpose in creating a universe with Jesus Christ. If the goal of our religion is to approach God as close as possible, as Kierkegaard said on his deathbed, we should try to imitate Lord Jesus as much as possible. The gospel clearly shows the extent to which Lord Jesus dedicated himself to bringing about justice in this world and also to saving both spiritually and physically the people living in lowliness. His last words were that He would use the sacrifice made by the smallest person as the yardstick for our loyalty to Him.[2]

In the Old Testament, God is portrayed not only as God of love but also as God of wrath, of punishment, and of vengeance. The image of God goes through a metamorphosis, however, with the coming of Jesus. The Old Testament is said to be meaningful as a supplement to the New Testament and thus has no meaning in and of itself. In my opinion, the parts of the New Testament pertaining to the gospel and the letters of the disciples should be read with some care. The letters of the disciples are noteworthy for their otherworldly orientation and the tendency to take bodily and material happiness lightly. In this age in which materialism dominates, we should use once again the spirit of the gospel to dispel certain misconceptions about Christianity both within and outside the church.

I am happy to note in Yun-soo's letter that Dae-hyun attends church with his wife. Actually, I feel sorry for Dae-hyun for a number of reasons. Since his graduation from high school, he has suffered a great deal of pain because of me. I am forever thankful, however, that he understands everything and cares for me. I hold his ability and attitude in high regard. You know very well the special esteem and affection I feel for his wife. I hope you will convey my thanks and best wishes.

2. The Gospel of Matthew, chap. 25.

It appears that three trips a week to Chung-ju are too burdensome for you. Besides, now that your house detention has been lifted, you must have more business to attend to. I want you to reduce the number of trips you make each week from three to two, or have Hong-il or Hong-gul make one trip for you. Make sure you do this so as to safeguard your health.

Do not be concerned; my health is holding up and I am managing as best I can. I am also trying to maintain peace of mind through faith and to develop my inner self. Because faith is not magic, it alone will not help me to overcome my weaknesses completely and all at once. Persistent effort, however, will lead to great accomplishments.

To Hong-il:

I read your letter dated the 15th. It is good that you are paying courtesy calls to the elders, but in the future, I hope you will devote yourself to self-improvement. I have now left politics completely and you should conduct yourself accordingly. The judgment you have demonstrated in the last two or three years is very pleasing and reassuring. I am watching with delight your faith, loyalty to the family, filial piety, judgment, ability, and attitude in overcoming adversity. I am hopeful about your future. From now on, you will have to grow and to work in your father's place because we now face unique circumstances. I want you to work hard to improve yourself in areas where you are still immature. (Be sure to read the books I have listed at the end of this letter, and read them many times until you have digested them. Do this with Hong-up.) Take good care of your wife and children so as to reward them for their hard work and longing for you all this time. Life boils down to challenges and to meeting them. No matter how difficult the challenge, there is always a way to respond to it. Every misfortune, no matter how great, can be changed into good fortune. Anyone who understands this truth and acts on it will surely reap success in life. I hope you will write often.

To Jee-young's mother:

I am so happy that Jee-young and Chung-hwa are rejoicing at the release of their father. I know a load has been taken off your mind also. I am glad you have weathered this trying period so well. In fact, your mother-in-law and Hong-up wrote often about how touched they were by your attitude.

As you know, Hong-gul is a rather detached child, but considering his frequent mention of her in his letters, he must be extremely fond of Jee-young. My wife wrote me that Chung-hwa now can speak well. I want to hear her talk. It may sound as if I am patting myself on the back, but my wife and I are blessed with fine children and have brought them up to the best of our ability. I say this based on the character and piety of Hong-il and Hong-up and their wonderful relationship with their mother, my good fortune in finding a daughter-in-law like you, and your relationship with your mother-in-law, which is like that between mother and daughter. Hong-gul has a good-natured and forthright disposition and is growing to be an independent person. I am thoroughly delighted and content with my children. I hope that you, our first daughter-in-law, will continue to grow and to try to promote friendship and love in the family.

To Hong-up:

Now that your brother has come home and your uncle has been released, you must be very happy and feel your strength renewed. Every time your mother writes, she never fails to mention she is concerned about you and pleased by your genuine and patient attitude. As I wrote you some time ago, it is important for you to remain calm in your present circumstances. If you quietly cultivate inner strength, others who have not undergone the kind of experiences you have will not be able to match your strength when opportunities come. I am not saying all this to flatter you; this has been my own experience. I have confidence in your character and ability. Be persistent once you have set your goals. It is good that you have gotten a driver's license recently, but I am worried all the time. Carelessness and adventurism are to be avoided in driving, and I want you to be alert and prudent.

To Hong-gul:

I wonder how your health is holding up since the examination. Be especially careful about your health. It may be prudent to drink vinegar, if your mother advises; it is supposed to be good for overcoming fatigue and also for preventing various diseases. I have been drinking it. In staying healthy and tough, a positive mental attitude is very important, and faith can also be very helpful. All this is from my own experience.

I am glad you are reading books on strengthening mental power. Stay with it. Do not stop in the middle but forge ahead with conviction. Do not forget I hope that Lord Jesus will always be with you, that you stay healthy, and that you will be able to enter the university of your choice. As the Bible says, move forward with the kind of aggressive faith in which there is the belief that even a mountain can be lifted and moved into the ocean.

I will never stop praying for you every day. Stay healthy and be happy, my beloved Hong-gul.

Religion

1. *The Debates and Decrees of the Second Vatican Council.*
2. Yu Tongsik, *Han'guk Chonggyo wa Kidokkyo* (Korean Religion and Christianity).

3. Walter Nigg, *The Christian Saints.*

4. *Hana ŭi Midŭm.*

History

1. Chindan Hakhoe, *Hanguksa* (7 vols.).

2. Edwin O. Reischauer and John K. Fairbank, *East Asia: The Great Tradition.*

3. Arnold Toynbee, *A Study of History* (an abridged version with illustrations).

Social Sciences and Economics

1. Alvin Toffler, *The Third Wave.*

2. J. J. Servan-Schreiber, *The American Challenge.*

3. W. W. Rostow, *The Process of Economic Growth.*

4. Peter F. Drucker, *The Age of Discontinuity.*

5. J. Kenneth Galbraith, *The Age of Uncertainty.*

6. J. Kenneth Galbraith, *Economics and Public Purposes.*

7. Pyŏn Hyŏngyun, *Han'guk kyŏngjeŭi chindan kwa pansŏng* (The Diagnosis and Reflection on Korean Economy).

8. Gunnar Myrdal, *Against the Stream: Critical Essays on Economics.*

These are books to be read more than two or three times in your lives, so each one of you should keep them as a part of your collection. And be sure not to neglect your own specialized fields or your study of languages.

The Road the Saints March

June 23, 1981

To you with respect and love and to my beloved children:

I am writing this letter as I thank God for the health and well-being you and the rest of the family enjoy. As you said, when the long-awaited visit is over, I am left with loneliness and a feeling of emptiness. Visiting hours are so short there is never enough time to finish one question I wanted to ask or one story I wanted to tell, so every day I anxiously await letters from home and count the days until the day—the only one of the month—I am allowed to write one letter. The letter goes home in my place, passing through the front gate, walking down the steps, entering the porch, and finally going into the living room to sit with the whole family.

It always takes me several hours to write one letter very carefully. It is my way of expressing my concern for you. It is also my earnest hope that our children may learn something from the letter. My health has not changed much since last time. Recently, my leg became swollen and painful for several days, but since yesterday it has begun to get better. Do not be overly concerned. I am jotting down the following thoughts for you and hope they may be of some help to the children.

We are prone to regard people of a century ago as anachronisms and those of one or two thousand years ago as primitive savages. The fact is, however, that mankind today lives within the limits and legacies of the thoughts of Jesus, Socrates, Confucius, and Buddha, all of whom lived sometime between 2,000 and

2,500 years ago. Muhammad lived about 1,400 years ago.

Although modern man has produced a dazzling array of scientific achievements and professional accomplishments, in terms of reflections on truth and happiness in life, he is as dim as a candle before the sun when compared to those of two thousand years ago. Modern scientists, including political scientists, economists, and sociologists, have not been able to offer any meaningful solutions to our problems. A secretary of commerce in the Carter administration in the United States once remarked that "of the countless number of theories advanced by American economists, none provides a genuine prescription for the American economy." This remark applies equally to any other country. There must be several reasons for the decline in the number of great men and the waning influence of professional knowledge in the modern world. I believe that one of the principal reasons has to do with ignoring the need to develop the all-around, whole person. In implementing our approach to life, we must remember both the appearance and the essence of all things, and we must see the parts in relation to the whole and vice versa. By way of analogy, in studying a river, we must understand both surface currents and undercurrents as well as the main stream and tributaries.

Modern man tends to be preoccupied with the surface of the river and with the tributary he has adopted to display his expertise. On this basis, he tries to formulate a judgment about the whole river. Therein lies his failure. We must be able to judge both part and whole, both noumenon and phenomenon, as well as whether a thing is heavy or light, fast or slow. In building our character, we must adopt such an attitude and strive to develop synthetic knowledge. So far as an economist is concerned, no workable policy can be formulated without the benefit of knowledge of politics, society, national culture, and history in addition to economic theory.

In relation to all this, you must remember my frequent advice to my friends: (1) they should read the newspaper thoroughly, from political to cultural and sports news; (2) they should comb through monthly magazines; (3) they should develop awareness of the world by digesting world news; (4) they should be well versed in classical literature in order to be able to absorb the great spiritual legacy of mankind; and (5) in addition to these basics, they should devote greater attention to their own fields of expertise. In the final analysis, a great man is a man with a great amount of knowledge; a great thought can be formulated only on the basis of broad knowledge.

I remember something of relevance to what I have just said. After I was elected to the Sixth National Assembly, I was often quoted as having argued for the need "to possess both the intellectual awareness of problems and the practical sense of a merchant." If we are going to succeed in any field, we must have both feet firmly grounded on principles, like intellectuals, while at the same time making free use of both hands, like merchants employing various methods. We must pursue a balanced development of both these aspects.

There are several paths to the mountaintop. Before we decide which path to take, we must consider carefully. Once a decision is made, there should be no further changes. During the course of climbing, the path we have chosen may seem to be the most treacherous, and the others may seem to be quite easy. There will thus be constant temptations to change course, but one should not succumb to them. Once on the mountaintop, there will be freedom to choose which path to follow on the descent. One who has become an expert economist can move into any other career, such as politics, education, culture, or diplomacy. This is because once a path has been conquered, other paths are found to share the same problems and can be dealt with by the same methods. Through my experience I have come to believe a specialist with ability can easily become a jack-of-all-trades.

In Plato's *Republic*, there is the famous allegory of the cave. It describes the philosophers who retreat into the cave to meditate on truth in perfect concentration. Here they vow to pursue truth alone and live by themselves. A true philosopher, however, descends from the mountain, reluctantly leaving his meditation because of his zeal to enlighten the ignorant masses and thus share happiness with them. Instead of accepting the truth, the masses deride, criticize, and persecute him. In spite of this, the philosopher cannot help but spread the truth. This is an appropriate reference to Plato's mentor, Socrates. Although Socrates was well aware that his effort to educate the morally corrupt citizens of Athens and lead them to truth would arouse their ire, he boldly marched forward. Buddha and Confucius were no exceptions to this rule. Even Buddha had absolutely no intention of teaching the truth after he had learned it. According to Jaspers, however, he could not bear seeing the conditions of the masses and finally rose up to "beat the drum incessantly in this dead world."

Confucius roamed the world in his desire to have his "way" implemented in politics. Even though he was scorned by the authorities of the time as a hangdog, he could not abandon his stubborn hope. It is utterly gratuitous to talk about Jesus Christ in this way. After all, He trod the path of crucifixion and resurrection to deliver mankind, moaning in sin. A saint is not someone who has had the greatest awakening but rather the person who shows great love, who cannot help but share his awakening with those who do not even acknowledge him. All this the saint does, even at the risk of self-sacrifice. What we have to learn from the saints or those who show enormous love is their self-sacrificing concern for neighbors and all people. Even though the masses may not appreciate the virtue of loving one's neighbors, or may be jealous or persecute those who do, the only way to bring our lives in harmony with the lives of the saints is to live only for the love of our neighbors and all people.

I learned from letters from you and Hong-up that the 150th anniversary of the establishment of the Catholic diocese was being celebrated. I agree with you that Catholicism in Korea had a beginning that is unprecedented in the world and that it has had a history of great martyrdom. While we still take pride in our past, we must examine whether we are truly carrying on the spirit of our ancestors, to whom we should feel obligated. According to Toynbee, when, after long persecution, Christianity became legalized by the edict of Milano in A.D. 313, Christians, who then comprised only 10 or 20 percent of the Roman population, brought the Roman Empire to its knees through the power of their great faith. When Russia fell to communism, however, the number of Christians was almost equal to the entire Russian population. Religion thus is a matter of quality, not quantity, which is a fact we should recognize and remember.

Every Christian has a responsibility to proselytize. Today there are great obstacles to carrying out this responsibility among people who are immersed in narcissistic arrogance, people who, because of their belief in the omnipotence of science, are certain of man's power. I shall present a hypothetical dialogue, based on my experience before I was imprisoned, that you and the children might find helpful when engaging in a discussion with nonbelievers. As Saint Paul said, when we confront non-Christians, we have to speak from their point of view to lead them to the path of faith. (A is a Christian and B is a non-Christian.)

A: Choose the right path of life by believing in Christianity!

B: What if I believe in God and He turns out to be nonexistent after I die? It is all the same.

A: That cannot be so. Suppose you did not believe in the existence of God, as you said. Even then, if you have lived your life believing in God who is the greatest entity man knows and who loves us so much and if you have been faithful to His teaching, then you will have lived a very substantial life. Historically, we have accepted great men as models. Why, then, should we regret following in the footsteps of a saint like Jesus? Not believing in Him is not a simple question of not going to heaven after death; it means wasting our lives today.

B: At any rate, there is no proof of God's existence.

A: When you talk about God's existence, are you basing your remarks on any critical thinking, say, at least as much as is required in preparing for a college entrance examination? Several billion people for over two thousand years have believed in Him, and a great number of disciples testified to having met him. A profound spiritual issue such as this cannot be judged on the basis of the incomplete and superficial scientific knowledge claimed by humans. Even Einstein said that a religion that ignores science is superstition, but a science that ignores religion is pure arrogance. If you are genuinely serious, you should be honest about the greatest issue in anyone's life. First, study the religious doctrines of the church. Before you make up your mind about God's existence, have a number of discussions with priests or ministers.

B: Christianity dwells on sin after sin. Why does it have to treat people like sinners and make them feel degraded? Is this not why Nietzsche criticized Christianity as the religion of the infirm?

A: Think about all the things you have done in your life openly or covertly and all the vicious thoughts you have harbored, such as jealousy, hatred, lust, deception, and greed. Just imagine that they were all flashed on a screen in front of you. Even your family would desert you. Human beings are sinners by nature and always harbor sinful thoughts. There is no exception to this, even among the saints. Christ died because of our sins; that is, he died to liberate us from sin so that we all could become free men and women. The proper word is not *degrade* but *liberate.* Nietzsche exerted a great deal of influence by stressing the philosophy of the superman with the will to power. But if you and I calmly examine our inner selves, we know we are too weak physically and mentally to become strong solely on the basis of might. It is only when we meet an absolute power that we can become superhumans. Witness the remarkable superhuman courage of all those men and women, both old and young, who calmly accepted death in the name of their faith in God when Catholics were being persecuted during the latter years of the Yi dynasty.

B: On one hand, Christianity promises salvation through faith, but on the other hand, God is supposed to deal with us according to our deeds on the Day of Judgment. Is this not a contradiction?

A: You would of course feel this to be a contradiction. It is true that faith alone will bring us salvation, regardless of our just deeds. Nevertheless, those who are saved because of their faith, assuming their faith is genuine, will be so thankful for the salvation they have been freely given that they will spontaneously try to live righteously to please God. If they continue their sinful lives, they do not truly believe in God but are only making a mockery of Him. It goes without saying that such behavior should be sternly judged.

B: After having heard all this, I am inclined to believe. But to be candid, I do not want to impose too many limitations on my life because of faith while I am young. After all, as heaven is a place we go after death, it should be all right to start believing in old age.

A: That is very human, straightforward talk. You are absolutely right—*if*, as you say, Christianity means a pass to heaven only after death. But Christianity is a religion that aims to create a heaven on earth by deciding how to spend this very hour freely and happily and how best to serve neighbors and society. The longer you delay your conversion, the more opportunities for freedom, peace, and service you will lose. In the past, some Christians mistakenly emphasized extreme stoicism. God wants us to enjoy a rightful amount of happiness.

To Hong-il and Jee-young's mother:

When I heard about the weak condition of Hong-il's liver, it reminded me of the acute liver infection I suffered in 1965. Overexertion is the worst thing for liver infection. Because your condition is not so acute, you should not be worried as long as you exercise moderately and watch your drinking and smoking. Read again all the letters I wrote while Hong-il was in prison, and find something helpful. As you wrote from Taejon, do not idle away time but continue to try to gain in some way. I hope you will live up to my expectations. As for Jee-young's mother, she should always consult my letters from Seoul and support your efforts toward self-realization. I read Jee-young and Chung-hwa's letter with delight. Wouldn't it be wonderful if we could be together? I am grateful and happy they are growing healthily and nicely.

To Hong-up:

It is well that you attend the minister's prayer meeting with your mother. As you point out, there is little difference between Catholicism and Protestantism in terms of the fundamental belief. The Second Vatican Assembly document, published in 1965, encourages active participation in such meetings. This is the very soul of the ecumenical movement. Be careful when driving.

To Hong-gul:

I am sure you are under a great deal of stress because of your studies. As only half a year is left now, I am praying you will do your best without impairing your health. Avoid excessive pressure and pray to Lord Jesus with faith in the conviction that He is always there to help you. Your father is also praying for you all the time. When you read books about reinforcing mental strength, mark the passages that impress you and read them over again. It might help. I pray that Hyung-joo will be as successful as you by studying diligently. Send him my words of encouragement. Also, send my congratulations to Yun-soo on her baptism.

To you:

Please give my regards to the families of Dae-ui and Dae-hyun, to everyone in the families on your side, and, finally, to everyone in our own family.

Toynbee: Intellectual Mentor

July 29, 1981

To you and my beloved children with love and respect:

I wish from the bottom of my heart for the health of our brothers and sisters, the friends who are staying with our family, and all the other lovely friends who are enduring this unbearable heat. Even though I have been struggling in this sultriness, my health is about what it was at the time of your last visit, so I make a special plea that you stop worrying so much about me and be careful of your own food and health.

By the end of this month I will have been here for half a year, a most difficult and slow-moving period. Yet even in the throes of pain, sorrow, loneliness, and despair, I have found comfort and light in the life of Christ. That comfort has sustained me until today and has restored my strength. I am sure too that the prayers filled with the love of family and friends have also helped.

In this difficult time, I have learned much and have discovered a conviction for Toynbee's philosophy of history. I have read most of his works, as you know. Their principal analytical perspective on historical understanding rests on the view that the colossal drama called the birth, growth, and collapse of civilization is determined by the relationship between challenge and response. Although he never taught me directly, I have always recognized him as my intellectual mentor. I am intending now to determine a response to the challenge of unprecedented adversity now confronting our family and relatives, a response we will not come to regret. While setting my thoughts down on paper, I am thinking of Toynbee's lessons. These notes are meant, first, to strengthen my belief and, next, to be of some aid to you all and the children.

Human beings cannot be dealt with by the natural science theory of causality. In the material world, the same cause will produce the same consequence, irrespective of time and place, but with human beings, because the human spirit can vary so greatly in the response to the same cause, different results occur. Human history is written in terms of examples. Consider two children born into a poverty-stricken family: one slides into the world of corruption and criminality, while the other pushes himself up the road of remarkable success.

Five or six thousand years ago, the rainfall that once covered all of North Africa moved northward toward Europe, leaving the Upper Nile area of Egypt to become desert. The inhabitants responded to this phenomenon in a variety of ways: some followed the rainfall into Europe, only to die from cold; some took shelter underground or started using hides for protection; some migrated to the island of Crete across the ocean; and others moved southward into the primitive jungle. The group that responded most successfully was that which later became the ancestors of Egyptian civilization. They plunged bravely into the swamps of the Nile, which were filled with mosquitos, crocodiles, and snakes. They began in the traditional mode of a hunting and gathering life, but through the laborious processes of measurement, irrigation, and cultivation, they soon developed an advanced practice of agriculture, characterized by sowing and harvesting, and made a unique contribution to building a prosperous and sophisticated civilization in ancient Egypt.

Depending on their imagination and courage, human beings can develop quite different results from a historical condition, and the history of mankind is no more than the stage for this drama of diversity. Nomadic cultures emerged in the steppes of Central Asia and the

Middle East, but there were no signs whatsoever of such cultures in the pampas of North and South America and Australia.

We can witness the same phenomenon in our own history of the Three Dynasties, namely, the success of Silla and the failures of Koguryo and Paekche. At the outset, the latter two held the advantage over Silla because of their proximity to the advanced civilization of the Chinese. The reason Koguryo and Paekche surrendered the laurels of victory to Silla, I believe, was the nature of their responses to Chinese civilization. They absorbed it indiscriminately and to excess, while Silla was not only selective in the adoption of Chinese civilization but also absorbed it within the context of its indigenous, shamanistic culture. Buddhism, for example, first was accepted by the people, then encountered opposition from the aristocracy, which, in turn, produced confrontation and division, including Yi Cha-don's martyrdom. In the end, Buddhism was actively assimilated into the Silla culture when the masses triumphed.

It is said that the universe came into being 15 billion years ago and the earth, some 4.6 billion years ago. Through this vast time, countless numbers of vegetable and animal life have appeared, then disappeared. What remains today is the result of successful responses to every challenge—even a single instance of an abortive response led to the extinction of many species. Humans appeared on Earth about 2 million years ago and *Homo sapiens*, about 30,000 years ago. Many races seem to have perished since, unable to cope with the unpredictable challenges of the environment. It is a historical truism that individuals and societies cannot evade unceasing challenges. Following a successful response, there may be a momentary relaxation until the next challenge, but there can never be a permanent respite. When one becomes a second lieutenant, there is the challenge to become a first lieutenant, and then, yet another challenge to become a captain. Intrinsic to human beings, however, is a tendency to react with an accomplishment once the challenge has been successfully met. In Goethe's *Faust*, when God is asked by Mephistopheles for permission to test Faust, He responds as follows:

> Human activities are prone to be followed by sleep, and human beings thirst for permanent rest. Therefore I gladly place in their world someone who will create work for them by agitation, incitation, and devilish methods.

It appears that humans are fated to weather the storm as an act of God's mercy.

Stability in everyday life is not to be likened to standing motionless in the middle of a living room. Rather, we must firmly remind ourselves that ours should be the kind of stability a passenger feels in riding a fast-moving train.

An expressive and creative response to a challenge does not necessarily guarantee an immediate successful outcome. The most noteworthy response since Adam was that of Christ seeking to grapple with the sins of mankind, but His response seemed in His lifetime to have ended in a miserable failure. The failure, however, was only our momentary misapprehension. Even in our own history, we cannot say that in their lifetimes the six martyred officials, Yi Sun-sin, Ch'oe Su-un, Chŏn Pong-jun, An Chung-gun, Yun Pong-gil, or the persecuted Christian martyrs were successes. Today, however, there is not one Korean who would consider them failures in comparison to others who might have been hailed as great successes in their times.

If these people had never existed, our history would be barren and destitute, and our pride would suffer an immeasurable loss. It is for this reason that we must cure ourselves of the myopic habit of judging the success or failure of our responses within the confines of our own historical moment, a woefully limited duration. Those who meet the challenge in accordance with

God's justice and human conscience may experience temporary setbacks but will never suffer permanent defeat. We have to live with that belief and hold to it as the basis for our lives.

Our responses to history's challenges cannot always lead to instant victories but will, and should, enable us to stay in command of things. For example, our children now face the harsh challenge of exclusion from all the kinds of social activities their peers enjoy. However, if Hong-up and Hong-gul devote themselves to the improvement of their intellectual capacity and the refinement of their personalities, something their peers cannot do because they are busy at work and preoccupied with socializing, they can establish more complete direction of their own fate and will find great success in the future. The history of the Chinese people is a most conspicuous example of how this works. The Chinese were ruled by the Mongols for one hundred years and then by the Manchus for two hundred seventy. Nevertheless, they never compromised spiritually, nor did they allow themselves to be assimilated into the conquerors' cultures. They continued the most marvelous initiatives by turning the given circumstances to their advantage, and as a result, they were able to expand their territory to Inner Mongolia and Sinkiang, while completely sinicizing Manchuria and the Manchu race.

The case of the Diaspora is identical. A rigid response is not necessarily always the most effective. Depending on circumstances, patience may be a more advisable response. The most successful statesmen in history are said to be Kaotsu of the Han dynasty in China and Augustus of Rome, both of whom demonstrated superhuman patience and persistence. This reminds me of Saint Paul, who says in the Bible that patience begets persistence, and persistence, hope.

When we are confronted by an overpowering challenge, it is important for us to have the wisdom and tenacity to wait patiently for circumstances to change. If the Jewish people had not challenged the Roman

Empire so recklessly in A.D. 66, they might have been spared their two-thousand-year ordeal. If the American Indians had not reacted so precipitously, as has been portrayed in movies, today they might have been one of the major ethnic groups in American society.

This has turned out to be an extended essay on challenge and response. You and the children surely understand why I have dwelled so long on this particular point. Let me repeat again that what I have written here is intended, first of all, to help me establish myself.

When you visited me at the military prison in Seoul, we pledged, first, to enrich our spiritual depth; second, to improve ourselves intellectually; and third, to fortify our health. For the half-year since then, I know we have followed through on these pledges. This is indeed fortunate, and I am grateful for the strength you have provided through your faith and love during this time.

My heart always aches when I think about the adversities I have brought on our brothers and relatives on both sides of the family. I was delighted to read in the last letter that you visited the families of our suffering friends. How is Hong-jun's father's ailing leg? A short while ago Hwe-young sent a letter that demonstrated her wisdom, strong belief, and concern for me. I felt like showing the letter to you.

Hyung-joo's father has come here occasionally to present me with certain items. From your letter, I learned about the growing faith of his family, for which I am very thankful. I feel greatly indebted to Hyung-joo's father. I cannot forget his affection for me as well as the sufferings he has experienced on my account since his graduation from high school.

To Hong-il:

I want to add how delighted I am to know that Jee-young and Chung-hwa are growing up to be healthy children. When I saw Jee-young's handwriting last time, I was deeply impressed by the remarkable improvement. Please devote yourself to improving your abilities with a well-thought-out plan. About the matter of the attorneys, please tell your mother not to be too concerned. There is no reason to overdo anything. You must continue to be strict with yourself. The greatest struggle in a person's life is always with oneself. I will say again that I have the very highest expectations for you.

To Jee-young's mother:

I was surprised to learn in your last letter that Hong-il has gained weight. You should be more conscious about his weight than he is himself. From my experience, a wife's frequent reminders are very effective. It is advisable to cut down on rice and meat and rely more on vegetables and fish. Vegetables, fish, rice cooked with mixed cereals, and seaweeds are the fundamental diet for longevity. Do not let up on studying. If a husband is to succeed, the wife has to provide half the resources. Do become a wife who is loved and respected by your husband.

To Hong-up:

I know today is your birthday, and I am writing this note with a congratulatory heart. You are always worrying about your father in your letters, and I am making every effort to lessen your worries about me. I feel pleased and assured that you feel confident about your own affairs. Cope well with everything. You have my confidence.

To Hong-gul:

I am praying every day about you, wondering how strenuous studying must be at this time. What delights me every time I read your letter is your attitude, bracing yourself for the difficult college entrance examination with the conviction that where there is a will, there is a way. As you say, there is no king's way in scholarship. It is best to continue your present level of efforts with this belief. I am waiting to see your face during the August visit. I can tell from your letters that you have good friends. This is one of the greatest assets in life, and it is especially important to have worthy friends when you are young.

1. Choe Namsŏn, *Chosŏn sangsik.*

2. Adam Smith, *Wealth of Nations.*

3. Yun Sŏngbŏm, *Han'guk sasang kwa kidokkyo.*

4. Yu Hongyŏl, *Han'guk ch'ŏnju yohoesa.*

5. Joseph Schumpeter, *Capitalism, Socialism, and Democracy.*

6. Ernest Hemingway, *For Whom the Bell Tolls.*

7. Margaret Mitchell, *Gone with the Wind.*

8. Shima Ryotaro, *Hurusatonatsukajikataku Kokyō wasureji Kataku Kō* (the story of Kojima potters who were kidnapped during the Japanese invasion of Korea in 1592).

9. Hwang Sŏgyŏng, *Ŏdumŭi chasiktŭl.*

For Life in the Twenty-first Century

September 23, 1981

With love and respect to you and my beloved children:

I wonder if all is well with everyone in the family and our friends. When I saw you during your last visit on the 16th, your face looked rather haggard. Have you recovered yet from the hay fever? I am about as well as I can be under the circumstances. I spend the days praying and reading. I am currently reading Bertrand Russell's *The History of Western Philosophy*, Yoo Heung-ryol's *The History of Catholicism in Korea*, J. K. Galbraith's *Life in Our Times*, and Chin Soon-shin's *The Compendium of Eighteen Histories*. As I told you in Seoul, I have read books in theology, philosophy, history, economics, and other areas and have learned a great deal. I am being truthful when I say that the more I read, the more painfully I realize how I have erred in thinking I was knowledgeable. I cannot but regret the months and years I have idled away.

Change that would have taken ten years in the past has now been accelerated into a year's time, and we are about to greet the twenty-first century, in which great changes totally beyond our imagination will no doubt take place. At this juncture, we must emphasize to our children the importance of being adequately prepared. Therefore, although it is certainly an incomplete conclusion, I am forwarding the following thoughts for your reference and also for the benefit of our children.

Let me first survey the history of mankind.

1. The universe is said to have been born about 15 billion years ago, and the earth was formed approximately 4.6 billion years ago. About 4 billion years ago, living organisms emerged on earth in the form of marine plants. Subsequently, through meteorological and other changes, numerous species of animal life and vegetation have evolved and perished. Amid all this, humans appeared relatively recently—only some 2 million years ago. According to anthropological findings, the birthplace of humankind is the eastern part of Africa, bordering on Kenya and Tanzania. *Homo sapiens* finally emerged about 20,000 to 30,000 years ago.

2. Following their evolution, humans first were engaged for an extended period in hunting and gather-

ing. Approximately 8,000 to 9,000 years ago, they brought about the great agricultural revolution. Through agriculture, humans were finally able to settle in one location, increase production, form cities, and build civilization. In order of development, agriculture began in the Mesopotamian region, the northern Nigerian area of western Africa, Southeast Asia, and Central America. The agriculture developed in Mesopotamia was diffused to Egypt, India, China, and Korea, among other places.

3. As agricultural production increased, so did agricultural surplus, which led to the formation of such nonagrarian classes as monarchs, aristocrats, priests, and merchants, which, in turn, was accompanied by the rise of cities. The first cities in history were established in Mesopotamia 5,500 years ago, in the Indus region and Egypt about 4,500 years ago, in China's Yin dynasty 3,500 years ago and, finally, by the Mayan and Incan peoples in the thirteenth century. As a point of reference, we often use the words *culture* and *civilization* interchangeably. But culture consists of the internal and external norms regulating human behavior since the evolution of human beings, and civilization had its origin in the rise of cities. Thus, we may refer to Old Stone Age culture, Copper Age culture, and agrarian culture while we discuss Greek civilization, Indus civilization, Yin civilization, and Western civilization.

4. Following the advent of the Iron Age, which was around the eighth or ninth century B.C., a spiritual revolution took place: the traditionally superstitious, repressive, and primitive religions gave way in one giant leap to a system of thought that was rational, open, sophisticated, and commonsensical. From the eighth century to the third century B.C., such spiritual revolutions occurred in four places, and their influence continues even today. In China, a variety of philosophical systems arose, including Confucianism

and Taoism. Earlier systems of thought from the era of warring dynasties maintained their intellectual vigor until the first century B.C., when the Wu emperor of the Han dynasty adopted Confucianism as the official state religion. The thought systems of China share an emphasis on internalizing the Tao through ethical practice.

In India, Buddha came forward to bring down the superstition and class system of the Brahmin religion. He carried out a religious revolution whose principal message involved rationality and equality and whose most distinctive feature was the belief in the possibility of passage to nirvana through speculative meditation.

In Greece, the Miletos and the Teles schools, with their focus on nature, arose in the sixth century B.C. Subsequently, in the fourth century B.C., Socrates and Plato formulated their philosophies of man. Aristotle synthesized these two philosophical traditions into a metaphysics that later became the most influential philosophy of the human mind. The nature of the ideal was the ultimate objective of this philosophical inquiry, which adopted empiricism as its methodology.

As the phrase "the Yahweh of all forces" indicates, the Hebrews regarded God as the God of War who protected them from external enemies. Their faith underwent a grave crisis with the collapse of the kingdom of Israel in the eighth century B.C. and the fall of the kingdom of Judah in the sixth century B.C. The question confronting them at that time was whether they should abandon Yahweh, who had failed to protect them from their enemies. About this time, prophets such as Jeremiah and Ezekiel came forward to say that the fall of Israel and Judah was God's loving test for their betrayal of Him, that God was the God not only of Israel and Judah but the universal God who built Assyria, Babylonia, and Persia and that God's love was always constant in spite of any adversities. (Of course, such prophets as Amos, Hosea, and Isaiah have already tried to prevent the destruction of their country.) They thus revolutionized the religion. This fresh beginning of Judaism was completed by the arrival of Jesus, and it subsequently became a universal religion.

5. The anthropological, agrarian, urban, and spiritual revolutions eventually gave birth to the scientific and technological revolutions of the seventeenth century. The Copernican theory and Kepler's three principles of planetary movement reached Galileo, who developed them further into the modern science that later made such great advances with Newton. Thus, mankind moved into the eighteenth century to experience the industrial revolution as well as the golden age of philosophy, then into the nineteenth century, which ushered in modern technological civilization, and finally into the twentieth century. The greatest scientific discoveries of the twentieth century are considered to be Einstein's theory of relativity and Planck's quantum theory; these two theories not only revolutionized physics but also shook the foundation of the world of ideas. The former changed the conception of time and space and forced the revision of the Newtonian theory of gravity. The latter established the significance of probabilistic necessity in the quantum world, rejecting the law of causation, which had hitherto been the conceptual basis for scientific explorations as well as the strongest weapon of atheism.

By any measure, scientific progress in the twentieth century has been dramatic and drastic, its pace and scope unprecedented in the history of mankind. In today's world we experience spiritual confusion and turbulence unknown to our ancestors. It is extremely important for us to understand accurately the character of our age and to be as certain as possible about our future prospects. Only then can we attain mental stability in this era of uncertainty and maintain the proper perspective on our lives.

6. My personal characterizations of the twentieth century include, first, the continuation of drastic changes, as exemplified by the fact that no new inventions, weapons, or fashions seem to have lasted more than a decade.

Second, we now possess, for the first time, the economic and technological capacity to create (should we desire) a world in which there is a proper distribution of wealth. For example, the nations of the world are spending a total of $460 billion every year for military purposes, while aid to the Third World amounts to no more than $30 billion. If global military expenditures were turned to promoting the welfare of Third World people, we would have more than sufficient capacity to overcome poverty and create a happy life for the entire human race by the end of this century.

Third, again for the first time, the highly developed transportation, communication, and information media have made everyone on earth feel that they are members of one community.

Fourth, these material and technological changes are abruptly and radically changing human values and ideas. Religion is faced with a grave challenge, and philosophy has shown a readiness to delve into the meaning of life and the mysteries of the universe on a scientific basis. The emergence of the scientific theories of noumenon, scientific empiricism, and scientific philosophy are all part of this trend.

Fifth, in the midst of all this, we face three tests that can determine our fate: the threat of nuclear holocaust, which, given the current nuclear stockpiles, can annihilate the entire human race seven times over; the population explosion, which will reach 6.3 billion by the end of the twentieth century and then double to 130 billion by the twenty-first century; and the depletion of natural resources and large-scale pollution of the environment. These problems will be largely, indeed decisively, influenced by our wisdom and, in particular, by developments in East-West and North-South relations. There exist a number of pessimistic views about the future, but confronted with the issue of survival, I expect the human race will arrive safely at the twenty-first century through mutual understanding, reason, wisdom, and public opinion.

Predicting the future is a hazardous task, needless to say; in the strictest sense, it is an impossible one. This is because, unlike the natural world, which moves mechanically, the history of mankind is not predetermined but flows according to unpredictable free will. It appears to me, however, that the following can be stated with some certainty. (1) The twenty-first century will welcome the age of the global village. Any place on earth can be reached in a matter of hours, and instant communications will become possible. The entire globe will be connected by a system of communications and transportation that will make it a reality. Any information about any place in the world will be obtained even more quickly and easily than domestic information now can be. (2) The twenty-first century will be the age of the global citizen. The human race will come to speak a common, universal language, and massive migration will result in the cohabitation of all races in any country. Interracial marriage will be a commonplace, and while the uniqueness of a race may be preserved and indigenous cultures respected, the age of our self-centered nationalism will give way to an age of universalism. (3) The monopoly of privilege and wealth held by the advanced nations today will dissolve, as will racial and regional discrimination. Such a trend will be attributable not so much to the goodwill of the advanced nations as to the power of the developing countries. (4) Hard work and long labor will be eliminated in all industrial areas and will be taken over by automation. People in the twenty-first century will face a critical task in deciding on the worthwhile use of leisure time. It seems possible that labor may even be considered the same as sports or hobbies. (5) The twenty-first century will become the space age that everyone expects. A large number of people and industries will be relocated in cities in space, and the question will be answered as to whether life exists on other planets, and if so, what types of life exist. Astronomy, which can observe only one-tenth of the Solar System today or view the distance of approximately one billion light years, will be able to bring the entire Solar System under its observation and unveil its deepest mysteries. (6) The twenty-first century will also become the maritime age. Cities built on water, mariculture, and the full use of marine resources will be developed on the oceans of the world like newly formed nations. (7) The twenty-first century will be a trying period for religion. We have to make sure that the church does not repeat the stupidity of trying to repress developments like the Copernican system or evolutionary theory. The church is obligated to accept all scientific progress as part of the evolutionary process according to the will of God, and it should provide moral support to all these advances. As a genuinely global religion, the church must be able to offer shelter to the human spirit that is unsettled in the vortex of material civilization and technological development. Most of all, it must entirely fulfill its role as the guardian of human freedom, justice, and peace and stand as spiritual precursor in making them accessible not partially but universally. This is the way to fully live up to the mission of the church in accordance with God's will. (8) In the twenty-first century there will be political and social changes that simply cannot be imagined at this juncture. It does not seem likely, however, that there will emerge a regimented society in which humans are destroyed by the machine and held at bay in slavery such as Aldous Huxley envisioned in his *Brave New World.* I believe it to be much more likely instead that an era of popular freedom and justice will come into being, an age in which, for the first time in our history, human beings will be able to make maximum use of their personal characteristics and abilities under conditions of equality of education and a secure economic life. It goes without saying that this will require our efforts and sacrifice, especially for posterity.

My intent in this letter is different from my intent in previous ones. It may seem somewhat remote from reality, but I am writing in the belief that to keep our eyes on the prospects of the distant future is to live more, rather than less, meaningful and faithful lives because it keeps our thoughts fixed on the future of our children. I hope too that the brief survey in these pages will help us to understand history in the proper context.

I can tell that Dae-hyun has been coming down here frequently by the sales slips for the items purchased for me at the prison store. Please tell him to find something worthwhile to do even under these circumstances so that his life can be meaningful.

I am spending each day here with the feeling that I have made an agreement with Hong-il, Jee-Young's mother, and Hong-up that we will keep pace with one another in terms of our progress in belief, learning, and health. I hope they are managing their affairs well. In one of the letters Hong-il sent me from Taejon Prison, he said, "It would be mortifying to have spent all this time here if I have failed to gain anything at all while here." At that time, I could not have agreed with him more. I hope he lives in the same spirit now that he has been released. Let us all try to gain something from this period.

I was extremely pleased with the high mark Hong-gul received on his athletic report. I am earnestly praying for him to attain his goals through conviction, diligence, and intelligent studying methods.

Please tell Jee-young and Chung-hwa that their grandfather is always thinking about them, that he wants to see them, and that they should learn a lot of songs and dances and should get along well with their siblings.

I received a letter from Hong-min. It was a fine letter that was mature in its tone, and it made me very happy.

I received two letters from Hwe-young. Learning that she could not accept an invitation to go to the beach because she was thinking about me makes my heart ache for the child. I hope all of you will not withdraw from too many activities on my account.

Please do send me the following titles:

1. Friedrich Nietzsche, *Ecce Homo*.

2. Raymond Aron, *Introduction to the Philosophy of History* (Hongsŏng-sa).

3. *An English-Korean Dictionary* (single volume) (Miguk Publishing Co.).

4. A world encyclopedia (single volume; anything recently published in Korea).

5. Yi Mangap, *Han'guk sahŏe* (Korean Society) (Tarakwŏn).

6. Chin Sunsin, *Chunggugin kwa Ilbonin* (Chinese and Japanese) (Tarakwŏn).

7. Ezra Vogel, Jr., *Japan as No. 1* (Tarakwŏn).

8. Sin Yongsŏk, *Yurŏp hapchunguk* (The Corporate Europe).

9. Charles Dickens, *A Tale of Two Cities*.

10. Stendhal, *The Red and the Black.*

11. Leo Tolstoy, *War and Peace* (in English; I have it at home).

12. Ernest Hemingway, *The Old Man and the Sea* (in English; I have it at home).

The Strengths and Shortcomings of Our Nation

September 30, 1981

With love and respect to you and my beloved children:

Because my August letter did not reach you, I asked the prison authorities for permission to write another. From your letter and from Hong-up's, I have learned that the climbing roses, the Rose of Sharon, and the other flowers in the yard have all blossomed. Their images are vivid, and I have the most urgent wish to see them. I hear also that the jujubes have ripened. Hong-gul must be very happy. I am sure he is sharing them with Jee-young and Chung-hwa.

On the exercise ground here, there is an elongated flower bed. These days, after their full bloom, the cockscombs and China asters are withering. Because I tended them with the greatest care during my exercise time, the flowers in my area were in fuller bloom than those elsewhere. This was the happiest part of my daily routine. My greatest anticipation these days is to see the chrysanthemums bloom.

In my letter of the 23d, I wrote about the history of mankind, but today I want to jot down some observations on the strengths and shortcomings of our nation, based on my reading of our own history. Our greatest strength has been the astounding ability to maintain independence for 1,300 years—from the time of the unification under Silla until the Japanese occupation in 1910. This record is unparalleled in world history.

Among the great nations in the world, China was ruled by foreign influences for several hundred years during the Yuan and Ch'ing dynasties. As for India, its entire history has been in the hands of alien races, except for several hundred years of autonomy under two dynasties, the Maurya in the fourth century B.C. and the Gupta in the fourth century A.D. Egypt also was chained to foreign domination for more than two thousand years, following the conquest by Alexander the Great in the fourth century B.C. We are also aware of the conquests of England by Rome, the Danes, and the Normans, the similar fate of France, and the foreign domination and internal fragmentation of Germany and Italy until their unification in the mid-nineteenth century.

We have been situated geographically such that we have been a target of continuing invasion by the Continental powers. The T'ang dynasty's imperialistic designs, the invasion by the Kuran, the troubles during the Mongol conquests, and the horrifying attacks by the Japanese in the year of Imjin and by the Chinese in the year of Byungja are only a few of the examples of foreign invasions. All this notwithstanding, we have been able to maintain our independence—a truly miraculous accomplishment. When we consider the sinicization of the Mongols and the Manchus, who once reigned supreme in all of China, it is indeed a miracle that we have not been annexed by China as part of its defensive rampart. This makes us realize once again the great reserve strength of our ancestors.

We tend to treat any signs of dependency on foreign powers as shameful. But one American scholar who has the benefit of an objective and broad view of world history has commented that such a tendency in Korea reflects the prudent wisdom to survive when faced with the pressure of the Continental powers. Even though our nation formally adapted to foreign influences, our people have stoutly preserved their identity. Despite the overwhelming influence of Chinese civilization, for example, we have retained unique characteristics in our culture. We have kept a distinct life-style in such things as clothing, food, language, and shelter and have completely prevented the penetration and domination by the notorious overseas Chinese. When we observe in many Southeast Asian countries that economic dominance is still in the hands of the overseas Chinese, we have to be grateful to our ancestors.

We also have to acknowledge our ancestors for their intense desire for learning. Although we belong in the hemisphere of Chinese civilization, we do not by any means lag behind China in terms of our levels of education and culture. Such a tradition of independence has given us the resourcefulness to join the ranks of the middle-tier nations, such as Hong Kong, Taiwan, and Singapore, all of which are also located within the sphere of Chinese influence.

Our nation has proven itself to be quite capable of assimilating others. For example, a great portion of Pyŏngyang and Hamgyung provinces was completely incorporated during the period of King Sejong, and other ethnic groups, such as the Yo, who once were settled there have been assimilated without a trace. Until a short time ago, the so-called social outcasts like butchers and shamans were segregated from the rest of society, and domestic servants comprised 20 to 30 percent of the population. Today, however, they have all been so thoroughly integrated that the former class distinctions are nowhere evident. This is a welcome national change from the standpoint of humanitarian and democratic concerns. Japan still discriminates against the Burakumin, their version of an outcast class, and they have not yet accepted as citizens the descendants of those of our ancestors who were forcibly taken to Japan during the Japanese Imjin invasion. When we compare ourselves to the Japanese, we have to feel proud.

There is little doubt about the intelligence and competence of our people. Take the examples of Saint Wŏnhyo or Master Yulgok, who synthesized from a Korean base the tenets of Buddhism and Confucianism, which originated in China. Such qualities are also manifest in the creation of the Korean alphabet, in the invention of printing, and in the autonomous development of pottery. Overall, the great potential of our people can be documented from a comparative ethnological standpoint in terms of our recent achievements at home and abroad.

We have shortcomings, however, that stand in rather shameful contrast to our strengths. First, our political culture is narrow-minded and lacking in magnanimity. The Confucian politics of the Yi dynasty were typical of this. Confucianism drastically affected Buddhism, a religion that had had a long tradition in our folk history; it crushed Tonghak, a newly emerging religion in the nineteenth century. Furthermore, Catholicism, which had played a decisive role in the modernization of our nation, was subjected to brutal persecution for nearly one hundred years, during which time some ten thousand Catholics were murdered. Even within Confucian circles, all but the narrowest orthodoxy was tightly suppressed. The heterodox were called unruly adversaries who were defiling the credo. In addition, the orthodox circle itself was divided by the most frivolous disputes about etiquette into the four-way strife among the Southern, the Northern, the Old Theory, and the New Theory factions. These factions engaged in the most vengeful eye-for-an-eye conflict right up until the very last day of the dynasty. Although this factional intolerance was not an attribute of the entire nation but rather the pernicious habit of the ruling Yangban class, those of us who share certain objectives nevertheless point with regret to the fact that such an unfortunate tradition has continued to poison our society today.

Second, although our nation has distinguished itself

in preserving its fundamental attributes, it is quite lacking in progressive tendencies. Our history abounds in conclusive proofs. For example, King Changsu of Koguryo moved the capital from Kungnaesŏng, located across the Yalu, to Pyŏngyang, which is on the peninsula. When Silla unified the peninsula, it voluntarily relinquished the eastern half of the Manchurian lands to the north of Taedong River and would not budge an inch northward in the location of the traditional capital city of Kyongju. Finally, even though Yi Sung'gye participated personally in the northward policy of the Koryo dynasty in its last years, he moved the capital south of Kaesong, misled as he was by the superstition against the north.

In spite of the fact that our country faces the ocean on three sides, we have refused almost completely to recognize this reality. This is why we have been bothered so persistently by the Japanese. If we were to try to identify great navigators or others engaged in maritime activities, Chang Po-go from the late Silla period is about the only one who comes to mind. Furthermore, even scholars of the Silhak school such as Yu Hyung-won, Yi Ik, Hong Tae-yong, Park Che-ga, Pak Chi-won, and Chung Yak-yong, men who were the intellectual pioneers of their times, left behind a great number of books but never thought to write them in the Korean language so as to make them accessible to the Korean people. Thus, we can clearly see how antiprogressive our orientations have been. It may be said, however, that our nation has been exhibiting substantial changes recently. You may remember that during my April 26 speech at the Kwanhun Club last year, when asked about President Park's accomplishments, I pointed out the infusion of a progressive spirit into our nation.

Third, we can take note of the formalist tendencies of our nation. We are so concerned with formal appearances that we quite disregard practical benefits, while our excessive sensitivity to the issue of losing face often leads us to pretensions that we cannot sustain and ultimately to waste. This sort of formalism only aggravates bureaucratic abuses and serves as a major suppressant of creativity.

Fourth, our nation lacks seriousness. We are a nation characterized by strongly optimistic traits, but at the same time we lack the desire to reflect seriously on life and things. As a result, we have a weak philosophical tradition. Even religion, whether Buddhism or Confucianism, tends toward a search for happiness and enjoyment in this world, which perhaps explains its readiness to form an alliance with shamanism. These tendencies and abuses can be observed commonly even in today's Christian faith.

I have thus far outlined the strengths and shortcomings of our nation as I see them. When we put them on a balance sheet, we can see that our nation has basic strengths that put it shoulder-to-shoulder with other nations but also that it is not a unique nation either. What we can conclude is that, in view of our overall qualifications, heritage, and abilities, we should endeavor persistently to reinforce our strengths while cutting down on our shortcomings. By doing so, I believe we will be able to join the ranks of advanced nations by the end of the 1980s and work toward unification with confidence.

Considering the historical disintegrative process that started in the middle period of the Yi dynasty, it is most imperative that we establish a foundation for national conciliation and mutual cooperation through our own temperament, magnanimity, and understanding. Without these, we cannot hope to clear the record so we can make a fresh beginning and move into the future with giant steps.

I write down the following fragments of my feelings of late.

Jaspers discusses the respective attitudes of Confucius, Buddha, Socrates, and Jesus toward sin.

Confucius admonished us to face good with good and evil with justice. Buddha preached patience and benevolence in the face of evil, and Socrates said that it would not be just to confront evil with evil. Jesus advised us to forgive and love our enemies and pray for them. Interesting and edifying differences, indeed.

Faith is a sort of decision, a willful decision. We know and feel the existence of God either through reason or emotions but cannot produce any scientific and objective proof of it, nor can we observe God. In the final analysis, it is necessary simply to wager one's own fate on the existence of God. But then it seems everything about life comes down to risky decisions. We can make only the best possible decisions about marriage, the choice of occupation, and everyday life. Faith appears to me to be the process of life whereby we live every day, making decisions and moving forward.

The theologian Paul Tillich suggested that faith seems to be devoting oneself to discovering the ultimate meaning of the self; in other words, dedicating oneself totally to appreciating how worthwhile living is. In this sense, everyone may be said to be faithful and religious. For example, one who does not have any religious belief in the normal sense nevertheless cherishes money as an object of faith if he is engrossed in money-making. Those who pursue power and glory must derive their faith from those attributes. One who intends to spend one's life in a roundabout fashion must have such an orientation as an article of faith.

As human beings, we are destined to search for the ultimate basis of life. If there are differences in this search, they lie only in matters of degree rather than substance. Viewed in this light, the way to feel happiness is to share with others a belief in the One who gave us the greatest example of love in the history of mankind.

According to Toynbee, God is the God of Justice and the God of Virtue. God cannot be omnipotent, however, because if God were indeed so, He could not have created injustice in opposition to justice and evil in conflict with good. To insist on divine omnipotence is to imply that God is not the God of Justice nor the God of Virtue.

Bertrand Russell made a similar statement in his discussion of Christianity in the context of Plato's philosophical theories. I am not able to compare a complete explanation of this matter and would like you to write to me about it later with your thoughts or the views of our minister or priest.

When we study or make plans, we often get interrupted and are apt to be disappointed and drop the plan. I have encountered many such failures. Since March 1976, however, I have changed my attitude and now remain unperturbed even if the plan gets interrupted. If my effort becomes suspended, I simply pick up where I left it when I can. This has become my practice now. For example, I have added new daily routines of reading, studying languages, and calisthenics morning and evening, and I have stayed with them consistently. What is important here is to maintain composure even when things go wrong and to have the tenacity to start over again and again.

As I wrote to you on the 23d, I have been worried about your hay fever. You are the pillar of our family and so you should take special care of yourself and stay healthy. I am very thankful and happy that Hong-il did such a wonderful job on your birthday on the 21st.

Please send me some appropriate titles in literary criticism of classical literature.

Of the two blankets you sent me, I have returned one because I did not quite like it. Please return it and send me another one, the kind that I mentioned during your last visit. I particularly did not like the color.

I imagine Hwe-sook will be married soon. Please convey my heartfelt congratulations and pray for her happiness. I feel saddened that I cannot witness the wedding.

Grandma Park,[1] Dr. Chang's wife,[2] and Grandma Soon-chun,[3] Hong-il's grandmother-in-law—to all these people I send my regards. I am grateful for their prayers.

I wonder if all is well with brother's family at Hawi Island.[4] I am certain that you communicated with them during Ch'usŏk. If you have any news, please let me know.

As there are only two months left until the entrance examinations, I anxiously hope that Hong-gul will do his best without losing his composure. I was delighted to hear from your letter that he is studying diligently.

Individual and Social Salvation

October 28, 1981

To you and my beloved children with love and respect:

Today is chilly again, and it looks as if we are going to have another cold winter. I am taking care of my health as the family wishes. My physical condition remains about the same as I described during your visit. My life here is taken up largely by reading—currently, the *Wealth of Nations*, Jame Cohn's *God of the Oppressed*, Bertrand Russell's *The History of Western Philosophy*, and *War and Peace*, all in English editions.

1. Madam Park Soon-chun.
2. The widow of Dr. Chang Myon.
3. An old woman who did everything to care for the author.
4. The author's oldest brother's family. The brother died, and his family was at the author's birthplace, Hawi township in Shinan County.

When I go out to the yard for exercise, I find chrysanthemums in full bloom but all in one color, yellow. The flowers I tended seemed to blossom with a fresh radiance and lasted almost a month longer than the others. It may have been because of my affectionate attentions, but I feel proud and thankful. Every time I tend the flowers, I remember working on the flower bed at home, and when you send me news about the flowers, I can picture them clearly. My yearning for them pierces my heart. There are times when I miss the dogs terribly, especially Smarty. It is such a help to me that you always manage to send the books you have selected with such care. More than anything else, I thank God for the good health you continue to enjoy. When I think about what we have gone through since last year, it is a miracle you are as healthy and mentally strong as you are today. I feel even more strongly that I am witnessing the proof of Christ's consummate love for us. I pray that you and the rest of the family will attain greater spiritual depth, further intellectual growth, and keep up your good health. I am very curious about how the Catholic conference on the 18th went. Please let me know. For a number of reasons, I think you should have attended it, setting everything else aside, since you received an invitation. I think you missed a good opportunity. Of course, I am not well informed about the state of things outside, and I do believe that you and the children exercised the best possible judgment. Keep me informed as fully as possible about Hong-gul's situation.

To Hong-il and Jee-young's mother:

You seem to come down with colds quite often. I hope you will be very careful. Children are particularly prone to catching cold when they are sleeping. You should check on them often at night to make sure that they are covered up. Judging from his letters, I am surprised and delighted by Jee-young's excellent penmanship. She may very well turn out to be the real intellectual in the family. Take good care of her. I hear that Chung-hwa has gotten prettier. I miss her a great deal. She will be loved by everyone and happy in the future. I am happy and thankful that Jee-young's mother and the rest of the family were baptized during Christmas. That has taken care of one of my concerns. I hope everything will work out well for Hong-il. Do not let go of books, and be stubborn if you have to in working to improve yourself. Send my regards to the old nun in Taegu, and give her pocket money as often as possible. She has retired and must be lonelier than she used to be.

To Hong-up:

I feel that I am always in your debt, and at the same time I feel concerned about you. It will be very good for you to start a family. I do know how you feel, and even though I am not around, I trust you will make a decision if you come upon the appropriate opportunity. No matter what your ultimate decision, stay with your plan. If your plans are thrown off course, pick yourself up and continue. Your father is in his present circumstances through that approach. It will help you in your studying if you choose the necessary subjects from your college days and read through relevant literature as if you were reviewing it for the end of the term. Never drive on a snowy day. Read the Bible, in particular, the Gospels. Pray to God, seeking His help in understanding the right causes. This is my experience.

To Hong-gul:

I see from your recent letters that your academic performance and your confidence have been improving.

Your mature, self-assured letters make me feel pleased and proud. I know it is no easy matter to feel that way with the examination only one month away, but your recent letters have helped me feel much more relaxed about it. Above all else, stay calm and do your best. Maintain your mental strength, and do not doubt that God is always with you and will assist you. I pray morning and evening for your success and Hyung-joo's on the examinations. Stay healthy.

When I reflect on all that has happened during the last year, when I read in your letters about your thankful prayers, and especially when I hear about the revelation of Lord Jesus that you described to me during your visit on the 16th, I realize even more keenly the boundlessly great and earnest love of Jesus. The more I love Lord Jesus, the more I love the church. The more I love the church, the more ardent my desire becomes that our church should demonstrate the existence of Jesus and become a place where, by witnessing our faith and by our actions, other people may come to know, love, and believe in Jesus. When we look at history, however, there are many instances in which the church has failed to carry out its mission completely. Among these failures, I can mention the suppression of reason by the church in the Middle Ages, the bloody struggle and confrontation between the old and the new churches since the Reformation, and the indifferent and uncooperative position of the modern church regarding humanitarian social reforms. These seem to be the main reasons for the precipitous decay of faith in the Western hemisphere as well as the great decline in the authority of the church throughout the world. Among these issues, social progress and reform still remain the most pressing questions for the church—questions that all peoples of the world, believers and nonbelievers alike, are raising. The church's position on this problem demands our most urgent attention at this point in history. I will note a few of my opinions on this problem in the space that follows.

As I have said on other occasions, the Christian has the dual mission of individual and social salvation. Historically, however, we have focused more on the former, following the proselytizing of the disciples, and such a tendency still prevails in many churches today. The church sometimes gives the impression of an entity that is totally sheltered from the world, a lone boat drifting away from the mainstream of society. When we read the Bible with care and with God's guidance, however, we readily find the great importance God finds in the material and physical aspects of this world. We also see the degree to which Jesus emphasized their salvation.

In the Old Testament we note the following. (1) In Genesis, when God created this world, He was delighted and congratulated Himself because it was a pleasure in His sight. In creating the body and soul of humans and in governing all things on earth, He established in His providence that happiness be a life dedicated to upholding God's will. For this reason, it would be a refusal to acknowledge the purpose of Divine Creation if we were to regard lightly the material and physical aspects of this world. (2) The central figure in the Old Testament clearly is Moses. God has Moses liberate the nation of Israel from their labor and suffering under the pharaoh. Further, He protected the rights of widows, orphans, and vagabonds and provided the Sabbath day and year even to servants and herdsmen. The realization of God's justice on this earth is an enterprise that has its origin in the Old Testament. (3) When social justice had been annihilated in the kingdoms of Israel and Judah, when the powerless were crying out under supression and exploitation, such prophets as Hosea, Amos, Micah, Jeremiah, and Isaiah arose, in turn, to declare that injustice was disobedience and indeed a challenge to God's will. They made clear that destruction would be the punishment. (4) As we know, the Old Testament contains virtually no references to the other world. God's words as well as all entreaties to Him center on grace and punishment in this world. It was only in the last days of the Old Testament period, long after the return from Babylon, that the question of the other world began to be raised in earnest. As you know, God is the God of history, a living God who is always with us. How can such a God disregard life in this world? Everything on earth acts out God's drama, whose stage is history and for which we humans are a supporting cast. This drama must have as its object the perfection of this world and of human beings.

When we read the New Testament, we can first witness the reason for the coming of God through the incarnation of Christ in human form. As Jesus Christ made unequivocal, He came to this world to perfect the Old Testament, that is, the Commandments. He came to repeal those clauses of the Commandments which are inappropriate and to revive and perfect the other parts that had been neglected. Consider, for example, Mary's songs (the Gospel of Luke 1:49–52); the reading of the letters of Isaiah by Jesus (the Gospel of Luke 4:18–19); the declaration of the kingdom of the poor (the Gospel of Luke 6:20); and those who are destined for heaven and for hell (the Gospel of Matthew 25:31ff.). There is little doubt that Lord Jesus came to declare the liberation of the jailed, restore sight to the blind, give freedom to the oppressed, announce the year of the Lord's grace, and propagate the gospel to the impoverished. He came to visit not just men but the guilty and not to be served but to serve the lowliest people. All in all, he came to fill this world with the loving gifts of God, which are freedom, justice, and peace. This is the very reason God sent His son out of His love for this world. Another reason for the coming of Jesus is His mission to invite human beings and their world to enjoy the freedom of the heavenly kingdom, transcending the earthly freedom, or historical freedom, à la Exodus. These two form the true reasons for the incarnation of Jesus, His suffering on the cross, and resurrection. He declared that His invitation places innocent people ahead of pretentious people and the poor, the guilty, and the prostitutes ahead of those who claim to be just.

Lord Jesus was born of humble origin, lived a humble life, befriended humble people, and died a humble death. Lord Jesus devoted His life to the people of earth. He cured countless sick, blind, and deaf people, lepers, cripples, and the possessed, and He forgave prostitutes. He not only cured their sickness but, in the process of curing, delivered to them the gospel of the heavenly kingdom and helped them perfect their humanity by enlightening them as to human integrity and freedom. Through the miracle of the loaves and fish, whereby He fed five thousand people, and His commandments to the rich to distribute their properties to the poor, He emphasized the importance of material life.

As you know, of the prayers the Lord himself taught us, the only one extant is in the Gospel of Matthew 6:7–15, which is as follows:

> . . . .
> may your Kingdom come;
> may your will be done on
>   earth as it is in heaven.
> Give us today the food we
>   need.

From the above, we can understand God's will as manifested in the Old Testament and the New Testament, that is, how much value He placed on our life and happiness in this world. Historically, Christianity has dismissed as vulgar this-worldly, material, and physical orientations. This prevalent tendency is not only a fallacy contrary to the gospel and remote from

God's will but also an obstruction, whether deliberate or unwitting, to social progress and the realization of happiness for the masses. This has become the greatest cause for criticism and rejection of the church and the defilement of God in modern times. It is inconceivable, after all, that one who cannot become a good citizen on earth, faithfully upholding God's will, could become a good citizen in the kingdom of heaven.

According to one prominent historian, mankind perpetrated four great sins when it entered into the civilized epoch: first, wars in which humans kill humans; second, humans enslaving other humans; third, humans exploiting other humans; and fourth, humans racially discriminating against other humans. He proceeded to note that from today's standpoint, except for wars, exploitation, slavery, and racial discrimination have either disappeared or are fated to be eliminated if the present trend continues. What he has to say after this is something that we Christians cannot hear without feeling great shame and pain. He notes that these improvements are the result of humanitarian, social, and political movements carried out in Western societies in modern times. Their moral foundation is derived from the Christian spirit. The motivating force of these changes was not the Christian church, however, but enlightened intellectuals and their followers, who were disenchanted by the state of the Christian church. We cannot write them off as inaccurate contentions when we look at history objectively. How much shame and disappointment has our church caused Lord Jesus? If our church had only carried out correctly the teaching of Christ, how could communism have expanded its power? How could the phenomenon of atheism have gained such widespread popularity in traditionally Christian countries?

A Christian believer will certainly transcend the secular world at some point, but he will be born again within the Holy Spirit to be involved in the improvement and perfection of this world and the loving care of neighbors, according to Christ's will. We dedicate our minds and bodies to Christ's purpose so as to facilitate the arrival of God's kingdom on this earth and the day of Christ's second coming. In this regard, I acknowledge the immense theological contribution of Father Teilhard de Chardin.

I know that this sort of awakening is increasing in the Protestant church. In the Catholic church, there have been great turnabouts since the Second Vatican Assembly in the 1960s, and John Paul II defined the church as the guardian of justice and peace. Seen against the backdrop of the urgent and irrepressible demands of the times, however, the positions of both the old and new churches leave much to be desired. The church should not be dragged into reform movements but should be a central force for reform.

It should be unequivocally stressed here that the church's participation in social freedom, justice, and peace should be regulated by spiritual and moral guidelines; it should never get involved because of its own political or social interests. This is taboo. If the church becomes engaged in political activities or allies itself with a particular political power, it will lead to the corruption and destruction of the church and spell disaster for society as well. Social reforms without Christ in view, however, can produce only misfortune and corruption amid affluence, as has happened in Europe. Affluence not accompanied by the moral perfection of society and the fulfillment of human potential by individuals cannot mean happiness.

I have written all this out of my restless mind, thinking about Jesus. In the end, however, Christ will triumph and paradise will be built on earth.

Send me the following titles:

1. André Maurois, *A History of France.*

2. Raymond Aron, *Introduction to the Philosophy of History.*

3. Karl Jaspers, *Philosophical Faith and Revelation.* (Ewha Women's College Press).

4. So Hŭngyŏl, *Nolli wa sago* (Logic and Conception) (Ewha Women's College Press).

5. Leo Lowenthal, *Literature and the Image of Man* (Ewha Women's College Press).

6. The world encyclopedia I got last time lacks maps on the provincial level, and its content is not satisfactory; please send another one.

7. Can I have a book on philosophy, economy, or sociology, perhaps structured like *The Great Literary Works and the Analyses of Their Protagonists* you sent this time? If possible, preferably in Japanese.

Three Pioneer Thinkers

November 27, 1981

To you and my beloved children with love and respect:

I am hoping that you, our family, brothers and sisters, relatives, and those who live with us will be blessed with health by the love of Jesus. I am always amazed and gratified that you have stayed healthy through the ordeal of the last year and have displayed such miraculous toughness in maintaining your mental stability. I am extremely curious about what Hong-gul's examination was like. On the day of the examination, I thought about Hong-gul all day and prayed for him and Hyung-joo.

I know from your letter that all the flowers in the yard have faded. Chrysanthemums here at the prison have already begun to wilt in the last twenty days. About twenty of those I have been tending, however, still display their beauty and are visited by bees. This makes me reflect once again on the significance of human care and love, even for one flower. Need we say more? The care and love for human beings is just as important.

As you know, while I have been reading a variety of scholarly works, I have also kept up with belles lettres as well. Of those I have read, the following titles come to mind right now: *The Old Man and the Sea, For Whom the Bell Tolls, A Farewell to Arms, A Streetcar Named Desire, Death of a Salesman, Wild Animals I Have Known, Gone with the Wind, Roots, Little Lord Fauntleroy, A Christmas Carol, Pride and Prejudice, Treasure Island,* various works of Shakespeare, *Corydon, Les Miserables, A Woman's Life, Gervaise, The Fat, Faust, The Marco Polo Papers, War and Peace, Anna Karenina, The Captain's Daughter, The Rich, Crime and Punishment, The Brothers Karamazov, The Idiot, The Devil, The Prosecutor, Doctor Zhivago, One Day in the Life of Ivan Denisovich, The Prisoner, T'oji, Chang Kil San, Nanjaengi ka Ssoaolin chaggŭn kong, Ŏdum-ŭi chasiktŭl, Irŏna pich'uŏra, Najŭndero Imhasosŏ,* and *Saban-ŭi sipchaga.*

Good literary works relieve our emotions and serve as an inspiration that makes our spirit vigorous and resilient. Especially for people like you and me, who are getting on in age, it is important to be able to adapt to this fast-changing world and stay open-minded to the thinking of the younger generation and the public. This requires the stimulation of our souls through reading fine literary works. I have listed some of the titles as a recommendation to you.

Hwe-young's mother wrote to me after the outdoor assembly of the Catholic church at Yeouido. Please tell my sister-in-law.

To Hong-il and Jee-young's mother:

You cannot imagine how worried I was when Hong-il was sick in bed. Any illness that starts with a cold has to be blamed on carelessness. As Hong-il says, we have a family tradition of long life and health since the days of your great-grandfather-in-law. Once Jee-young begins to find studying fun, it may be advisable to let her develop on her own instead of supervising her closely. About Chung-hwa, it may be good for her education to help her find friends so that she will not be lonely. Also, it is imperative to guide and encourage the two sisters to play together part of each day. I am sure you will take good care of these things on your own, but children's character formation is greatly influenced by playing with good friends, by being close to their brothers and sisters of similar age, and by affectionate relationships with their parents and families. As husband and wife, you two should develop a habit of engaging in worthwhile and productive discussions. Man and wife should not live together simply on the basis of emotions but should communicate intellectually and share the same ethical viewpoints.

To Hong-up:

I was greatly comforted by your reply to my earlier letter, in which I expressed concern about your well-being. It is a priceless blessing that you have not lost any of your mental reserve or your hope for the future, even under these circumstances. Confidence like that will surely reap victory. Make weekly, monthly, and yearly plans for your life, and try hard to live purposefully, constantly checking on your performance. Do not break down if things do not go as planned; make up your mind to start anew. This is the recipe for self-development and success. Such is your father's experience.

To Hong-gul:

It has been three days since your examination, but your father has absolutely no inkling of how it went. I am brimming with curiosity. I am completely perplexed. Your father was fully aware that you had to push yourself beyond your physical limits to prepare for the examination. My heart aches when I think that you were not able to study sufficiently because of me. When you wrote in your letter that you would do your best for your father, I was deeply touched and grateful. This is all still too much of a shock. At any rate, you have done your best and there can be no regrets. Make sure that you do your best in the remaining examinations in high school. In life, what you become is not as important as how you live. The process is more important than the consequence. When you are through with your examinations get unwound gradually. Let me know how Hyung-joo did in his examination.

As you know, I hold King Sejong, General Yi Sun-sin, and General Chŏn Pong-jun in high esteem and consider them among the preeminent figures in our history. That these three men compare favorably with anyone in world history in terms of their greatness is not just a personal bias. King Sejong stood out not only as a ruler but also as a leader and innovator in the fields of politics, economics, science, and culture.

General Yi Sun-sin is an example par excellence of the greatness and perfection that human beings can attain. He was a spiritual giant who reached the top as a military strategist, a commander on the battlefield, a great inventor, a leader who loved his people, a literary figure, and a statesman. His like is almost impossible to find.

General Chŏn Pong-jun is a sort of miracle. He was a simple tutor in a private school for Chinese classics in a small town. Nevertheless, he was able to mobilize and organize instantly hundreds of thousands of people. Furthermore, he demanded and implemented the kinds of policies that were appropriate and desirable for our nation at that time, that is, a populist, anti-feudal government that resisted foreign influence. This is ample evidence of his versatile qualities as a leader. Today, however, I want to write a few words about three pioneer thinkers who are different from the above three mainly in intellectual and spiritual terms. These are Wŏnhyo, Yi Yulgok, and Ch'oe Su-un.

When we review our history, we find only a few men who were engaged in profound intellectual inquiries. As I see it, this was due to the following factors: the optimistic, easygoing nature of our people, whose orientation is happiness here and now; the dominance of Chinese intellectual and cultural influence, which inhibited originality; the diversion of scholarship from inquiries into truth to service in government and attention to the advancement of one's career; and repeated foreign invasions and social instability that have precluded the mental attitudes needed for reflection. These three men, however, stand out as towering figures in spite of all the adverse conditions. They are not great simply as thinkers but also as doers. Indeed, they are outstanding and shining personalities.

With my limited knowledge, it is impossible to comprehend adequately the thoughts and personalities that enabled these men to attain such heights and depths. I am putting down a few thoughts, however, on the basis of what I have learned from several sources, to understand our roots correctly and also to provide you and the children with something to think about. Because of lack of space, I will be concise and hope that you will fill in the details by reading the relevant books.

Wŏnhyo

Wŏnhyo can be considered an ideal, prototypical Korean. He was handsome, intelligent, and carefree—truly a man of real quality. There has not been another like him. Buddhism first took root in India, but it blossomed and branched out into all its ramifications in China. It was Wŏnhyo who brought Buddhism to maturity in Korea and helped it fructify. His writings served as an indispensable guide for Buddhism in Japan and China as well as in Korea.

Wŏnhyo's concept of Buddhism was developed on the solid basis of universalism. His view was akin to the idea of universal salvation espoused in Christianity. According to this, all people possess the spirit of Buddha and can become bodhisattva if they repent their sins; thus, there is no differentiation between Buddhism and secularism.

Wŏnhyo was a thoroughly practical man who rejected legalism and formalism and would not tolerate such obstacles. For example, he committed a cardinal sin when he slept with Princess Yosuk in order to save her, and when necessary, he ate fish at Pohang beach and did not hesitate to frequent taverns in downtown Sorabul. All these actions were congruent with the way of Buddha and the essence of the Buddhist credo.

Wŏnhyo championed the reconciliation of all disputes and strove for the unification of all Buddhist sects. He was never chained to any one particular sect but represented Buddhism as a whole in the Silla dynasty.

Wŏnhyo's Buddhism was completely dedicated to the salvation of all people. His life span covered the twenty-year period following the unification of the peninsula by Silla. At this time, the Silla people were mired in despair and emptiness just like the peasantry during the height of the Roman Empire. The peasants were the main means by which the Silla dynasty achieved dominance, since they played the dual role of soldiers on the battlefield and producers of military provisions. In spite of their enormous sacrifices, all the fruits of unification were appropriated by the ruling classes of Song-gol and Chin-gol, who left the peasants wandering in despair and indignation. It was during this period that Wŏnhyo sought them out, taught them the piety of Buddha's salvation, and helped them to learn about nirvana by reciting Buddha's Prayer with them. Although it might be argued that Wŏnhyo was talking the masses into inertia, this is a shallow view if we consider that period in history and Wŏnhyo's earnest and genuine concern for the salvation of the masses.

Devoting his soul and body to comfort the masses and to deliver the hope of Buddha to them, Wŏnhyo befriended people of lowly origin, such as snakecatchers, and carried the body of his mother on his back when she died. No matter what, Wŏnhyo was an uninhibited, proud example of a Korean.

Yi Yulgok

Yi Yulgok is known as a high-ranking official of the Sŏnjo period who argued for the recruitment and training of one hundred thousand soldiers—the sign of a foresighted leader. Many people have negative feelings about the Confucianism of the Chosŏn dynasty, blaming it for, among other things, the fall of the Han dynasty. Nonetheless, Yi Yulgok should be accorded high respect as one of our historical representatives, and he should also be revered as a man of great character who possessed both wisdom and virtue.

First of all, Yulgok was an outstanding protégé of Kudojangwŏn'gong. He was, nevertheless, a paragon of practicality whose life's goal was to cultivate saintly wisdom that never relied entirely on intellectual ability.

Yulgok endeavored to enlighten the monarch and the public through his numerous writings. He made every effort to promote the welfare of the people and was an unparalleled precursor of the Silhak during the late period of the Chosŏn dynasty. He struggled to eliminate the causes of factional strife and cultivate the spirit of conciliation.

What makes Yulgok most valuable from a contemporary standpont is his original and distinctively Korean interpretation of Confucianism. According to authorities, Yulgok established a great philosophical system that focused on the element of spirit. His system was the product of synthesizing the mutually exclusive theories of Chang Hwaeng-gu, that is, the spiritual monism of Su Hwa-dam and Chuja and the spiritual dualism of Yi Toegye. In integrating the theories of humanity and heaven then prevalent in Korea and China, he elevated them to a new creative pinnacle.

Yulgok's philosophical ideas revolved around the spirit, of course opposing corruption and favoring reform. What are reason and spirit? For Yulgok, they can be thought of as equivalent to a pantheistic god in Spinoza.

Ch'oe Su-un

The birth of Ch'oe Su-un marks a turning point in our spiritual history. He is thought of as an example of the originality of Korean thought. Even though some have compared his philosophy of life to that of Nietzsche or to modern existentialism, fundamentally he represents the autonomous development of Korean thought.

Ch'oe was the son of a fallen aristocratic family. Coming from poverty, he became a traveling drapery peddler and experienced the hardship of the underprivileged. The masses were the origin of Ch'oe's life path. His basic idea was to build a paradise on earth by restoring human well-being and straightening out present reality. According to him, this meant eradicating greed and uniting humans with heaven.

The principal thrust of the Tonghak, founded by Ch'oe, was never more succinctly stated than in the Tonghak prayer, "Serving God will determine harmony, and forever remembering God will lead to the natural understanding of all things." The God to whom Ch'oe refers was a God with a human character and will. This was a pagan idea for the Confucians of his time, but it was an idea akin to the Catholic concept. In fact, Ch'oe was executed for practicing Catholicism in disguise. Despite his public denial, there were strong indications that he was under Catholic influence. Tonghak was a religion of the oppressed and was directed solely toward the peasantry. It was antiestablishment, nationalistic, autonomy seeking, and defiant. Finally, Ch'oe's Tonghak was a religion that was unique to the Korean nation, based as it was on traditional Korean shamanism. It incorporated some elements of Christianity, however, and also took into account Confucianism, Buddhism, and Taoism. Although he died only three years after he first promulgated the Tonghak, Ch'oe Su-un's spirit and accomplishments have been permanently etched into our history.

1. Joseph Hoeffner, *Christian Socialism* (Pundo Publishing Co.).

2. Gustavo Gutierrez, *Liberation and Change* (Pundo Publishing Co.).

3. *The Thoughts of Von Hofe.*

4. *Pŏpchŏn.*

5. *Sonja* (Sun-tzu).

6. Leo Tolstoy, *Resurrection.*

7. Alexandr S. Pushkin, *Eugene Onegin.*

8. Charles Dickens, *David Copperfield.*

9. Sŏ Insŏk, *Sŏngsŏ ŭi kananhan saramdŭl* (The Poor in the Bible).

10. Georg Simmel, *On Individuality and Social Forms.*

11. John Dewey, *Experience and Nature.*

12. John Dewey, *Logic: The Theory of Inquiry.*

The Birth of Jesus and the Copernican Transformation

December 16, 1981

With love and respect to you and my beloved children:

I am getting the Christmas spirit and preparing for an enjoyable holiday as I read the cards you send every day. Because I have no way of sending you Christmas cards, other than this letter, I am writing this month's letter earlier than usual so that the family can read it before Christmas. I send my heartfelt greetings on the birthday of our Lord Jesus to you, Hong-il, Jee-young's mother, Hong-up, Jee-young, Chung-hwa, and those helpers who live with us. I also send my yuletide greetings to the brothers and sisters on both sides of our family, priests, nuns, ministers, and our many caring friends. I am fervently hoping they will be showered with the love of Jesus. This year has been a year of hardship and sorrow, just like the year before. Hasn't it been a year when our hearts have been filled with so much grief that we could not stop the hot tears from streaming down our cheeks?

Even in all this turmoil, Lord Jesus has stayed with us and saved us from despair and destruction. Lord Jesus blessed me last January by saving my life for the fourth time, and then he brought home to the bosom of their families Dae-hyun, Hong-il, General Park Sung-chul, Han Hwa-gap, Ham Yun-shik, Kim Ok-doo, and others.

Our family has gathered around you in good health and has overcome the adversity with unity of mind. Furthermore, everyone in the family has kept up his or her efforts toward self-development. God has looked after us by having our many friends pray for us and remain concerned about me. I thank God that I have been able to rise above loneliness and grief, thanks to the bountiful blessings of Lord Jesus, and enrich myself religiously and intellectually. I remember with a grateful mind that this past year has yielded a great deal in terms of striving to improve myself as a human being.

As Christmas draws near, I am writing about the significance of the birth of Jesus and its impact on the history of mankind. I will also reflect critically on our current situation. I will try to put together my thoughts without repeating what I have written in the past. I think that this letter can be regarded as a balance sheet of my life of faith during the past year.

The Incarnation of Jesus

The birth of Jesus is the greatest event in the history of mankind because it was the incarnation of God. With this event, the history of mankind took on a totally new meaning and objective. First, Lord Jesus was born as God's child and as such had a unique status as the true God in terms of essence and as a perfect human being. Even though Lord Jesus was born in the lowly circumstances of the impoverished family of Mary and Joseph, in essence he embodied the richest love of God.

Second, the incarnation of Jesus meant the secularization of God and at the same time made this world sacred. Thus, heaven and earth became united in one kingdom, and God and man became one as well. Therefore, the incarnation of Jesus was the declaration and beginning of God's project of salvation. All in all, sacred and profane became merged in God's love.

Third, the birth of Jesus was God's way of retrieving the correct image of God, which had been distorted by Judaism, and also of completing the prophecies of the Old Testament. In the time of the Old Testament, the Jews saw God as a God of Wrath and Vengeance, which left humans no alternative but to flee from Him.

With the incarnation of Lord Jesus, however, God unveiled His true image of love, forgiveness, and reconciliation and thus endowed humans with hope, joy, and peace.

Fourth, Lord Jesus was engaged throughout His life in activities that showed beyond a doubt that God was a friend of the oppressed and poor and that God's salvation begins with the realization of justice and liberation in this world. I am not going to dwell on this point any longer because I touched on it in my October letter.

Fifth, the incarnation of Jesus attained its fullest meaning through His actions while He lived among others and by his death on the cross and subsequent resurrection. We often understand the death of Lord Jesus on the cross as an act of unquestioning submission to God for the redemption of our sins. This is true, of course. We should pay more attention, however, to a fact made clear in the Bible: He was executed as a political prisoner by the Jewish ruling class and the Roman Empire for standing up for the rights of the oppressed and the poor. His resurrection, therefore, should not be interpreted simply as a hope for eternal life in heaven. It should be seen as God's approval and confirmation of Christ's actions on earth, that is, as a sign of God's approval for Jesus' struggle and advocacy of justice and peace in this world, which should be made unconditionally accessible to the oppressed and the poor.

The Influence of Jesus

The incarnation of Jesus influenced the history and spirit of mankind in the Copernican era. It is universally recognized that both the orthodox Christian community and the non-Christian world were greatly influenced, tangibly and intangibly, by Jesus and Christianity. Let us consider the impact of Jesus on the history of mankind.

First, the Jews thought of God as exclusively a God

of the Jews, but the incarnation of Jesus revolutionized this by restoring the original concept of God as the God of all peoples. This introduced a new era and the gospel was spread to the end of the earth for the salvation of all people.

Second, the revolutionary idea known as eschatology came into being. Originally, the understanding of history was based on the repetition of the four seasons, the recurring cycle of birth, growth, and death of plants and crops, the life and death cycle of human beings. From this concept, the notion of Yin and Yang developed in China, the idea of eternal cycles in India, and the Greek understanding of philosophical revolution. In both the West and the East, life and the universe were understood as endless repetition and eternal revolution. With the spread of Christianity, however, an eschatology arose whose aim was to await the reincarnation of Lord Jesus while living a genuinely faithful and ethical life. This implied that tomorrow would not be just another day. Rather, a great transformation in the concept of life and the fate of all things in the universe took place and pointed toward progress and development; that is, moving with hope toward the ultimate destination, where eternal life and paradise were assured. All this brought great hope and courage to a world mired in stagnation and despair because of the cyclical view of history, and it had immense influence on the course of history. This is proved by those Christians who keep their faith no matter how great the hardship or sacrifice and by the spiritual and material development of the Christian community.

Third, one must note the idea of overcoming the everyday world through love. Before Christ, force reigned supreme, and resistance to force amounted to no more than passive denial or withdrawal, or spiritual escape into nirvana—a flight from reality. Since Christ, however, the world has begun to repudiate and resist evil's unjust rule by force and domination. This has been accomplished with the help of the living God. At the same time, protecting and serving our struggling and weak neighbors has been unmistakably identified as the greatest religious virtue.

The means of struggle against injustice and evil lay in the idea of conquering the world through love, not force. The idea was not to approve evil in this world or to confront it with hatred and violence. Neither did it mean sidestepping evil. Instead, it was boundless love, the love of Jesus and God that could embrace this world, even those who were committing evil deeds. It is this kind of love which has had a decisive impact on mankind and its history up to today.

Fourth, we have won freedom and liberation, thanks to Jesus. In our belief in Jesus we have gained freedom from sin. Moreover, no temptation, persecution, or oppression can deprive us of this freedom because we live in God's truth. Gaining such freedom was not forced on us, not even by God, but was the result of our own volition. A philosopher noted the great influence of the majestic statement in the Gospel of John (10:18) on the history of thought and politics:

> No one takes my life away from me. I give it up of my own free will. I have the right to give it up, and I have the right to take it back.

God's greatest gift to us is this spiritual, psychological, and secular freedom that we have acquired out of our own desire.

Fifth, the most conspicuous transformation that Jesus brought about is the idea of equality. In the past, whether in the West or in the East, slaves, children, and women were not treated fairly as human beings. We can see this throughout history. Even Plato and Aristotle left writings that tended to view them as inferior, and it was not any different in Chinese, Indian, Egyptian, and Jewish society. Can you imagine the sadness and pain of those who were treated as subhuman? After the incarnation of Jesus, however, mankind began to firmly repudiate and struggle against this attitude, which is the greatest sin and shame in history. Slaves could participate together with aristocrats in worship, and they could call one another brother. Love and respect for children came to be seen as one of Jesus' great commandments. There is no one in the world who has benefited more from Jesus than women, because it was only after the advent of Christianity that women's rights were protected within the monogamous framework. In the West, as in the East, and even in the Jewish community in the time of the Old Testament, polygamy was a commonplace and divorce was the privilege solely of men.

Jesus established the system of monogamy and forbade divorce. These were the most urgent and appropriate measures for the protection of the weak. Today, the status of women has improved, and the freedom of divorce is often granted. In the Catholic church, controversies have arisen over these issues. I read in your letter that the church would be sanctioning divorce after next year. Although I did not know any details, this appeared to me to be a truly decisive action. It should be noted in passing that the church did oppose divorce on principle until the eleventh century but after that, recognized it in a limited way. At that time, the church approved marriage spontaneously arranged by man and woman on the basis of love, although the aristocracy looked on such marriages with disdain and disapproval. Freely arranged marriages based on love became common among the people at large, who became the principal force in pressuring the church to impose a wholesale ban on divorce.

At any rate, the justice of Christ continued evolving and became the spiritual foundation for the abolition of slavery, the elimination of racial discrimination, and economic equality. As I pointed out in my earlier letter, it is a cause for shame that these were brought about by non-Christian reformers instead of people following the Christian ethic. This makes us realize, however, that God has the right to use forces outside the church if it is necessary to carry out His purposes.

Sixth, we have to grant credit fairly for the many spiritual accomplishments with which the church has graced this world. It goes without saying that the church has been guilty of a great number of errors, but it is also true that the church has made enormous contributions to the spiritual salvation of mankind and to the realization of human rights and equality. This particular point is brought out in Toynbee's *A Study of History* or André Maurois's *A History of France* and even in the writings of Bertrand Russell, an acerbic critic of the church. We know that the churches in Jerusalem in the early period, and their counterparts in Rome during the persecution, served as the source of great hope and comfort for the oppressed. After the fall of the Roman Empire, the church protected the masses from rampaging savages and also played a role in maintaining the Roman system of law and civilization, transmitting them to medieval Europe. The Benedictine convent became a leading force in revitalizing European agriculture, which had been ravaged by the barbarian invasion, and the church not only advocated human rights and the economic rights of the peasantry but also threatened and admonished the feudal lords on these matters. Furthermore, the church established centers of medieval culture and education in the University of Bologna in Italy, the University of Paris in France, and Cambridge University in England as well as dedicating itself to education in convents. The popes were scholastically inclined, and without their support and encouragement during the medieval period, some argue that the Renaissance could never have taken place.

We know very well that the Protestant church played an important role in the development of modern economics and the establishment of democracy after the

Reformation. In spite of these efforts by the church, however, the Catholic church and the Protestant church stood for the protection of the interests of the feudal aristocracy and big capitalists and turned away from the rights of workers or the popular struggle. In taking a position that was diametrically opposed to the teachings of Jesus, they frequently caused the loss of popular faith in the church and the defamation of Lord Jesus. We have to make a fresh beginning by repentance and seeking absolution before Lord Jesus and also by critically examining our past mistakes. Fortunately, since the latter part of the nineteenth century, especially since the beginning of the twentieth century, both churches have made progress in critical self-examination and new programs. This phenomenon has become quite conspicuous since the Second Vatican Assembly and the creation of the World Council of Churches.

Critical Examination and a New Start

This is a time of drastic changes in the history of mankind, who has been wandering in spiritual confusion. This is the time, therefore, when the church must act expeditiously to assume a strong role as salt and light. The direction of reform has to be toward the real Christ and away from the doctrinaire tenets that surround the Christ of faith. First, the church will have to be a spiritual center in the salvation of today's world by reinforcing the religious teachings of Christ as outlined in "The Incarnation of Jesus." There has to be unity between individual and social salvation and also between the high priestly teachings and prophetic faith.

Second, the church has to move away from its traditional conservatism and its favoritism for the rich and develop an eschatological position that points to progress for the common people as well as strengthens an evangelical position that befriends the oppressed and the poor.

Third, what is most lacking in our church is the ethos that characterizes a communal body based on love. If praying to God is all we demand, there is no need for a church; it can be done as well at home. The fundamental reason for the church is the need for a community of love among fellow churchgoers. This, in turn, would function as the loving hand reaching out to the whole society. One reason for the popularity of fraternal Christian gatherings is that there are those who have not felt the sense of affectionate belonging in the established church but have been seduced by the call for absolute oneness.

Fourth, I believe there is much room for reform in our Christian prayers. We tend to think of prayer as a solitary ritual to be performed in a quiet place. Is it not true, however, that genuine prayer can be among people? I read that Lord Jesus often looked up to the sky and prayed in the middle of a crowd. In my opinion, genuine prayer is realized when we meet with our neighbors and relate to them in the presence of God and work with them with God's love. Praying in a closet is likely to give rise to desultory thoughts. It is advisable sometimes to look, instead, for themes of prayer in surveying a newspaper that may have some news about the country or neighbors one should pray for. Solitary prayer away from the secular world is said to have been instituted by some disciples who retreated into the Arabian and Lybian deserts and prayed in seclusion because they were dissatisfied by the legalization of early Christianity, which placed the church under the protection of the state.

I have jotted down my thoughts just as they poured out of my mind. Therefore, they are not well organized. I hope that you or others will correct me if there are mistakes.

Korean History

Yi Kiback, *Han'guksa sillon.*
Yi Kiback, *Silla chŏngch'i sahŏesa.*
Pyŏn T'aesŏp, *Koryŏ chŏng'chi chedosa.*
Ch'ŏn Kwanu, ed., *Han'guk sanggosa.*

Eastern History

John K. Fairbank and Edwin O. Reischauer, *East Asia: The Great Tradition.*

World History, etc.

Arnold Toynbee, *A Study of History.*
André Maurois, *A History of France.*
André Maurois, *A History of America.*

Economics

J. Kenneth Galbraith, *The Age of Uncertainty.*
Alvin Toffler, *The Third Wave.*

Literature

Choose from the list I made last month. Try Sartre, Camus, Kafka, Saint-Exupéry, and Franz Fanon. Above is a rough list of recommended readings drawn from those I have already read. (This does not include materials related to American history.)

For Moral Reconstruction

January 29, 1982

To you and my beloved children with love and respect:

This month's letter has been delayed because I have been waiting for news about the two boys' entrance examinations. I learned yesterday from your and Hong-il's letters that Hyung-joo has passed the examination and that Hong-gul also is certain to pass. I send my heartfelt congratulations to Hyung-joo and pray that Hong-gul's case will turn out all right in the end. I cannot but feel mortified that I am the only one who has been so tantalized, waiting for this news that was decided two days ago. It was a very commendable thing for the family members to limit themselves to offering advice and leave the final decision to Hong-gul. Even if such an approach has undesirable results, the outcome is secondary in importance to the fundamental attitude that one has to make responsible decisions regarding one's problems on one's own.

The condition of my health has not changed much since I told you about it during your last visit. Although the last two or three days have been terribly cold, I do not want you to be overly concerned about it because I can manage. As usual, I spend each day reading. Lately, I have read *Philosophical Faith and Revelation* by Jaspers, *The History of Korea* in five volumes put out by the Chindan Hakhoe, *The Choice of America* by the Hoover Institution, and an English edition of *Gone With the Wind*. They are all very useful.

I do not know how to express my gratitude to Reverend Park Choon-hwa for his visit last Christmas and to my compatriots for their visit on my birthday. I was greatly comforted even though I did not get to meet everyone. Reverend Park has come to our home every week to lead prayers and also has expressed concern over Hong-gul's academic career on numerous occasions. When I think of what he has done, I am inclined to believe that the reverend is indeed the kind of Christian worker who is a servant of the humblest people. To my compatriots who have known nothing but suffering on my account, I can only be grateful, but I do not know how I can meet them face-to-face.

As I reminisce about the days and months as well as

the things we are undergoing even today, I am forever indebted to you for having overcome so many rugged mountains and rocky seas. I feel nothing but gratitude and pride for my children, who are trying to live righteously and prudently while still respecting their father and his goals in spite of countless adversities.

To Hong-il and Jee-young's mother:

When I read in Hong-il's letter the other day that "the three brothers are determined to live in fraternal love that will be the envy of all," I could not help but feel joyous and proud. Judging from your attitude, as the eldest brother, and the righteous characters of Hong-up and Hong-gul, I have no reason to doubt that things will turn out just as you say. In particular, there is an old adage that a good wife is a necessity for keeping fraternal love intact. Jee-young's mother certainly has a kind and understanding personality, which makes me believe that both of you will carry out your intention splendidly. I sincerely hope so. I hear that Jee-young is learning piano and can skate very well. I can visualize her doing all this, and at the same time I am aware how fast time is passing. I am truly happy that Jee-young and Chung-hwa are praying diligently for their grandfather. God will receive their prayers with special consideration. Tell them for me that they should get along better than ever before.

To Hong-up:

I read in your letter that you have a whole slew of questions about belief and whatever—simply a lot of things you wanted to discuss with me. Your father keeps thinking how wonderful it would be to be able to study with you three brothers and engage in a discussion with you. You are not alone. Your father also has a mountain of questions I want to discuss with someone who has extensive knowledge of theology. Some of these questions I can answer through reflection, but there are also some I cannot answer at all. Actually, so long as we continue learning and thinking and do not abandon the project of self-improvement, we are bound to be burdened with doubts and unresolved problems. So we have to make a meticulous list of doubtful questions and try with patience and persistence to find answers. You may find it useful to read your father's letters over again.

To Hong-gul:

I am ambivalent as I write this letter because, not knowing the result of your college entrance examination, I have no idea whether to congratulate you or not. No matter what the outcome, your father is very pleased with your attitude in two respects. One is that you have followed through on your decision in spite of all the risks. Once when you came to visit, your father expressed the opinion that even if you had to brace yourself for another try, you should apply to the school of your choice. At your age, with so little experience in life, however, it is only natural to waver, but according to your mother's letter, you did what you wanted to do all along without ever blinking your eyes. How splendid! Even though it may not turn out as hoped, from the standpoint of a long lifetime, only those with conviction can live their own lives.

You were very remorseful that you had not made greater efforts during the past year and expressed a new determination for the future. It was certainly a very necessary and appropriate reaction, and I hope you will sustain your new resolve. Your father has wetted his eyes more than once thinking of how much your study has been hampered by the pain that has been inflicted on you because of him. Every time I have prayed to God. My child! Overcome!

In a letter from Hong-il the other day, there was a reference to a macabre incident in which a teacher murdered his student because of gambling debts. He asked my opinion on it and also hoped that I would explain it in terms of Confucian morals. Our society today faces a great number of tasks, among them the most fundamental one of restoring spiritual health; that is, the moral rehabilitation of our people, who are the masters of our country. You know very well that this is one point I emphatically stressed before I was imprisoned. Because of lack of space, I am jotting down my thoughts in skeleton form. I think it will be helpful to use this letter at a family gathering as a resource material for critical debate.

The Assessment of Confucian Morals

There is a tendency among those who lament the status of today's morals to consider reinstating Confucian morals as a remedy. There was a massive movement at one time to revitalize loyalty and filial piety. In principle, however, we cannot return to Confucian morals, nor is there any need for them. Confucian morals are feudal vestiges that do not allow for human rights. How can we adhere to them in this age when we are striving for democracy and an industrial society? Loyalty and filial piety in Confucian morality boil down basically to the idea "Even if the ruler is not being a ruler, the subject must respect his status. Even if the parents are not behaving as parents, children must stay in their place." These cannot serve as the basis of a democratic society that is founded on the integrity of individual character and the idea of a social contract. Loyalty and filial piety in the context of the present should be based on mutualism, that is, "government should act like government just as people should act like people. Parents must be deserving of their title just as children must be of theirs."

Another great pillar of Confucianism is order. The core of Confucian morality consists of the following feudal attitudes: the hierarchy between old and young, according to which the latter should obey the former unconditionally; male dominance over female, which prescribes a wife's obedience to her husband, and the distinction between man and wife, with the former enjoying absolute superiority (e.g., he enjoyed the right to disown his wife if she was guilty of the seven violations such as jealousy or infertility); the dominance of bureaucracy over the people; and bureaucratism, formalism, and a class system discriminating between nobility and the masses.

Many of those who speak of reinstating Confucian morals confuse our own traditional moral system with Confucian morals. We have to be able to distinguish accurately between them; otherwise, we will be negligent in our present task of rooting out the vestiges of Confucian morality, which not only suppressed our people during the five hundred years of the Yi dynasty but also led to its downfall. Furthermore, such confusion would bring about ignorance and self-contempt by making it seem that before the advent of Confucian morals our nation was nothing more than savages without anything resembling a system of morals.

Reacknowledgment of Our Indigenous Morals

From the words of Confucius, the formulator of Confucian morals, and from many Chinese historical documents, we can learn what moral people our ancestors were. In the Analects of Confucius, Confucius himself says that he "had the urge to leave Chinese society where truth did not have a place and travel on a raft to Ku-I (The Pyŏngyang and Hwanghae region in those times) and settle there, in a country of men of virtue. This was 2,500 years ago.

In Chinese topographical documents that date back

1,500, 1,600, or 2,000 years and also in Chinese historical writings, we find the references to the morals of our ancestors during the period of the tribal states before the era of the Three Dynasties (i.e., Ryo, Koguryŏ, Ko-chŏsŏn and the Three Kingdoms). "There are no thieves, wives are chaste and faithful, and people are benevolent, gentle, and of a humanitarian character." "Beyond the eastern sea, there is a land of men of virtue, where people are properly dressed, carry swords flanked by two large tigers, and have the kind of personality that makes them inclined to yield to others rather than dispute." "As in China, people are reverent of white clothes, worship their ancestors, and mourn deaths. Wives cover their faces with veils and do not adorn themselves with jewelry." "It is a country where men of virtue never die." "It is a country in the east where decorum reigns supreme." All this refers to a time before the formulation of Confucian morals in China. We know, then, that before the advent of Confucian morals our country already had an indigenous system of splendid morals such as honesty, female chastity, benevolence, peace, politeness, courage, humility, filial piety, funeral rituals, and frugality.

Subsequently, during the final years of Silla, Ch'oe Chi-won wrote that our country had had from ancient periods a mysterious Way. That is, immanent in our Old Divine Way was the Way of Graceful Pursuits, which already included the laments of the three religions of Confucianism, Buddhism, and Taoism. In the Tan'gun mythology, which stressed the idea of benefiting the common people, we can discern the sacred spirit that is consistent with the Benevolence in Confucianism, the Kingly Way in Mencius, and the social justice of contemporary democracy. Even though the moral precepts of our nation were partly influenced by Buddhism until the final years of Silla, the ancient morals of the period before the Three Dynasties subsequently prevailed. But the era of the Koryŏ dynasty came under a strong influence of Buddhism, while that of the Yi dynasty came under a pervasive Confucian influence. As pointed out above, however, our indigenous morals have been stubbornly retained, harmonizing themselves with those of Buddhism and Confucianism. I do not know exactly the origin of all this, but it seems that we are a people with a high caliber of moral and cultural fiber from time immemorial.

The History and Morality of Mankind

Morality is the principal criterion separating good and evil and right and wrong in human behavior. Morals are also the regulatory norms of human social behavior. Human beings pursue the true, the good, the beautiful, and the sacred, and morality has as its object the good. In terms of principle, the true and the good are unchanging spatially and temporally. Their methods, however, are bound to vary in time and place.

As pointed out earlier, the loyalty and filial piety of the feudal period are at great variance with those of the contemporary era, which is necessary if they are to have any effective results. Have morals, then, progressed or regressed as a result of these changes? They have recorded immense progress. We can easily recognize the progress that they have made when we suppose that we have to live in a society based on Confucian morals, which used to be the dominant type of society. As I mentioned some time ago, Toynbee stated that of the four great sins in the history of mankind, that is, slavery, exploitation of men, racial discrimination, and war-related killing of humans, the first three with the exception of wars have either disappeared or are disappearing. This should corroborate the above point.

Any historical era witnesses a crisis in morals. Especially in times like these when unprecedented, catastrophic changes are taking place, morals cannot but be shaken to their very foundations. This kind of situation inevitably causes revivalism to be in vogue. This is as foolhardy and harmful an undertaking as trying to force on a child clothes that he wore in his infancy. Especially in modern times when alien moral systems are swarming all over, panic naturally sets in. As a result, some adopt the zealot approach (in the manner of zealots in ancient Israel), which rejects everything unconditionally, or the Herod approach (in the manner of King Herod of Israel), which unquestioningly incorporates everything. Both are hazardous and harmful. As I will explain later, we have to select carefully what we are going to incorporate into our morals and endeavor to blend it with our native thinking in a careful and realistic way. This is the lesson of history.

The Crisis in Morals and Its Causes

I have never wavered in my faith in our people and their potential. Today, however, the status of our morals is at a critical point and leaves much room for concern. As shown by the Roman Empire or the various Chinese dynasties, countries throughout history—no matter how strong or prosperous they might be—have all, without exception, collapsed when they became morally bankrupt. It should be noted, however, that if nations can maintain their moral fiber as strong as it was in the beginning, they can find their way out of adversities into prosperity. The reasons for the current crisis in our morals are complex.

1. Today our society is experiencing confusion that arises from having to deal simultaneously with the three stages of social morals that Riesman discusses in his book, *The Lonely Crowd*. These are the tradition-oriented morals of an agrarian society, the self-oriented morals of the industrial phase (i.e., immersion in work, escape from society by satiating pos-

sessive desires through consumption and recreation), and the other-directedness (i.e., the loss of self through tailoring one's behavior to meet the expectations, values, and tastes of others).

2. The continued emphasis of money as the top priority has resulted in the negligence of spiritual values.

3. The colonial mentality that accepts foreign culture without reservation has to be mentioned.

4. The polarization between a tendency to hold our native morals in absolute contempt and the tendency to overemphasize traditional morals have produced conflict and confusion.

5. The prevalence of opportunism and careerism and the destruction of conscience and traditional values in our current society allow malicious and dishonest people to succeed instead of honest and conscientious ones.

6. Leaders have failed to set an example of honesty, consistency between action and words, frugality, probity, diligence, and service; instead, they frequently act in ways that refute these values. This is a major reason for the onset of the moral crisis.

7. The crisis in morals with which Western societies are beset today is an inevitable phenomenon accompanying the process of transition from industrial to postindustrial society. It is also the result of a long-term accumulation of improper practices.

These factors are finding their way into our society like waves. The crisis in Western morals can be traced to the following elements: negligence with respect to spiritual values and the tendency to regard material things and technology as omnipotent; the urbanization of industrial society; the declining role of Christianity, which has been the basis of Western morality; mechanization; the loss or alienation of human values as a result of the division of labor; lack of confidence and vision for the future; loss of leadership on the part of American leaders in situations like the Vietnam War, Watergate, and the Iranian hostage crisis; the incompetence of Western leaders, that is, their inability to achieve political integration in spite of economic cooperation and cultural similarities, which has led them to give in repeatedly to the threats of the great powers, thereby resulting in the disillusionment and rebellion of their own people, especially the young. Many of these factors are true in our case.

The Way for Us to Go

Our moral path has to be compatible with our politics, economy, and society. This is the only way we can avert confusion and conflict, build a healthy and vital moral society, and enable each individual to build his or her own moral society and lead a worthwhile moral life. Without such harmony, insistence on morality alone can never generate development.

The direction for us to take is toward democracy, social justice, economic development, national security, and the unification of our fatherland. When our social morals correspond with our national goals, individuals can live morally, with motivation, a sense of worth, and hope. I will put down a few concrete things within the framework of this broad principle.

At first glance, this may sound contradictory to what I wrote earlier, but as individuals we must have the attitude that we will defend our morals to the bitter end, even if the whole world is morally bankrupt. As long as we possess free will and human integrity, which we have acquired from God, we cannot be deprived of our autonomy because of what happens in the outside world. We cannot, however, expect this from everyone. We have to accomplish the moralization of our society through cooperation between the government and the people, and we must overcome the causes of the crisis in morals pointed out in "The Crisis in Morals and Its Causes." It is only when both the individual and society have been uplifted that the consummation of morality can be expected.

The choice of which of the traditional moral precepts to retain and the formulation and promotion of a new system must be decided by broad national debate and participation. As we have often seen, the enthusiasm or the insistence of the leaders alone cannot bring about morality. Even if one could drag an ox to a river, there is nothing one can do if the ox does not want to drink the water. What is most important is for the leaders to take the initiative by setting moral examples. Otherwise, we cannot expect the moralization of the entire society and people, even though a great moral sage such as Confucius might appear in the midst of the chaos. In light of the moral character of our people, we can achieve great success if the leaders will lead and voluntarily set examples that show the right direction.

Western values should not be accepted uncritically, nor should they be rejected categorically. It would be nonsense for use to accept Western politics, economy, society, and the rest. We must try to adhere to our indigenous morals, which, after all, emerged from the total context of politics, economy, and society. We can assimilate those Western morals that served as a spiritual incentive for modernization and democratization. These include respect for the individual, the sense of independence, nationality, aggressiveness, adventurism, civic-mindedness, a sense of justice, diligence, pragmatism, and respect for human rights.

The following is a list of our morals that we should preserve and refine: filial piety, love between siblings and relatives, extended family relationships, humaneness, the spirit of cooperation and reciprocity, cheerfulness, magnanimity, peacefulness, humility, hospitality, and respect for dignity. Also, we have to restore frugality, courage, and honesty, which are some of the traditional morals that have disappeared recently.

Reminders to My Beloved Children

We have to read good literary works throughout our lives. They serve as a spiritual fountain that never dries up.

One who thinks rationally expects the same from others; likewise, one who is conscientious expects others to be the same. One acts on the basis of these expectations, which is a principal reason for one's failure in the world.

We have to be able to distinguish between what is important and what only appears to be important. When we look back on our lives, we wonder if we have not wasted a great deal of our time clinging to frivolous matters because we mistook them to be important.

If we are to become genuinely free, we have to chain ourselves to God. Only the followers of Christ can be liberated from the enemies that enslave us. Among these enemies are death, glory, fortune, temptation, adversity, anxiety, and crisis.

We should not hesitate when we have to forge ahead and should not be restless when we have to be patient or despair when we have to regret.

People of little value will come to us, but we have to seek out and befriend good companions.

I heartily recommend the following books to you three brothers:

1. *A New Choice of America* (remind yourself that in the U.S. there are people who might disagree with the content of this book).

2. *The Poor in the Bible* (an excellent book; the only flaw is that it scarcely deals with the New Testament, especially Jesus Christ's life).

3. *The Zero-sum Society* (an admirably good book; helpful if read concurrently with George F. Gilder's *Wealth and Poverty*).

4. *The Church* (wonderful insights).

5. *The Korean Society* (some articles that prove to be interesting).

Please find the following books:

1. Rudolf Bultmann, *Theology of the New Testament.*

2. André Maurois, *A History of America.*

3. Pierre Augustin Caron de Beaumarchais, *Figaro's Marriage.*

4. Alexandre Dumas, *Count of Monte Cristo.*

5. Karl Jaspers, *Nietzsche: An Introduction to the Understanding of His Philosophical Activity* (Pakyŏng Mungo).

6. Friedrich Nietzsche, *The Anti-Christ.*

7. *Simp'al sayak* (1–3 vols., but a single version is preferred).

8. Kang Kukchin, *Ko Ki-pong ŭi saengae wa sasang* (The Life and Thoughts of Ko Ki Pong).

9. Hans Kelsen, *Vom Wesen und Wert der Demokratie* (Hongsŏng-sa).

10. J. Kenneth Galbraith, *The Nature of Mass Poverty* (Hongsŏng-sa).

11. Erich Fromm, *To Have or To Be?* (Chŏnmang-sa).

12. Ch'ŏ Chunmyŏng, *Kyŏngyŏngin* (The Businessman) (Tarakwŏn).

13. Kaionji & Shiba Taidan, Nihon rekishi o tenken suru (An Examination of Japanese History) (Kodansha Co.).

14. Kaionji Chōgoro, Shi-king (The Book of Songs).

15. Japanese history (a complete collection).

16. Chinese history (a complete collection).

Our Proud Family

February 23, 1982

To you and my beloved children with love and respect:

When you visited yesterday, I could not see you very well because of the glass partition, but you appeared more haggard than before. There was so little time that I could not even ask you about it. How are you?

Visits are so brief that we rarely get to talk enough, if at all, about the things we want to say, so they always end with a sense of frustration. They are, nevertheless, the happiest hours of the month. No sooner does a visit end but I start counting on my fingers the number of days until the next. There are four great joys in life around here: visits, letters from the family, reading good books, and tending the flowers in the flower beds from spring to fall. During the winter, when the flowers are gone, I do not find it much fun when I go outdoors for exercise. Now that spring is approaching, I am filled with great expectations.

I am gratified and pleased to read in a letter from Jee-young's mother that she is "grateful to be serving such wonderful people as my husband's parents." I feel the same when Hong-up says in his letter that he is "happy to be respectful of his parents in times of adversity and to be part of a harmonious family." Actually, I think you and I are fortunate in this regard. I feel proud and fulfilled to see Hong-il and his wife manage to have such a wonderful family, which far surpasses my expectations at the time of their marriage. I hear that Jee-young is very kindhearted and makes great efforts to be helpful to her mother, which leads me to believe she must have grown up quite a bit. As you mention in your letter, Chung-hwa seems to keep to herself, which is in marked contrast to Jee-young. When I was reading in her mother's letter that she has a very tenacious streak, I was grinning to myself, thinking she might have gotten that from me.

As you wrote, I feel concerned and sad about Hong-up, but I feel thankful and relieved that he is handling himself so well. I pray to Lord Jesus that this will be a good year for him. I still cannot keep myself from smiling happily over the fact that Hong-gul has successfully passed the entrance examination for Korea University, the school he has dreamed about since early childhood; and that he was solely responsible for the decision to apply there. But this is not simply a miracle. Ever since last year I have been isolated from the outside world and forced into a confounding situation. Hong-gul, however, has had to face his teachers and classmates every day in school but has endured without ever murmuring a word of vexation. Every time I thought of this, I felt sorry for him and cried in gratitude for his stalwartness. I have read over and over the poem, "The Pathos of a Journey," which describes his state of mind. I consider Hong-gul's success this time as God's gift for his kindheartedness, marvelous patience, and triumph over adversity. Even families with wealth, fame, and glory are often plagued by problems, but our family has achieved respect, love, and harmony despite extraordinary difficulties. We should take limitless delight and happiness from this. All this is the precious fruit of the efforts of everyone in the family to live a life of faith in God, loyal to conscience, neighbors, and history. You have played a large part by guiding our family with your strength. This letter is turning out to be full of half-baked self-praise and seems to gloss over our shortcomings on which we should reflect. Be that as it may, being truthful does not simply mean emphasizing only one's faults; it has to do with analyzing oneself without prejudice, sometimes taking into account one's merits as well. As usual, I am going to write a few words for you and the children. No matter how tiny I make my handwriting, I just cannot put everything I have in mind in the space of one postcard, which is very frustrating for me.

The Historical Background of the Polish Situation

Currently, the Polish situation has become the center of worldwide attention, and I suppose it would be the same in our country. No matter how it is resolved in the short run, this is a phenomenon similar to situations that have occurred in Hungary, East Germany, and Czechoslovakia, countries having the long-run potential of becoming the Soviet Union's Achilles' heel. A complete understanding of the Polish crisis requires a correct appreciation of the long history of conflict between Poland and Russia.

First, there is the history of religious conflict. During the medieval period before the Reformation, the confrontation between the Roman Catholic church and the Orthodox Christian church was very intense. At the time, Poland was guardian of the Catholic church in the East, while Russia became in essence the birthplace of the Orthodox church when Greece fell under the Ottoman domination after the collapse of the eastern Roman Empire in 1453. Russia thus came to take the place of Greece, now under the rule of heathens, and started its own Orthodox church. Around this time, Poland and Russia were divided over religious differences and repeatedly fought against each other. Poland was at one time a great power that annexed Lithuania and ruled western Russia, even occupying Moscow for two years at the beginning of the seventeenth century. Behind these Polish actions was the great desire of the Vatican to expand the sphere of Catholic influence to Russia.

Second, we can cite the long history of brutal Russian invasions of Poland. Through the notorious division of Poland, Russia partitioned and swallowed Poland three times during a twenty-year period in the latter part of the eighteenth century. Russia did this either with the help of Austria and Prussia, with Prussia alone, or by itself, but the outcome was the same. It wiped Poland from the face of the earth. During the following 150 years, until the end of World War I when they regained independence, the Poles staged anti-Russian independence struggles whose ferocity was almost unprecedented in the annals of oppressed peoples in the world. The Russians, however, retaliated with barbaric repression. We have only to recollect our own experiences under the thirty-six-year rule of the Japanese imperialists to imagine vividly enough the degree of the Poles' antagonism toward the Russians.

Third, in August 1939, immediately prior to the September 1939 invasion of Poland by Germany, the Soviet Union concluded a nonaggression pact with Hitler. When Germany invaded Poland, the Russians moved into Poland from the east and divided and annexed the country in cooperation with Germany. Moreover, just before the end of World War II, the Russian army massacred tens of thousands of Polish nationalist guerrillas who had fought against Germany. Also, there was an exiled Polish government in London whose forces, numbering tens of thousands, engaged the Germans in the Middle East. This government had the enthusiastic support of the Polish people, but its return to the homeland was finally blocked by Stalin despite Churchill's insistence.

Fourth, the Poles, like other East Europeans, feel a sense of cultural superiority vis-à-vis the Russians. In fact, the Russians had been near-savages until their acceptance of Christianity in 989, and they lagged far behind Poland culturally even when Tsar Peter was aggressively importing Western civilization. The gap still remains; East Europeans continue to hold the Russians in contempt, which can easily be understood when we recall our feelings toward the Manchus of the Ch'ing dynasty.

Fifth, after World War II, the Soviet Union pillaged industrial facilities in the East European region as it did in North Korea. Subsequently, the East European countries were subordinated to the economic domination of the Soviet Union and were exploited to promote Soviet economic interests, which gave rise to internal dissension. I have written my thoughts above for reference.

The Cycle of Dynasties

When we read our history, we are struck by the longevity of each dynasty, which is rarely matched in world history. First, Silla lasted for ten centuries, from 57 B.C. to A.D. 935. If we do not count the early period of tribal alliances and treat it as a bona fide dynasty from the King Namul period when it finally assumed the typical dynastic features, it still existed for 500 years. Second, the Koryo dynasty lasted nearly 500 years, from 918 to 1392. Third, the Yi dynasty also persisted more than 500 years, from 1392 to 1910.

The long duration of the Korean dynasties is markedly different from the history of Chinese dynasties. The succession of Chinese dynasties is as follows: the pre-Han period lasted 200 years; the post-Han, 200; the T'ang, 300; the Sung, including both North and South Sung, 300; the Yuan, 110; the Ming, 200; and the Ch'ing, including the Manchurian period, 300.

As for Japan, the reigns of emperors were long, but they were only figureheads. Those governments with real power were very short-lived. The Tokugawa Shogunate, which was the most durable regime, lasted 260 years.

In the Middle East, the Arsaces kingdom in Parthia, in what is now Iran, lasted approximately 470 years, an Islamic kingdom founded by Abbas lasted for about

500 years, and the Ottoman Empire in Turkey for 600 years. Seen in this light, the Korean dynastic history has no parallel anywhere, except for some of the Middle Eastern countries.

As a rule, dynasties go through a complete cycle in two hundred to three hundred years. In the first third, they progress with vigor and pioneering spirits; in the next third, they gradually slip into stagnation; and in the final third, they plunge into an irreparable stage of decay. In our case, the second and third stages of stagnation and decay tended to be unusually long.

In 1170, a revolt by the warriors in Koryŏ lasted about 250 years. That was the time for a dynastic change that should have occurred at the latest when the Mongols invaded. Strangely enough, the Koryŏ dynasty survived both the warriors' revolt and the Mongol invasion.

In the case of the Chosŏn dynasty, the Japanese invasion in the year of Imjin took place in 1592, exactly two hundred years after the founding of Chosun. The dynasty should have changed then, or in 1636, at the time of the Chinese invasion in the year of Byungja.

When a dynasty loses its innovative spirit and vigor, it resembles a large, dying animal that keeps gasping for breath and rolling over in the grass. In this condition, it is only the grass (i.e., the people) that is trampled and sacrificed. If the Chosŏn dynasty had been replaced at the optimal time, it would not have been so abysmally lethargic, corrupt, and bankrupt in its final years, which invited the invasions by Japan and Western powers. At least there should have been a more adaptable government that could deal with the situation and possibly avert the sad fate of national disintegration. We just might have been able to survive.

What I want to discuss here is why the dynastic cycles were so uniquely long in our history. As you know, I have read a number of works on our history but have not come across even one that refers to this phenomenon. I have been thinking about it in a number of different ways and feel I have come up with a few causes, but none is very convincing. If you have a chance to seek explanations from experts, please let me know. An accurate answer to this puzzle would provide invaluable material for understanding our past as well as the unique characteristics of our nation. (I should note that Japan was going through a period similar to the final period of the Chosun dynasty when it confronted Western powers. Had the Tokogawa Shogunate not been succeeded by the Meiji, there would not have been any progress and development in Japan.)

The Self-inflicted Punishment of the Chosŏn Dynasty

The spiritual constitution of the Chosŏn dynasty's ruling class was remarkably consistent in its aloofness. From the beginning of the dynasty, the governing class hurried along the road of exclusiveness, and it persisted on this course until the day of the national collapse. It discarded the system of coexistence between Confucianism and Buddhism that had existed in Koryŏ and proceeded to repress Buddhism methodically. Even within Confucianism itself, all the various schools of thought, with the exception of Chujahak, were rejected. Things reached such an extreme that even within Chujahak, a single typographical error was sufficient grounds for accusing someone of violating Confucian tenets. It goes without saying, then, that the spiritual climate was not suitable for recognizing Catholicism and the Tonghak.

The nobility, at first, was strictly differentiated from the commoners. Later the nobility was divided between the eastern and western factions, and still later, into the four factions of the old and young schools, the eastern, western, southern, and northern. Divided as they were, they continued habits of murder and expulsion until the last days of the dynasty. They severed all social contacts with members of different factions in the same Confucian school and forbade marriages between families of different cliques. Even on such occasions as death or marriage, there were no exchanges of courtesy calls.

The ruling class of the Chosŏn dynasty first excluded those from the northwestern region from political participation and then added to this list people from the Honam region, after the revolt by Chong Yo-rip. The people from Yŏngnam and Kiho were also involved in bloody regional rivalries and went so far as to proclaim the deceased Yi Toegye and Yi Yulgok as their respective gurus, in obvious defiance of their lifelong ideals. Then they tried incessantly to besmirch the integrity of one another's spiritual and philosophical leaders.

During the reigns of the queen's relatives, the Kims from Andong, the Chos from P'yŏngyang, and the Mins from Yohŭng, the limitations on access to political power became even stricter. Now only those who resided within the four great gates of Seoul could vie for power. It was absolute exclusivism and absolute self-enclosure. It cannot be too strongly emphasized that such patterns of behavior led to the disintegration of our nation and had a devastating effect on the spiritual and cultural life of the entire people. But then the leaders of such factionalism had inflicted on themselves a most brutal kind of self-punishment for five hundred years. They created a barren and destitute spiritual environment in which there could be no discourse, magnanimity, or coexistence. They dug themselves into their little enclaves like shellfish, and spent their lives in hatred, distrust, and conspiracy.

Insofar as their mistakes are material or identifiable, they can be remedied or healed without much difficulty. The legacy of more subtle, spiritual vice, however, lies latent in our psyche and, in most cases, we are either totally unconscious of it or unable to understand it even when we are aware. The saddest fact about ourselves today is that we have not been able to free ourselves from the poisonous spiritual legacies of the Chosŏn dynasty.

If the climate of hatred, vengeance, misunderstanding, and distortion takes precedence over the ethos of tolerance, coexistence, understanding, and cooperation, clearly there is no hope, no matter what is built up or how much progress occurs in other aspects of life. Mostly, it is the lack of mutual understanding that creates the climate of hatred and denies the possibility of an atmosphere of tolerance, and so we are trapped in the former. Lack of understanding, in turn, is brought about by inadequate communication. Suppose, for a moment, that during the Chosŏn era there had been a candid exchange of opinions between Confucian and Buddhist schools, that the Confucianists and the government engaged in a dialogue with the Catholic church and the Tonghak and thus understood correctly the essence of each, and suppose the state of affairs in the Western world and the intolerable conditions of the masses had been explained. Can you imagine how different we would be today? If there had been a dialogue between the nobility and the commoners, if political participation had been allowed without regard to provincialism or regionalism, and if the factions had talked to one another, there would not have been such murderous factional struggles or popular revolts. In addition, contrary to what we read in our history books today, the fate of our nation and the state of our politics would have progressed on a much brighter track.

Lord Jesus exhorts us to love our enemies, which is a near impossibility. We can, however, come closer to that goal. Before loving, we have to forgive. Forgiving, in turn, requires understanding the situation of others and their state of mind, which cannot be learned without communication. Forgiving and loving cannot take place when there is no dialogue and mutual understanding. All there can be is much misunderstanding and ignorance. Unconditional forgiveness and love are indeed possible, but they are rare in human beings. You have known for quite some time how I feel about these things, and so you should know that what I have written above is not something that just struck me suddenly.

My dear Hong-gul and Hyung-joo:

As both of you whom I dearly love are about to enter college, which is an important stage in life, I am writing the following, hoping to provide you with just a little bit of assistance in making college life worthwhile and productive. I want you to keep it in mind as you make plans and psychological preparations, most of which you must have made by now. Whenever you try to make something your own, be sure to draw on your own judgments in absorbing and digesting it. Also, you would do well not to treat this advice as something of immediate value but as something you should reread several times in the future, whenever you have an opportunity to do so. I hope that what follows is what Hong-gul had in mind when he asked for my advice.

1. The modern view of universities as a place for scholarship should be modified. They are not merely places for learning but also for creating an all-around individual, emphasizing the cultivation of character, sound physical strength, and other matters. When we consider the history of educational philosophy, we see that Kant's idealistic philosophy of ethical education prevailed in the eighteenth century. In the middle of the nineteenth century, however, the philosophy of education began to stress pragmatism, scientism, and empiricism and has continued to do so into the present. Its drawbacks have become so

apparent, however, that a synthesis of Kantian and modern approaches has been determined to be the best pedagogical framework. Nevertheless, education today has not changed its emphasis on knowledge and pragmatic utility as all-important. I want both of you to realize this and strive to complement the shortcomings of college education by developing your character and body.

2. A university is not a place for learning professional skills but for nurturing a basic cultural background so as to become a potential leader. Professional studies can be undertaken at graduate schools or workplaces. I hear that Harvard University offers only electives for the entire four years of the undergraduate program. I want both of you to work for a broad cultural basis so that you can become future leaders, that is, public servants. Instead of getting bogged down in your major fields, try to learn the fundamentals of the social and natural sciences. You cannot master contemporary scholarship without understanding both. For example, philosophy as a whole is so intimately tied to science that it may even be called the science of sciences. There is even scientific philosophy.

3. Set an ambitious goal for your future. Even when you have big ambitions in youth, they are bound to become gradually constricted. How can you shoot for great success unless you start with giant aspirations? Keep lofty ideals and goals such as graduate school, study abroad, and serving people and society meaningfully and devote yourselves wholly to realizing these goals.

4. I want you to develop independence, which will enable you always to live according to your own spirit. I also want you to preserve an attitude whereby you will never fail to evaluate critically what professors or any intellectual authorities tell

you and make sure that whatever you accept will be completely yours. But listen to everyone with an open mind. You must also have an open-minded attitude toward changing your position willingly when you have been corrected, and admit your mistakes.

5. Both of you should consider English and Japanese as absolutely necessary foreign languages. The need for Japanese may be somewhat difficult to comprehend, but there are good reasons for studying it. First, whether you like it or not, Japan is our close neighbor and will have great influence on our destiny. Second, Japan's strength, which derives from its economy, has an enormous amount of influence in Asia and the world, and it will grow even greater. How can we ignore it? Third, of necessity, Japan is entering an age of original creation after a period of imitation, because the West has been exhausted as a model of learning. This holds true for technology, culture, and scholarship. One of the most important issues for your generation is how to synthesize the relations between Eastern and Western cultures. Japan is several paces ahead of us. In Hyung-joo's case, both languages will be prerequisite to the practical application of his major interest.

6. You should treat your professors with respect. Teachers were revered in the old times because they were considered equals to the king and the father. This notion still has an important message. If one does not respect a teacher who guides one from ignorance to a learned state, one does not know the meaning of being indebted and cannot become a person who can lead others and expect to be respected by others. Learning critically from what professors teach is a separate issue from respecting them.

7. How one relates to friends who can have a decisive influence on one's life is an important question. Further, if one has three genuine friends, one has suc-

ceeded remarkably well in human relations. When it comes to choosing friends of the opposite sex, the person who is selected should be someone who can be respected, who has positive goals in life and works consistently toward those goals, and who has concerns and affection for others. Do not consider anyone your true friend unless he or she meets these criteria, even though the person might share your interests or give you positive feelings. If you do not find that person to be as described above, you should just socialize and wait until you can find the ideal companion.

8. Be sure to read every page of a newspaper with care, and also read magazines in the same manner. This is necessary to acquire knowledge, to become a cultured person and citizen. Hyung-joo should keep reading good literary works, and Hong-gul should continue to study Chinese characters. This is because Eastern and Korean classics are required for majoring in either literature or philosophy.

9. Make conscious efforts to talk with the family. It is part of the growing process that, at your age, you begin to create distance between yourself and the family. You have to suppress the urge, however, and consciously attempt to communicate with the family. There are several reasons. First, we find a sense of belonging in family, love, and understanding. Therefore, staying close to the family is an effective way of overcoming alienation and loneliness, which are common in industrial society. Second, through engaging in discourse with the other members of the family, you can assimilate the thoughts, habits, and worldviews of those who are different from you in terms of age and sex. Third, family members are your lifelong partners, those to whom you are most intimately linked. Furthermore, your parents brought you into this world, and your siblings are the only people among 460 million on earth who

share the same parents. How can you expect to live in a loving and understanding relationship with others if you cannot form an understanding, cooperative, and loving community with the people who are most closely related to you?

10. You will live in the twenty-first century and must prepare yourselves for it. As for the various prospects for the twenty-first century, consult what I wrote earlier.

11. Finally, be grateful to God and endeavor to become a responsible being in God's presence. Also, express yourselves with total candor so that you can receive God and neighbors, and demonstrate God's love by loving neighbors. I want to bless you with a happy college life and hope that you will strengthen the friendship that began in early childhood.

To you:

As I mentioned during the last visit, I suggest the following titles to you and the children as *must* readings.

1. *History and Interpretation* by An Pyŏng-mu (a really good book for understanding both Old and New Testaments; extremely worthwhile).

2. *The Church* by Hans Küng (a very inspirational book; a must for us).

3. *Japan as No. 1* by Ezra Vogel, Jr. (The author is the gentleman who had invited me to Harvard in 1979, and the book makes many interesting points about modern-day Japan. Moreover, the attitude of Americans to acknowledge Japanese as "No. 1," restraining national pride, and to try to learn from them is admirable.)

4. *Cardinal Suhwan Stephen Kim: Collected Conversations.* (Once again praise the Lord for giving us such

a brilliant leader as our shepherd. We can peek into his precious thoughts and boundless love through this book. Especially touching is the discussion with Dr. Kang Wŏn Yong.)

Loving Our Fate

March 25, 1982

To you and my beloved children with love and respect:

It feels as if spring is here in full force. Azalea buds in the flower bed here are beginning to open and reveal their reddish top parts. When I see the flower buds that will soon be showing off their victorious bloom after having overcome the wintry cold, I can only feel awe-struck reverence. It seems as if they are quietly saying something to us as we find ourselves in our current adversity. When I read in your letter that lilacs and magnolias in our yard are on the verge of blossoming, I am overcome with such yearning. The scent of lilacs is something I have always cherished so much, and the magnolia was such a favorite of Hong-up.

You could not imagine how happy I was when I learned from your and Hong-il's letters that there was nothing wrong with your health. As I have said during our visits, we have to take special care to avoid any more misfortune while we are already facing a predicament. Otherwise, even a jolt that can be managed with ease in normal times can become a lethal blow.

Many people go down to defeat because they get so preoccupied with the first misfortune that they either invite or cannot prevent a second and a third. In my opinion, it is very important wisdom in life that we remain alert to the chain reaction of misfortune and try to prevent it.

Now that Hong-gul's college entrance has been resolved satisfactorily, I am worried about Hong-up's problems, with which we have to deal immediately. As for Hong-il, he and his wife are very solid and enjoy a stable family life. Also, Jee-young and Chung-hwa are both healthy and growing up to be good-natured children. I can only feel fortunate and grateful.

As you wrote in your letter, however, I feel sorry and heartsick about Hong-up. In Hong-up's most recent letter, he expressed his determination to "try to shake free from a habitual tendency to rationalize about myself, which stems from the fact that I have not been able to be socially active like others." This woke me up in more ways than one. It is true that our two sons have not had a role in society for the last ten years since their graduation from school, and one of them still remains a bachelor, although he is now past the age of thirty. Last night, as I was mulling over in solitude the state of our two sons, I kept wondering who would give my sons jobs with the situation being what it is and who would allow their precious daughters to marry into our family. My heart felt wretched, burdened by the thought that my guilt toward my sons was simply too heavy. In addition to our children, there are our brothers and sisters, relatives and friends, who have all been inconvenienced by me. How can I not feel sorrowful and guilty?

On top of all these troubled feelings, my heart has been afflicted for the last two years by the sorrow, humiliation, and lamentation that made my blood run dry and pierced my heart with pain. Coupled with the solitary and isolated life that has perforce continued since 1976, all this seems to have aggravated further my mental stress. Just as you express your concern about this problem and provide encouragement in your letters, I am constantly trying my best to overcome it. At times, however, I lament the inadequacy of my faith and the lack of fortitude and culture in my character. But I shall prevail to the end, with the help of Lord Jesus and the prayers of many supporters. We have to love our fate, which we have to accept because we are born with it and can neither run away from nor reject it. Therefore, even in the midst of ordeal and despair, we have to put up the best fight we can so as to discover new possibilities and move forward.

As we read the Bible, we can learn that Lord Jesus loved His fate. He gladly accepted His destiny to be in this world for the benefit of those who were suffering and to become their friend. He did not turn away from the fate of having to die for human sins, and so he was nailed to the cross. Yi Sun-sin, An Chung-kun, Yun Pong-gil, the six Yi dynasty officials who were executed—all those martyrs who perished from persecution as well as those who reaped success in spite of poverty and misfortune—all these people loved their fates in their own ways.

I hope that you, our children, and I love the fate that has been bestowed on us and earnestly hope that we acquire faith, morals, and wisdom, which can be attained only as fruits of the kind of ordeal we are undergoing. Even as I write this letter, I would like to convey my thoughts more fully to my children and enjoy more opportunities to talk with my siblings and nephews. I feel helpless, however, because I cannot write more frequently.

I am relieved to find in Hong-gul's letters indications that he will adapt himself well to college life and that his thoughts are sound and profound. If you can let me know the course titles, the professors, and the textbooks this semester, it will not only satisfy my curiosity but also enable me to offer some pointers.

Today, as usual, I am sending you some of my thoughts, as follows.

The British People Who Learned from History

Recently I have been reading a short essay by Toynbee entitled "Is History on the Side of Man?" There are a few very moving stories. First, in the middle of the seventeenth century, England experienced the internal turmoil known as the Puritan War, and, in 1649, executed Charles I. Such extreme punishment of political adversaries produced considerable repercussions, such as radical internal division and the emergence of the even more dictatorial regime of Cromwell. The British people learned a great deal from this bitter experience and, during the Glorious Revolution of 1688, drove James II from the throne.

The son of Charles I, who, like his father, supported the absolute rights of monarchy, surreptitiously aided James in his escape to France in disguise. One ignorant fisherman spotted James II on the run and reported him to the authorities in expectation of a generous reward, only to be reprimanded. For three generations, James II, his son, and grandchild harassed the British government by establishing an exile government in France and staging a struggle to restore the monarchy. This struggle lasted three-quarters of a century. The British government anticipated this, but decided to ignore the nuisance, judging this line of action much preferable to direct reprisal or the political and social aftermath of a political vendetta.

The lesson the British people garnered from history still influences them today. Proof of this is that they exercise moderation; they do not force extreme confrontations. The virtues of magnanimity, dialogue, understanding, and coexistence which the British have attained are the fruits of the bone-wrenching experience of the execution of Charles I.

What comes to mind in relation to this is the fate of the Chartist movement among the British workers in the middle nineteenth century. Initially, the bourgeois government in England repressed and crushed it, but in less than thirty years, Disraeli, a member of the Conservative party, played a leading role in giving the workers the franchise. Such a magnanimous posture on the part of the rulers was a principal reason for the emergence of a peaceable British society with the Fabian Society as its leading force. Furthermore, a political party formed by the workers has been permitted to rule since World War I, and this change was accomplished peacefully.

The British political policy, which eschews extremism and practices tolerance and understanding, has strengthened the foundations of the British crown, a feudal vestige; kept intact the respectability of the system of nobility; and succeeded in creating a climate in which even the leaders of the Labor party gladly accept knighthood on their retirement from politics.

France offers a sharp contrast to this. French monarchs and aristocrats were unwilling to make a compromise with the citizenry before the revolution or in the postrevolutionary period of monarchical restoration. They continued in their hate-filled and vengeful ways. The bourgeoisie was not any different when it executed the monarch, the queen, and many aristocrats. Its bloodthirsty madness eventually resulted in a pandemonium of murderous purges among the revolutionaries themselves.

Subsequently, there arose a class struggle between the bourgeoisie and the proletariat, the Paris Commune. The battle among the royalists, the bourgeoisie, and the proletariat continued without any conciliation for 150 years until World War I, hurling the French political situation into fearful chaos.

Leaving aside the experience of other countries like France, we know that the pernicious spiritual legacy of the tragic factional strife during the five hundred years of the Yi kingdom (Chosŏn) still hovers over us. I referred to this in my letter last month.

Another historical lesson that the British have learned, according to Toynbee, relates to the American War of Independence. At the time of this war, unfortunate events could have been avoided if England had responded with even a modicum of magnanimity. In fact, according to John Adams, the second president, only a third of the Americans endorsed the Declaration of Independence; another third supported the British crown; and the final third advocated neutrality. Historical records show that even those who had espoused the Declaration of Independence adopted a conciliatory attitude, expecting benign action on the part of the king. The king and Parliament, however, acted rather imprudently. War followed as a result, and the American colonies won independence. England learned from this unprecedented setback and came to realize that repression is no solution when a colony is ready and determined to have independence.

Therefore, Britain granted autonomy to Canada in 1849 and subsequently to Australia and New Zealand. While France and the Netherlands were engaged in an armed confrontation with the liberation-seeking natives in Indochina and Indonesia, after World War II, England peacefully liberated most of its colonies, starting with India in 1947, followed by Pakistan, Ceylon, and other colonies in Asia, Africa, and Latin America. It is for this reason that most of the former colonies still remain members of the British Commonwealth.

The crimes enacted by imperialist nations in the colonial areas will be a permanent part of history, but the actions by the British, which testified to their insight and virtuous self-restraint, will also be recorded in history. England is no longer a superpower; it is a second-rate power, and its economic conditions are not very sound. The living conditions of the British people, however, have seen an all-around improvement, compared to any time in the past, and the British are maintaining ideological stability and vigor.

Today, mankind is experiencing an unprecedented ordeal and fluctuation. As we seek wisdom to help us find a way out of our cul-de-sac, I think the inspiration may come not from the superpowers of the United States and the Soviet Union but, instead, from England, which has shown us a wise and prudent course.

The Reason for the Defeat of Mao

I often read in Hong-il's letters about great purges that have been taking place recently in China. Judging from the self-criticism and downfall of Hua Guofeng and the sweeping purges of the remaining Maoist forces, the Maoist faction has clearly been dealt a lethal blow only a few years after his death. Mao became the chairperson in 1931 when he established a Chinese Soviet government. He ruled China for nearly half a century as its deified leader, with substantial popular support. How could anyone ever imagine that his heirs would collapse like a house of cards before the reactionary forces that came to life after his death?

It must have been due largely to his human and policy mistakes. First, he stubbornly adhered to policies that ran counter to the aspirations of the Chinese people. Since the Opium War of 1839, the Chinese people had wanted nothing more than the expulsion of foreign imperialist forces and repossession of the lost land. This enduring aspiration was almost completely realized except for the southeastern region of Siberia around the Amur and Usuri rivers (Taiwan is treated here as an internal problem). There is no way Mao's enormous contribution can be minimized.

Actually, the Chinese people saluted him with gratitude and respect, regardless of his ideology. Having attained their primary goal, however, they turned their attention to the next objectives, which were to improve the living standards of the people, pushing economic reconstruction at the fastest possible pace; to strengthen national security, especially against the Soviet Union; and above all, to restore China's status as a world power, in accordance with the traditional ethnocentric orientations. Incidentally, such party bureaucrats as Liu Shao Chi, Zhou Enlai, and Deng Xiaoping pushed for these objectives.

Mao, however, repudiated the policy of assigning top priority to economic growth, saying it corrupted the revolutionary spirit. He denounced Liu Shao Chi as a revisionist and stirred up the Red Guards into what is called the Great Cultural Revolution. Mao's objection to economic development as the top priority suggests an underlying and ulterior motive having to do with his power struggle against Liu Shao Chi. At any rate, his position drew the distrust and criticism of the Chinese people, who had fostered the above objectives as well as a vast array of modernization efforts in such areas as the military, the bureaucracy, and the industrial sector.

Another mistake was due to human error. Mao mobilized the Red Guards, who were in their teens or early twenties, and turned them against the top echelon leaders of the party who had been his revolutionary comrades for several decades and also against the leaders in other fields, such as the military, education, factories, and administration. He had these youths inflict bodily injuries and attack their character, until he finally drove his former comrades out of power. Granted that we are talking about a Communist society, we are still dealing with a society having a strong Confucian tradition of decorum and justice as well as saving face. In the sphere of the Confucian influence, we can easily imagine the kind of psychological reactions Mao's actions would provoke.

That Mao was forced to carry out the Great Cultural Revolution shows, in effect, that he had run into a wall of tenacious resistance and had begun to retreat step-by-step. The cadres of various ranks in diverse fields who had once been purged as revisionists, therefore, began to make their way back in large numbers under the leadership of Zhou Enlai. Finally, even Deng Xiaoping, one of the leading figures in the revisionist faction, could be restored to power. Even though Deng was purged yet again in Mao's lifetime, it was not sufficient to turn the tide.

It may not be an exaggeration, therefore, to state that Mao's defeat could have been foretold before his death. What, then, was the motivating force that gave the anti-Maoist forces such a dramatic and overwhelming triumph? It was the several-million-strong bureaucracy that blanketed Chinese society from top to bottom. Modern society is a bureaucratic society. As Max Weber explained so lucidly in his influential sociological works at the beginning of the twentieth century, bureaucratic management reigns supreme in modern society, not only in government but also in business, the military, the university, and in social and religious organizations. Like it or not, bureaucracy is an indispensable factor in administering the complex and enormous machinery of modern society. In both democratic and dictatorial systems, no organizational heads can ever rule and manage successfully without the cooperation of bureaucrats.

Weber views bureaucracy positively, but he also recognizes its drawbacks. Nevertheless, he values very highly its rationality, efficiency, democratic character in terms of nondiscrimination (i.e., impartially treating everyone according to rules), functional neutrality, and systematic way of supervising the whole efficiently.

Peter Blau in his *The Bureaucratic System in Modern Society* acknowledges the merits of the bureaucratic system but points out its shortcomings as well. These include its depersonalizing nature, formalism, inefficiency, antidemocratic bias, and manipulability as an instrument of dictatorship.

At any rate, bureaucracy is the monster of modern

society. It can render impotent even presidents or cabinet ministers and make a scarecrow of entrepreneurs. It appears that Mao was done in by bureaucracy because he underestimated its power. We may say that a revolutionary who accomplished the monumental task of changing the world brought his fate on himself through overconfidence, underestimating the chances of an ambush.

The Correct Acknowledgment of the Value of the Ch'unhyang Folktale

One of the shortcomings of the Korean people is their uncaring attitude toward what is uniquely theirs. The Ch'unhyang folktale, for example, should receive much higher acclaim and be cherished more dearly than it is today. I think it has to be made accessible to the whole nation. As you know, it was originally written as a traditional musical drama during the period of Kings Yŏngjo and Chŏnjo in the eighteenth century but was recast in its present form during the time of King Kojong in the middle of the nineteenth century, by one Shin Chae-hyo from Kojang in the Chŏnnam region. There have been numerous alterations in its content thus far, but its major plot continues to revolve around the fatal love affair between the young master Yi and Ch'unhyang. We often hear that it is the Korean version of Romeo and Juliet, but there is more substance to the Ch'unhyang folktale than to Romeo and Juliet, as I will explain below.

First, the process by which the Ch'unhyang folktale reached its present form involves ordinary people. There was no written script per se. It was the combined product of the masked actors, people of lowly class who first appeared in the King Sukjong period in the seventeenth century, and the ordinary people who made up the audiences. As a masked actor would improvise a story in the marketplace, when the mood warranted the audience would react with such humming refrains as "All Right!" or "There You Go!" The masked actors would then continue their improvisations according to the audience's responses. The traditional Korean opera, therefore, was a work of both the singers and the audience. In a similar way, the epic poems popular in medieval Europe were developed. In the case of the epic poems, however, troubadours recited, often with musical accompaniment; in the traditional Korean opera, the masked actor not only sang but also made up the story, acted, and danced. One person, in other words, performed three roles, which made it a colorful affair indeed. There are twelve varieties of the traditional Korean opera which were all the art of the people. The best known are Ch'unhyang; The Story of Hungbu and Nolbu, the two brothers; The Undersea Palace; and The Story of Simch'ŏng, the virtuous daughter. The Ch'unhyang is the best of all.

Second, the Ch'unhyang folktale was not simply a love story. It is the tale of a great struggle for human rights, involving a woman whose integrity under the feudal system was ignored. It is the story of a daughter of a lowly *kisaeng*, or woman entertainer, who defended her chastity for her lover, even risking her own life. She challenged Governor Pyon Hak'to as to whether a kisaeng had indeed no right to preserve her chastity and whether the *Daejun Tongpyŏn* (a bill of rights at that time) legalized the rape of a married woman, which she was. These passages enable us to get a glimpse of our ancestors in an introspective mood regarding contemporary values during the latter period of the Yi kingdom.

Third, the Ch'unhyang folktale is a representation of the people's resistance to, and strong satirical awareness of, the corruption of power. Because the masses could not interfere with the officials directly, they called on the government emissary, Yi Mongnyong, who composed a poem about exploitation by corrupt government officials and the pleas of the ordinary people. Yi proceeded to use his power as emissary to fire the corrupt official, Pyon Hak'-to. Resistance against corruption was not by direct action, however. It had to depend on the power of Yi, the government emissary; and the fight against corruption was not directed against the whole system but only against one government official in a town called Namwŏn. Furthermore, the firing of this official was all that was required for a happy ending. These details reveal the limits of popular consciousness at that time as well as the constraints under which these operas were placed because they were performed in front of aristocrats.

Fourth, because I am a layman in the field of art, I do not think I can offer anything of value concerning the artistic quality of the Ch'unhyang folktale. I can simply note again the unique form adopted by the traditional Korean opera to attain its consummate status in popular art. I can also call to mind the bold and progressive nature of Ch'unhyang's love on the first night; the tense dialogue between Ch'unhyang and the governor; the unaffected jubilation in the scene when the Namwŏn peasants meet the emissary; the stately humor of the part where Emissary Yi, disguised as a beggar, visits Ch'unhyang's mother; and the satirical realism in the abject behavior of the governor and other low-ranking officials when the emissary reveals his identity. I hope my thoughts on the Ch'unhyang folktale will inspire you and our children to study even more deeply what is uniquely ours.

The Economic Success of Japan and Germany

When I read in your and Hong-il's letters that Japan has proposed to the United States a loan of $10 billion to help cover its trade deficit, I thought that the world had indeed changed quite a bit. Who could have predicted the economic recovery of Japan and Germany, which were so thoroughly destroyed in World War II? Who could have anticipated that the American economy, which once almost monopolized the entire world trade, would find itself in such a troubled position as it occupies today?

Human thoughts cannot be predicted because human beings possess free will and do not react mechanically. Individuals react differently even to an identical stimulus, which makes predictions futile. There are many instances, however, in which necessary causes can be clearly identified. This happens sometimes when, once a result has been obtained, its causes are traced. The causes for the success of Japan and Germany fall into this category.

First, in light of the unfortunate consequences of the war reparations the Allied Powers demanded from Germany, no such action was taken against Japan and Germany after World War II. Furthermore, the United States, with its enormous wealth, did not withhold assistance to these two countries and created a market for them in special supplies that were needed in the Korean conflict and the Vietnam War. These were very lucky breaks for the two countries.

Second, the Japanese and German people made the most of their tragic defeats. When they became unnerved by the postwar uncertainties, they called upon their unique attributes of diligence, saving, frugality, and cooperation between labor and management and responded to the anxiety-ridden situation with everything at their command. In addition, the complete destruction of production facilities forced them to install new ones. Thus, the most modern, superior machinery was installed which made them highly competitive. Recognizing that their management system and technology lagged behind those of the United States, they studied American industry with almost fanatical zeal. We have to give a great deal of credit to the wisdom and crafty determination of both governments and peoples for having turned the misfortune of defeat in World War II into positive advances.

Third, another reason for their success is their economic policies, which concentrated totally on export trade, following the trend of the world economy that was expanding thanks to the extended forty-year peace after World War II. Exports have been the motivating factor in the economic growth of Japan and Germany.

Fourth, although there are slight differences between the two, both countries could rely on the United States for their national security and thus avoid heavy military expenditures. In spite of this, the Japanese tendency to shirk their own security responsibilities must be judged highly inappropriate considering that Japan has developed into a great economic power.

Fifth, it is most important to note that the two countries adopted democratic systems after the war. As in the Soviet Union today, there was economic growth in prewar Japan and Germany, but the fruits of production were not fairly distributed. Fair distribution is possible only when there is a guarantee of human rights under a democratic system, especially freedom of the press and labor activity. After they became democracies following World War II, these two countries effected a fair distribution of wealth benefiting the working class and the ordinary people, which, in turn, helped them realize social stability, a prerequisite to economic growth. Fairly distributed income was subsequently converted into savings or purchasing power, thus forming a basis for economic expansion.

I have thus far outlined the causes for the economic success of Japan and Germany. How does their future look? Although it cannot be predicted with certainty, this much can be said: foreign demands for an open market and balance of trade, pressure on the government for military spending, and the pursuit of hedonistic pleasures by the postwar generation who know little of earlier hardship will emerge as obstructing factors.

Until now, all they have had to do is follow in the footsteps of the United States. But they have surged to the front now and will have to solve problems, such as relations with the developing countries and the improvement of management science and technology, through their own creativity. Whether or not they will succeed in meeting these challenges is something to be watched closely. On the basis of what they have been able to accomplish, there is no reason to doubt they will succeed. What is clear in all this is that the economic success of Japan and Germany has given a great boost to the confidence and security of the entire free world.

Reasons for the Economic Stagnation of the United States and Other Countries

Why is it, then, that the economies of the victorious United States and England are mired in stagnation, if not failing outright? It should first be pointed out that they were the victor nations, unlike Japan and Germany. They could not demand from their people diligence, savings, frugality, and cooperation between labor and management. The climate was not conducive toward these ends. Moreover, they could not overhaul production facilities overnight because they were not damaged. As for management and technology, their frontrunner status made them feel rather relaxed about these issues and also negligent in their efforts to improve them. These internal factors played a major role in driving the American economy into stagnation. If the American economy is to revive, the Japanese should not be hysterically blamed for its problems. Rather, there should be a new whirlwind of movement toward the rationalization of management, technological reforms, and incentives for work. A new determination will be required.

Second, the chronic trade deficit can be cited as another factor, and it is attributable largely to the import of oil. The United States has enormous oil reserves that can be tapped, but it still imports half of its oil needs. In 1980, for example, the cost of U.S. oil imports was $32 billion, more than the year's trade deficit.

Third, American exports have been lagging because of its weakened economy and especially the declining value of the dollar. The inaccessibility of the Japanese market also must be considered a contributing factor. But today's situation has been brought about by American industries, which spent the 1960s and 1970s blindly pursuing monopolistic profits from military provisions without strengthening their international competitiveness through technological and management innovations.

Fourth, a major reason for the inflationary trends in America today stems from the rise in the price of domestic products. This has been a result of the curbing of imports by putting pressure on such countries as Korea in an effort to protect domestic industries that are not internationally competitive, for example, textile and footwear industries. It is only natural that prices will not go down unless the dying industries are converted into something new and the door is open to cheap imports. The problem, then, is the inability of the American economy to withstand the temporary pain of unemployment, thus making the decline of the competitiveness of the American economy inevitable.

Fifth, it is well known that the reckless, protracted involvement in the Vietnam War and excessive war expenditures ran the American economy aground. Further, American aid of such great magnitude has not been of much value for the economic reconstruction of the developing countries, but instead it has been misused by corrupt government leaders for their own purposes. As a result, the United States has not been successful in creating a market in the Third World, despite efforts to promote its economic development.

Sixth, a significant spiritual problem in this regard has to do with America's younger generation and, in particular, the leading group of middle-class people who feel hostility and hatred toward economic and technological omnipotence and consider economic slowdown or standstill necessary for the recovery of alienated humanity and the protection of the environment. Such thinking is supported by many people. Undoubtedly, these are demands to which we have to pay heed. However, there is strong opinion in America that the glory of the country and its confrontation with the Soviet Union require the economic revival of the United States. This cannot be ignored, and the best example of it is President Reagan. Regarding the future of America, I believe that it still possesses dynamic vitality and an ability to solve its problems.

Does God Exist?

April 26, 1982

To you and my beloved children with love and respect:

I received the letter you sent after your visit on the 19th. I felt very hurt when you wrote that your heart was torn at my appearance and my situation. Through a countless number of severe ordeals, you have managed to hold your own in the eyes of others. In your heart, however, how could piercing pain have stopped, even for one day? I know only too well that it is you and the family, rather than I, who deserve to be comforted. God will surely be with you, be proud of you, and love you.

How can I deny that I have held up as well as I have because of you? I thank you and pray all the time for you and the family from the bottom of my heart. Let me beseech you not to be too preoccupied with my condition. I wish the children would work with single-minded dedication for their future.

You told me during the last visit that Dr. Chong Il-hyŏng appeared to be nearing death. Given the gravity of his illness, there does not appear to be any hope. I think about him every day. He has led a truly remarkable life, consistently maintaining the proper attitude from the time of Japanese colonialism right up until today. It is not uncommon that many of our elders whom we respected highly destroyed their reputation and lifetime accomplishments because they were unable to preserve their commitment in the twilight of their lives. Dr. Chong has been an outstanding exception, and I believe that, in addition to Dr. Chong, Messrs. Chung Ku-yong and Hong Ik-pyo have also lived admirable lives. We all know that as ingredients for his success, Dr. Chong has had not only his own greatness but also Dr. Yi Tae-yong's outstanding cooperation as his spouse and partner.

To Hong-il:

Every time I read your letter, I can tell how much you care about your father. You know very well what kind of expectations I have of you. Work hard without stopping and with strong resolve and firm plans. Nothing is more important in making a successful life than aggressive desire and persistent efforts. I want you to live faithfully each and every day, determined never to dawdle away time and waste your life in a worthless manner. Take Jee-young and Chung-hwa to such places as historical palaces or the Minsok Village once or twice a month. This can be educational for children. Never hesitate on my account, but see to it that the children grow up to be admirable persons. I am deeply mortified that I did not provide good care for you.

To Jee-young's mother:

I am very delighted and satisfied to learn from your letter that you are managing a happy household with your children. How fortunate it is that your kids are bright and gentle. It seems that I already said what I wanted to say to you now when I wrote to you from the military prison in Seoul. Always read that letter over, and use it as a reference in cultivating a successful life. Keep in mind that half the responsibilities and credit for a husband's success belong to his wife. There is no greater stimulus for a husband than his wife's encouragement and occasional criticism. As I always say, try to become a wife who is respected as well as loved. And try to be a helpful wife.

To Jee-young:

Jee-young, your grandfather was surprised by your penmanship when reading your letter. What a splendid child you are! You listen to your father and mother, run errands for your mother and look after Chung-hwa, and you are making good progress in your piano lessons. Your grandfather is always thinking of you. I want you to eat plenty of rice and grow healthily.

To Chung-hwa:

Chung-hwa, from your mother's letter, your grandfather knows, much to his delight, that you are very kind. Your grandfather used to hold you on his head and play a peddler's game. You used to love it, but I wonder if you still remember. I am very thankful that you always pray with your sister for grandfather. Have fun playing healthily.

To Hong-up:

About you, my heart feels sorry and worried. But, as your mother says, because of your kind heart, you will certainly have a life that is blessed by God. What is most important for you is persistence; never fail to push a plan to the end, with firm resolve. Persistence is one of the most important ingredients for success in life. It is imperative to set up a feasible plan, divide it into weekly, monthly, and yearly segments, and then work at it step-by-step. This has been my experience. I am praying this year will be a good year for you. Always be prudent and careful when you drive. I know that you are taking the bus to come to Chŏngju. I am happy that you look healthy.

To Hong-gul:

When I read your letter, I can sense that you have grown up a lot, spiritually and intellectually. Your father is very pleased. When I picture you in your school life, my heart is gladdened immensely. Your plan to endeavor to cultivate all-around and high-level knowledge in addition to the required academic work in school is a good one. Further, I want you to strive for character development more than anything else in college life. Scholarship that is not founded on character is nothing more than shallow intellectual technique. I also want you to always listen to conscience, never hesitate to do good, seek balanced judgment, and serve others and society. I want you to possess such a character. Think about a plan to spend the summer vacation with friends with whom you share ideas, and travel around the countryside to learn about our country. When you read books on philosophy, do not leave out Kim Chun-sŏ's *Introduction to Philosophy*. Your father is not well versed in philosophy but has found his thinking to be very similar to mine.

Reflections on Easter

This year I could not go to mass on Easter but spent the day praying and meditating. What can be the basis for our belief in the existence of God? How does the death of Christ on the cross absolve us from our sins? Is resurrection something feasible? Why does evil run amok when God is omnipotent? Do prayers really get answered? There are many interested non-Christians as well as Christians who do not dare speak out but have doubts in their minds about these questions. Many theological works, however, focus on issues that are partial and technical in nature and not on these fundamental problems. For us general laypersons, it is not urgent or of primary importance.

Any issues beyond these are so overwhelmingly large that I cannot write lucid answers, based on the level of my knowledge of theology. Several months ago, Hong-up wrote, "If God exists, how could such a thing as the genocide of several million Jews happen? There are too many doubts that I would like to discuss with father." When I read this, I wanted to write something back but did not have the self-confidence to do it. This has been bothering me ever since, however. I decided to write this letter when I read yours of the 19th, in which you put down your anxious feelings following your visit, about answers to prayers. Undoubtedly what follows is unsophisticated and imperfect, but it represents a record of a journey to faith. I want you and the children to use it as a reference and respond if you have any opinions.

I once read an impressive book by a British author named Robinson. In it, he warned Christians against the hypocrisy of faith into which they could unwittingly fall so easily. Even if we commit that fallacy at times, we must march with sincerity on the road of honest believers. (I learned much of what is here from *One Faith*, a joint religious confession by Protestant and Catholic theologians.)

The Issue of God's Existence

This question has been a focal point of inquiry by philosophers for over two thousand years, from those before Plato up to Hegel and others. There are a variety of proofs regarding God's existence: first, the cosmological proof, which speaks of God's existence as the first cause, based on the theory of causation which originated with Aristotle; second, the teleological proof offered by Socrates, Plato, and Augustus and subsequently taken up by a number of scholars, which is the view that God is the cause of teleology that endowed nature with order and harmony; third, the God discussed by Descartes, God as the perfect being, leads to the noumenal proof that the perfect being must have the essence of existence; and fourth, as Kant argued, as long as there is nothing that corresponds satisfactorily between a good man and good results or between a bad man and bad results, there is room for the moralistic proof that God must exist in order to guarantee such a corresponding relationship in the other world.

There are difficulties with these contentions, however, as follows: first and second, they have the fallacy of abusing the theory of causation that can be proven only in the empirical domain by applying it to noumenon and third and fourth, there is a shortcoming in the definition of what must be and what is. (I wrote briefly here because I have written about this before.)

Because God is a transcendental being, a noumenal proof appears forever impossible. However, if in-depth psychology ever develops enough from its present kindergarten stage, there might come a time when God's existence can be conclusively demonstrated scientifically.

What appears rather plausible to me at this point is Toynbee's theory of God. According to Toynbee, all human beings, whether devilish men or illiterate barbarians, have instinctual concepts of good and evil, right and wrong, and they display them publicly. Such a common human phenomenon can be comprehensible only when the existence of good, justice, and God is taken into consideration.

From a theological standpoint, the deistic contention, as outlined above, can serve as a partial basis for understanding God, but it cannot be the complete key to it. Reason reaches a certain level of faith and demonstrates the compatibility between God's message and reason, which aids faith. Reason alone, however, cannot answer all the questions pertaining to faith. It is natural that rather limited human reason cannot explain all the messages concerning God, who far transcends reason. God's existence as discussed in religion cannot be shown by objective proof but only through individual experience. According to Pascal, we encounter God when and where we open up our minds to God and receive Him.

There are several ways to experience God. First is when we pray. When praying, we can listen through our conscience to the words of God concerning certain problems. God is said to be experienced directly through such a human dialogue with Him. Second, we can experience God when we read the Bible. As we directly participate in the Bible scene and receive the words of God as a direct statement to us, we experience God without even realizing it. Third, we experience God when we put into practice the love of neighbors. When we carry out God's love—that is, sacrifice ourselves unconditionally at the scene where our help and participation are needed—we are said to meet God.

As shown above, it is not through objective evidence that we come to know God. It is possible only through human dialogue and contact with Him which are brought about in our religious life. This is possible for anyone with genuine faith.

The Cross and Our Absolution

Before we talk about why the death of Jesus means the absolution of our sins, we need to consider what sin and original sin are. Sin is said to be a perverted, selfish state preoccupied with ego. When we quietly meditate, it becomes clear that greed, jealousy, hatred, stealing, murder, and all other kinds of sin are rooted in self-centeredness. It will be difficult for anyone to avoid sins that stem from such a state of mind. It must be only a symbolic expression to say that we all have become sinners because of Adam's sin, but we cannot deny that we are destined to commit sins from the moment of birth. Therefore, when we believe in the existence of God, we cannot avoid God's punishment for the fatal sins and cannot rest peacefully even for one day because of remorse for our sins. This is self-evident.

As we wander around with the remorse of conscience and the certainty of destruction, we find ourselves helpless, with only our own power. It is at such times that the absolving intervention of Jesus occurs. Christ's act of absolution is His acceptance of punishment on our behalf so that we may be saved. This is the decision of God's limitless love for us and the result of Christ's spontaneous and unconditional obedience to God's will. The life of Jesus, particularly His death on the cross, represents a form of existence that is exclusively for others. Therefore, we have come to be absolved of our sins by nothing more than the belief in God. What, then, is faith? It is said to be joining in the mission and the fate of Jesus. It is to live for others as Jesus did and follow in his footsteps, carrying the cross on our backs for the sake of God's love and justice. This means to become a disciple of Jesus on the basis of a new pledge to live a life patterned after Jesus. It is through all this that we can comprehend the true meaning of salvation and taste freedom, peace, love, joy, and true humanity. This is the salvation of the cross.

The Meaning of Faith in the Resurrection

How can a dead man come back to life? This is something that cannot be explained by human knowledge. It is not something, however, that cannot be comprehended. If we believe in God, omnipotent God cannot be limited in His activity because someone has died. It cannot be denied that God can take someone's life if He so desires and that God can also bring back to life a dead person.

If this is true, it is only natural that God would resurrect Jesus. After all, God sent Jesus to this world to fulfill His mission as the executor of God's will and, finally, in compliance with God's will, he died like a guilty man although he was not guilty. So Jesus became the first man to be resurrected. But the resurrection of Jesus cannot be fully understood by our reason. It goes without saying that in the final analysis it is through our faith that we can understand it.

Through resurrection, God made Jesus his equal and raised and increased His glory. But it was by no means an action to reward Jesus in personal terms. By making Jesus one with Him, God showed that what Jesus taught us was true and that those who would follow the teaching would be resurrected. This is said to be the fundamental meaning of the resurrection of Jesus and the evidence of God's endless love. So to believe in the resurrection of Jesus is to believe in our own resurrection and to gain great comfort and hope. Belief in resurrection is a prerequisite to becoming a good Christian. As I said earlier, it is through faith in resurrection that we make a choice between Jesus as God's son and accepting some other sage who came and left this world.

What difference will there be between the resurrection of Jesus and our own? As long as we have faith in resurrection, the question of when man will be resurrected after death is not an important issue. As proofs of the resurrection of Jesus, we can consider first the change of mind, at the risk of their lives, by His disciples, who had abandoned Him and run away at the time of the crucifixion; second, the conversion of Saint

Paul, who had considered Jesus his enemy and persecuted his disciples but later spent his life as an evangelist, defying the authorities who would put him to death; and third, in spite of the wretchedness of His death (which was a disquieting event for the Jews but a stupid death to the Hellenes), He was worshipped as God immediately afterward; an unprecedented fact in the history of world religion. Because I have written about these things before, I am not going into any detail here.

The Omnipotent God and the Triumph of Evil

Protestant and Catholic theologians state that Christianity has not fully answered the question, "When God is omnipotent why is there evil, and why does it frequently triumph while good men are defeated?" An answer to this query is very urgent for us and indispensable for relieving our anxieties and doubts about faith. Kant stated that proper reward and punishment for good and evil, which cannot be realized in this world, will be accomplished by God in the other world. As I wrote before, Toynbee argued that God is good and just, but not omnipotent.

In the religious community, one of the traditional explanations is that evil exists together with God as a protection for our free will, which was your answer to my questions some time ago. There are valid reasons for this, but there are some problems as well. First, to protect free will, would competition among good not be sufficient, rather than having to contend with evil? Second, there are situations in which free will has no chance to operate: when hundreds of thousands of people perish in a flash when an atom bomb explodes, when there is instant destruction due to earthquakes or typhoons, when a robber murders a child, when a child is born handicapped, and when the forces of evil, which cannot be coped with by individual powers, go on the rampage.

I have reflected a great deal on this issue and have agonized over it from the standpoint of faith. The problem is not completely resolved, but recently I am of the opinion that it can be generally thought of in the following manner. I have consulted *One Faith* (mentioned earlier) and other theological discourses.

Although God is omnipotent, He is not a computer operator who intervenes in everything that happens in this world. If God is thought of in that way, it is tantamount to considering Him a devil who deliberately gives us evil and even deliberately gives helpless children disease and misfortune. If God unilaterally decides everything, human free will loses its meaning. We have to repudiate such a God.

Then what is the relationship between God and secular affairs? Even though God exists in reality as we do, He does not carry out our responsibilities for us. After God created the universe, He entrusted the management of this world to us human beings. Furthermore, He revealed everything about how He wanted us to live and what His love consists in through many prophets since then and also through the life and death of his son, Jesus, whom He finally sent. Therefore, while human beings carry out their responsibilities entirely on their own, they progress toward the ultimate day, the day of the Second Coming. This is what God expects.

Human beings, however, are forever fostering evil by repeating sins and ignoring or betraying God's teaching. The responsibility for the predominance of evil in this world devolves on human beings. Hitler's massacre of the Jews was a breach of God's commandment of love. Instead of saying "human beings" I should say Christians. How many German churches were mobilized in support of Hitler? In all its long history, how much persecution has the church instigated against the Jews? Has the church, Protestant or Catholic, failed to take the part of the oppressed and argue for and bless them in accordance with God's commandment to befriend the poor and the troubled? At least before World War II, the church had stood firm amid such mistakes.

God neither creates nor confers evil. Most of it has been caused by human abuse of freedom. Disease can also be attributed to the carelessness of human beings—their negligence and their lack of effort to eliminate disease, instead channeling money and energy into such things as war. It should be seen that God will make up for all other small misfortunes as well as the evil for which human beings are responsible, in the other world if not in this.

So, is God totally indifferent to the evils of this world, and does He ignore them? This is absolutely not the case. God is always around us and constantly exhorts us to join in the life of His love. When we accept His invitation, He will encourage us in our endeavors and answer our questions. He will also guarantee, beyond any doubt, that our loving efforts, our efforts to participate in the purpose and destiny of Jesus, will succeed, although we, ourselves, may not be able to see this. He promises that our lives will be successful and happy and that we will attain eternal life in heaven.

We can believe in the eradication of evil and the triumph of justice and also in the perfection of this world and our eternal salvation only when we are at one with God. The key question here is whether we human beings, especially Christians, become the true disciples of Jesus and fulfill our mission or whether we wind up merely as hypocritical Christians. Fortunately, since the Second Vatican Assembly in 1965 and the Geneva Conference of the World Council of Churches (the theme was church and society), the church has taken a giant step toward implementing the ideals of freedom, justice, and God's love. We must pray for its success and actively participate in it.

Answers to Prayers

The problem of evil leaves much room for controversy and will arouse doubt. First, if God does not watch how we discharge our responsibilities, what good would it do to pray to God for assistance? So then one might even say that prayers are unnecessary.

I think there are two kinds of prayers through which to ask God for help. One leaves the solution of a problem entirely up to God. Those who believe in the results of such prayer may very well pray in that way. But there are certain dangers. First, it is easy for a human being to shift his or her responsibility onto God. Second, if the prayer proves futile, God may be blamed or faith weakened. Third, faith can be easily corrupted. Another way to pray for help is to place the problem before God and ask what one should do to, plead with Him to work with one, provide encouragement and the ability to cope, so long as one's efforts are according to His will. I think this kind of prayer avoids the dangers described above.

Fundamentally, prayer is an attempt to engage in a dialogue with God rather than to supplicate God. God communicates with us and waits for our response, so we have to pray to hear the words of God. When we raise certain problems, God will surely send a message to our conscience. There is the possibility that He may send messages before we raise the issue. True prayer is a human dialogue with God, and the last words of our prayers should be "Lord Jesus, we believe in you." This is a statement that confirms our belief in the justice, promise, and love of God. Our prayers must always be a dialogue with "You."

Prayer must therefore become a part of daily life, because in our daily activities we constantly encounter problems. We have to listen to God's words and respond by putting His love into practice. (I cannot write other things I really want to say because of lack of space.)

The Falsehood of Common Knowledge

May 25, 1982

To you and my béloved children with respect and love:

The month of May, the most bitter month for us, is now almost over. It has been two years of sorrow and loneliness, two years filled with grief. Even now, I do not want to remember these times. I have prayed for the family every day during the last two years, without missing a day. As I said during our visit, I could never have endured as I have if it were not for the comfort and encouragement I have found in dialogues with Lord Jesus and the belief that through Lord Jesus we can discover new possibilities even in the midst of all sorts of ordeals and despair.

Actually, I think my gains in terms of faith, intellectual growth, and character formation have been greater in the past two years than at any time in my life. I am thinking again with sorrow about the torments and worries our family, brothers, and friends have endured during this time. I am grateful and happy that, thanks to your love and sacrifices and those of the children, I have been able to wade through all the loneliness and ordeals, feeling at one with the family.

I dedicate all our efforts to the reunion of our family, which is, as you put it, our "minimum aspiration." Let it be realized as soon as possible.

I was truly delighted that you visited Mrs. Park Soon-chun, Dr. Chang Myon's wife, the Reverend Moon's parents, Professor Lee's mother, and Mrs. Lee Tae-young to comfort them. I can never forget them, and I wish them good health and comfort. I was very happy that you did not forget, that you took the trouble to visit them. I hope you will visit them often when the opportunity arises.

I hope Mrs. Lee Tae-young will step up her activities from now on, with firmer determination, remembering the spirit of the late Dr. Chung. Wise as she is, maybe she is already thinking about this. It would be very nice if, as Max Weber's wife did, she would write a wonderful memoir about her husband. Having been Dr. Chung's lifelong companion, Mrs. Lee could record his life since the days of Japanese colonialism. In those turbulent times, Dr. Chung exemplified a great nationalist and democratic spirit. I think such a project would be more than just a personal memorial; it would provide sorely needed testimony and a lesson to our nation, which will be growing up in the future.

Congratulations once again on Jee-young's mother's baptism. I hope she will grow and serve spiritually, under God's love. I am sending the following for guidance.

Human Civilization and Two Tasks

Today we seek the causes of the collapse of the Roman Empire in the downfall of the yeomen, the complacency with the vast slavery system, and the privileges and corruption of the nobility. The fall of the Ch'ing dynasty, however, is attributed to the static feudal system and the corruption of officials. Supposing today's world were to be ruined. Where could we find the causes? It is not an overstatement to say that our civilization depends on the establishment of a world government and equal distribution of wealth.

First, when we examine the question of establishing a world government, we can see that we have reached the stage when we cannot avoid the task. Stupendous development of communication and transportation systems has eliminated distance on earth. Contacts among all nations and states have increased in both regularity and frequency in the last 100 to 200 years and have unified and changed the political, economic, social, and cultural systems of all countries, generally along the lines of Western cultures. As for the economy, no country can possibly have a self-sufficient economy, and almost all countries are staking their fate on export and import. Population movement has become so frequent that in the last twenty years alone, about one million Koreans have migrated to North and South America. This is reality. There is an urgent need for the world to coexist in all aspects, under one global government. In view of the nuclear threat that could wipe out all of mankind, the need for world government is especially urgent.

Considering facts such as the U.S.-Soviet confrontations, the disorderly behavior of some 160 countries, and the untrammeled nationalistic selfishness, the argument for world government sounds like a dream. No matter how it may sound, however, history is ready and willing to mete out reward or punishment, depending on our attitude. Judging from history, when a nation reaches the stage when unification is inevitable, its response invariably was followed by appropriate reward or punishment.

Greek city-states had to form a unified state within the framework of one nation, one culture, and one economic domain. This was the only way to survive the threats from its northern neighbors and the ever-expanding Roman power. Nonetheless, the Greek state was engaged, from beginning to end, in shortsighted factionalism and was dominated, in turn, by Macedonia, Rome, and the Ottoman Empire (Turkey). Thus, for two thousand years until the nineteenth century, it was forced to live under the rule of foreign nations and heathens. Even today it is not able to free itself from the fate of being a small power in the world. In contrast, the Chinese people attained a unified state after the conflict-ridden 550 years of their early history. They were united in 221 B.C. by Emperor Huang Ti and have consistently preserved their unification and status as a great power. Punishment and reward are unmistakable, and we do not have to look elsewhere for examples. Even in our own history, such lessons are evident.

Because the unification of the Three Dynasties was brought about by a foreign power (i.e., the T'ang dynasty) instead of by ourselves, unification was limited to the area south of Pyŏngyang. We had to abandon the vast territory of the Koguryo dynasty and be satisfied with the status of a small country whose territory was only a fraction of Koguryo's. This is where we are today. Examples of this kind abound throughout the world, and we cannot avoid the monumental task of creating a world government and, finally, the complete unification of all mankind. How could we achieve this?

In the past, unification generally was brought about by the last surviving victors in armed conflicts. Given nuclear weapons that threaten the extinction of mankind, world unification by force cannot be imagined. How can we resolve this problem when the Communists, led by the Soviet Union, are attempting conquest by force? Most of all, the Soviet Union must first be convinced of the impossibility of conquering the world by force. Dissuading them depends on the unity of the free world and nonaligned nations. Such unity requires belief in, and expansion of, democratic freedoms, which are our greatest weapons, and the concentration of superior economic strength in the free nations to improve the quality of life for the people of the non-Communist countries. Only through such freedoms and the realization of justice can we dissuade the Soviet Union from its ambition and force it to agree to a genuine dialogue concerning peaceful coexistence and world unification. If the Soviet Union reaches this point, the concrete methods and step-by-step process of world unification can be figured out through mankind's wisdom. It should be added that the establishment of a world government by no means implies destruction of each nation's autonomy. World government repudiates only self-centered nationalism and would encourage and help develop unique national character. It is unification within diversity; no other way is feasible.

Second, the issue of the distribution of wealth is twofold: it involves equal distribution among rich and poor nations as well as among rich and poor within nations. This is vitally important.

When we scrutinize history we see that about twenty civilizations have disintegrated for the same reasons. One is war, and the other is internal class struggle. In the past, the limitation of productive capacity made plausible the excuse that not everyone could be rich. Today, however, modern industrial and superindustrial nations all enjoy a miraculous productive capacity that gives them the power to rescue the entire human race from poverty. Nevertheless, the gap between rich and poor is widening each day. How can we rationalize this? Moreover, poor people in developing countries have become wise to the extent that they will not tolerate this artificial unfairness.

All the countries of the world are confronted by situations that require them to make a choice, for example, the question of world government, and reward or punishment will depend on the choice. It may be said that at no other time in history has there been greater need for critical reflection, consideration, and decision by all of mankind. For while the potential reward is brighter than ever, punishment would bring truly dreadful results.

We Get the Treatment We Deserve

Ham Suk-hon has frequently said that "the treatment one gets is commensurate with one's caliber." I recently read *The Adventure of a Bystander* by a prominent American economist, Peter Drucker, and *Escape from Freedom* by Erich Fromm, which reminded me of Mr. Ham's words. Drucker is Austrian. He went to America to escape from Hitler. In his autobiographical work, he mentions three types of evil that helped Hitler. Everything he wrote was from his own experiences.

First, one German reporter who worked with him on the same newspaper dearly loved his pretty Jewish wife and joined the Nazi party to advance his career. Later, he was promoted to commander of Hitler's bodyguards and massacred hundreds of thousands of Jews and Germans (who were retarded as a result of genetic causes). Before he joined the Nazis, the man told Drucker that he would not go very far in his newspaper job, given his ability (or lack of it), nor would he be able to go abroad because he lacked knowledge of foreign languages and other talents. He did not like living as poorly as he was then, however, so he had no choice but to join the Nazis so as to get a piece of the pie. Joining for the sake of career advancement was the turning point. He became a heinous villain, and after the defeat of the Nazis, he committed suicide.

Second, another person he met was a correspondent for a famous Berlin newspaper. He was stationed in America, but his reputation was well known in Europe and the United States. When Hitler came to power, he invited this man to take control of the newspapers the government had expropriated. Drucker met the man in London on his way back from America. He told his friends who tried to dissuade him from returning to Germany:

> Hitler will have to rebuild the economy to maintain his power, which requires loans from the United States. To secure loans from America, he needs my influence in America. Therefore, he will have to listen to me. To catch a tiger, I am walking into a ti-

> ger's den. I am going to join hands with Hitler and will prevent his dictatorship with my power. Hitler will have to listen to me to survive.

When he returned to Germany he was given a big welcome. Two years later, when he had outlived his usefulness, however, he was discarded, never to be heard of again. (When I read this part of the book, I was struck by the similarity between this man's behavior and that of Yi Kwangsu, who feigned friendship when he first joined hands with Japan during the period of Japanese colonialism.)

Third, there is a story about a college professor. He was not only a renowned professor in the university where Drucker was a lecturer but also a man of high reputation in the German scholarly community. When Hitler grabbed power, an education official came to the university, called together all the teachers, and, using threats and foul language, fiercely attacked the anti-Hitler prejudice of university intellectuals. He then commanded anyone who wished to speak out to do so. All eyes were focused on the eminent professor. Knowing his integrity and his feelings about nazism, everyone expected that he would say something poignant. When he was given the floor, the professor stepped forward and said, "I have heard clearly what you have just said. My department of anthropology, by the way, is suffering from an inadequate budget. Could you do something about it?" The Nazi, who was expecting an attack, immediately acquiesced to the request. Everyone at the meeting was disappointed, but so long as no harm was being done anyone at the moment, no one dared say a word. According to Drucker, the kind of people who made the greatest contribution in support of the Nazi's pernicious acts in Germany were not the first type, the careerists, or even the second type, the well-meaning idealists, but the third type, who kept quiet about evil, even when their consciences rebelled.

When we recall the period of Japanese colonialism, we see this is a truism.

According to Erich Fromm's *Escape from Freedom*, modern man can be grouped according to authoritarian and automated types. Authoritarianism has two dimensions, sadism and masochism. The former simply tramples on anyone in an inferior position; the latter is obsequious and surrenders completely to superiors. This was a conspicuous phenomenon under Nazi rule, and Hitler himself was no exception. Since there was no one to whom Hitler had to be obedient, he subjugated himself to an imaginary entity he called the soul of the German race and was immersed in serving and worshiping it.

The automated type is outwardly oriented and, like a chameleon, gives up his or her own identity, private judgment, and independence of character. This type follows eagerly all the news of the world as it is reported and evaluated by the media. He imitates others in life-style or fashion and tries to mingle with the crowd by socializing with others at work or in his neighborhood on their terms. Even Sartre, in his existential philosophy, portrays the other-directedness of modern man in the imagery of a lost soul living in the constant awareness of how others see him. The majority of men today suffer from the loss of self typical of modern man but will change into the authoritarian type whenever an opportunity arises, just as the German people did under Hitler's rule.

In this age, the twentieth century, these two characteristics of modern man are reflected in the single fact that such systems as nazism and communism, which enslave human beings, have become possible. We must give critical thought to the qualities of the individual who could lead us to a fundamental realization that our individual characteristics are God-given and cannot be surrendered to anyone. Without this conviction, we cannot become masters of this age. Especially since we are locked in a life-or-death confrontation with communism, we should reject escape from freedom under all circumstances and stoutly defend our rights. I believe this is the way to prevent Communist domination.

We should consider anticommunism from a fundamental standpoint and examine our position critically and with a great sense of urgency, as both the government and the general public do.

The Falsehood of Historical Common Knowledge

When we read history, we have to be aware that there is a great deal that requires the reevaluation of common concepts. Reports of certain individuals and events that appear conclusive and thus form the basis of common knowledge need to be reevaluated. Because of lack of space, I will cite only a few of the more outstanding examples.

History tells us that everyone considers Alexander the Great and Napoleon as the greatest heroes in Western history and Sparta as a solid, model state. However, we deem Emperer Qin Shih Huang-di and Cao Cao as the great villains in Chinese history. This view, held by many people, is considered common knowledge. This may be valid if we define a hero or a great man as one with great accomplishments, right or wrong. But if we base our definition on whether a man made positive contributions to progress or helped the people, then this common knowledge needs a great deal of revision.

Let us first discuss Alexander the Great. He started at the young age of 21 and in only ten years established control over the Greek city-states, swept through Asia Minor, the Middle East region, Egypt, Babylon, Iran, and the Persian Empire, and, finally, even conquered the western part of India. His victories, however, inflicted death, destruction, and pain on countless people and made little contribution to the well-being of any group or to the progress of history. Alexander's historical mission was not the conquest of Asia, which was risky and impractical, it was first to attain the solid unification of Greece, to give peace, rest, and prosperity to his people, and to be ready to compete with Rome, which was growing stronger to the west. Even in terms of expeditions, Alexander should not have gone beyond the Mediterranean region, the hemisphere of the Greek states. The most worthwhile, albeit unintended, gain of Alexander's eastern expedition was the propagation of Greek civilization, which led to the development of Hellenism, without which the Greek civilization would have been almost entirely lost.

Bertrand Russell described Alexander by quoting from "Aristotle, Teacher of Young Alexander" in A. M. Ben's history of Western philosophy. He says, "He was an arrogant character, liked to drink, was cruel, very vengeful, and highly superstitious. He possessed both the cruelty and the craziness of an Oriental despot." (Hegel, however, thought that Alexander's life proved the usefulness of philosophy.) The laudatory assessments of Alexander were influenced greatly by Plutarch, who praised him very highly in his book on heroes.

Second, I will write about Napoleon. He was a genius. He excelled not only in strategy but also in insight and the capacity for action as a ruler. In fact, Napoleon played very positive roles until he became emperor in 1804. From 1799, when he became corporal, until 1804, he restored peace and order for his people who were struggling in war and internal chaos; strengthened national defense by crushing threats of foreign invasion; successfully stabilized the economy, including the value of currency, which had plummeted; maintained a balance between the new, rising bourgeoisie and landowning peasantry by promulgating the Napoleonic Code; and created a system of law that reflected the modern, democratic spirit, that is, equality before the law, the inviolability of property ownership, and freedom of religion.

Once he became emperor, however, he changed abruptly from a defender of the French Revolution to its betrayer, from guardian of freedom to its destroyer, and from republican to despot. In the ten years after he ascended the throne until his fall, Napoleon was the source of all that brought death, destruction, and subjugation to the people of France and Europe. When we speak of Napoleon, we must always distinguish between the great Napoleon who, as corporal before 1804, stood on the side of the people, and the Napoleon who, as emperor, became corrupt and betrayed them.

The providence of history is great, however. In spite of the ills he brought, Napoleon's war of conquest against all of Europe yielded enormous, unexpected benefits. His victory over several European monarchs violently shook the foundations of the feudal order and catalyzed the germination and growth of democratic forces. The greatness of a democratic polity established by the French Revolution was proven through his successful wars of conquest, which stirred the nationalism of each nation and thus implemented the creation of the modern nation-state. The defeats of Spain and Portugal brought about liberation and independence of their colonies in the Caribbean and South America. The feverish glorification of Napoleon occurred after his death as a result of the influence of romanticism, which swept through Europe in the middle of the nineteenth century. It is true that, among the several Greek city-states, Sparta possessed the most courageous military force, and its culture was predominantly characterized by frugality, perseverance through ordeal, courage, and the pursuit of glory. Therefore, it attained political stability because of the modest and austere lifestyle of its people and received commendations from the people of other Greek city-states who were fed up with the persistent disorder and corruption at home. Sparta's reputation later became as distinguished as it was particularly because Plato, in his theory of state, praised and imitated it and also because Plutarch gave it a high mark.

But the truth is that Sparta was not faithful to progress at that time, and it failed to bring happiness to its people. It contained grave weaknesses. Around the eighth century B.C., other city-states built colonies on the shores of the Black Sea on the Italian peninsula, near the island of Sicily, and they solved the problem of food shortage by sending manpower or other exports to Sparta. Sparta alone conquered neighboring Messina and forced it to provide food. At home, it exploited the oppressed, who outnumbered by twenty times its own population of 25,000. Strong military force, therefore, was a logical necessity. To overcome the incessant rebellion of the conquered, it became heavily militarized. Examples of this were the prohibition of labor by citizens and their total dedication to military duties; maintenance of secret police to watch the conquered; declaration of war against the conquered once a year, followed by massacre of suspected subversives; abandoning of sick and infirm children; regimented life and military training until the age of 20; encouragement of robbery during training; prohibition of intimacy between man and wife until the age of 30; joint training of boys and girls in the nude; suggestion of sexual intercourse with other males if unable to beget a child and similar instruction when the husband is sick; humiliation for wailing over the death of a child in war; overreaction against cowardice; and persecution of deserters. From a historical standpoint, Sparta, along with Assyria and the Ottoman Empire, represents a prototype of a methodical and inhumane militarism. This is not something we can imitate or praise today.

A summary of my overall assessment of Sparta is as follows.

1. In an effort to solve its food and population problems, Sparta did not rely on effective and sound methods such as trade and the opening up of colonies abroad. Instead, it attempted to solve its problems by exploitation of its neighbor, whose productive capacity was poor. This was a very crude policy.

2. Sparta pursued policies that ran counter to human nature. They brought about the destruction of families and a rapid decline in the population. Thus, its policies were self-destructive.

3. The ultra-dictatorship under the pretext of national defense inevitably led to the corruption of the ruling class and thus accelerated the deterioration of national strength.

4. The exclusively military nature of education imposed on the Spartans made them abnormal individuals who had lost the ability to adapt to reality. In the latter part of the fifth century B.C., therefore, Sparta emerged as the reigning power in the Greek world by triumphing over Athens in the Peloponnesian region, but it soon became an object of contempt by other Greek city-states and finally crumbled under their resistance because it lacked the political capability to govern. In 371 B.C., Sparta was defeated by Thebes, and its glory was shattered.

5. The exclusive, ignorant attitudes of the Spartans made them incapable of understanding correctly the flow and demands of history (e.g., to be prepared for the threats of the northern race in the fourth century and, later, Rome on the west). This led them to oppose and crush the movement to unite the Greek city-states, a decisive mistake.

In our society today, there are many individuals who do not recognize the ahistorical and inhumane nature of Spartan politics and its humiliating failures. They entertain the dangerous idea of idolizing Spartan politics and education. I want to emphasize the danger of easily accepting history as common knowledge.

Fourth, I want to change the topic and examine Emperor Qin Shih Huang-di, who has been denounced as the most objectionable despot. I shall critically evaluate the falsehood of historical common knowledge.

Emperor Shih Huang-di repressed freedom of speech to further his policies (during the period of warring dynasties, the greatest freedom of speech in the history of China was allowed). He also treated Confucian scholars, who opposed him, with extremely harsh retaliatory measures, such as burning their books and burying them alive. Even though there may have been some exaggeration about this later, these things did happen. Furthermore, he adopted a very radical and hasty approach in an attempt to root out in one stroke the thousand-year-old feudal system. He made the mistake of lumping the deeply entrenched feudal elements together with his enemies. His greatest error was in whipping them into building the Great Wall and digging canals when the people were already taxed to the limit, were utterly starved by the 550-year war of the period of warring dynasties, and needed to rest and recover their strength. In addition, he started ill-conceived civil engineering projects such as Afanggong and Yaoshannung, which, although superficially justifiable, alienated the people and thus sowed the seeds of destruction of the Jin dynasty after his death.

In spite of these errors, however, he brought enormous benefits to China and the Chinese people. As stated earlier, he brought the interminable war to an end and completed the task of unifying the entire land, which formed the basis of the unified state that he built and the Chinese have maintained ever since. Above all, he liberated the people from the agony of turmoil.

He terminated the feudal system that had persisted for 1,000 years under the Zhou dynasty and set up a centralized, bureaucratic state based on county and provincial units which determined the political form of

China for the next 2,000 years or more. (Our country also adopted this system after the unification by Silla.) He either refined or established a measurement system, a monetary system, laws, an almanac, wheels, etiquette, and Chinese characters, and he opened canals. All these accomplishments had a great influence on Chinese society and economy, not only then but later. Pursuing the ideology and policy of a school of thought that emphasized the need to make the country rich and strong, he adopted and promoted rationalism, legalism, scientism, and national wealth and military strength. This was 2,100 years ago. The spirit this exemplifies is congruent with the spirit underlying the modernization of the West. In a sense, he was born 2,000 years too early.

These great accomplishments notwithstanding, he is called the incarnation of despotism. This is because Confucian scholars who had participated in government for 2,000 years since the Han dynasty denounced him over and over in retaliation for his repressive policies against Confucianism. There has been a reassessment of Emperor Qin Shih Huang-di and the benefits he brought to his people by Eastern and Western historians alike, and he has been highly esteemed.

Toynbee strongly advocates such an interpretation. In view of the reevaluation of Emperor Qin Shih Huang-di, we again realize the importance of revising our historical judgments.

Then, there is Cao Cao. I mention him here not because he had any remarkable accomplishments as emperor but because I want to point out the falsehood of historical common knowledge, which treated him as such a villain, and thus stress the need to judge history with caution and on the basis of the two principles mentioned earlier. The reason Cao Cao was treated as such a conniving figure was that according to the traditional mode of thinking in the Confucianist mind, Liubei of Zhuhan was regarded as the rightful heir to the Han dynasty because his surname happened to be Liu.

As a result, Cao Cao, who was fighting against Liu, had to be considered a villain. According to Sanguozhi, which is official history, however, this is not necessarily true. The decisive factor that made Cao Cao a villain was the glorification of Liubei, Zhugelliang, and Guanyunzhang in the novel *Sanguozhi.* In reality, there is sufficient reason to give Cao Cao great credit. Although he failed to unify the land because of the defeat at Chibi, he brought peace and stability to Zhongyuan, the heartland of China, and enhanced the power of the people through the policy of enriching and strengthening the nation by using the military to aid in agriculture.

As discussed above, I believe that we should not be swayed by common knowledge but refocus with correct historical insight to achieve an independent assessment of history. It is from this perspective that we have to reevaluate and criticize our history. Already such popular leaders as Ch'oe Che-u and Chŏn Porgjunchun and the realist scholars like Yi lk, Yu Hyangwŏn, Hong Taehŏn, Pak Chiwŏn, Pak Chega, and Chŏng Yagyong are being reevaluated, and such folk art as masked dance and the traditional Korean opera are now being reexamined from a new perspective. But this is only a beginning.

Love that Gives and Love that Takes

June 25, 1982

To you and my beloved children with love and respect:

Today is June 25. Fresh in my memories is the anti-Korean, savage behavior of the Communists which gave rise to the national tragedy of thirty-two years ago and the ensuing events. When I think about our situation today, I cannot but feel the precariousness of our nation. The treacherousness and severity of my personal fate was precipitated by the June 25 Conflict. Since I miraculously broke out of the Communist imprisonment on June 25, I have been involved in political life, hoping to contribute to establishing a sound democratic system in which such a tragic fate would not be repeated, but I have had to endure innumerable ordeals and four brushes with death.

I can only feel frustrated because I and our country cannot yet enjoy genuine safety and freedom. When I think about the energy of our nation in overcoming the June 25 Conflict and the very real education that we had from the Communists during it, and the inextinguishable aspirations of our people for democracy, I want to look ahead with hope and belief, although there are still many sad and perplexing problems.

Although I have walked a trying path since June 25, hurdling over four encounters with death, I believe that my life has been worthwhile. If what to become were life's goal, I would be said to be a complete loser. If how to live were life's purpose, however, I can console myself in thinking my life has been of some value. On this day, I pray earnestly to Lord Jesus who oversees history, liberates us, and leads us in the path of justice and peace that He will give our nation the strength and wisdom to bring about the security of our country and people, the realization of freedom, peace, and justice, and the peaceful unification of our fatherland.

I have learned from your letter that our compatriot, Lee Hyup, has been safely released from prison. I cannot find words to comfort him for his trials and cannot pay enough respect to his unusual conscience and the way he acts on it.

My greatest pastime in recent days has been going

out to the flower beds to tend the plants—the common marigolds are already wilting. Petunias, globe amaranths, hollyhocks, yellow cosmos, maidenhair ferns, and balsams are blooming now. Yellow cosmos, maidenhair ferns, and small-petaled petunias are my favorites. When I read that you are tending the flowers at home, thinking of me, and that trees there have grown beyond recognition, I have a great longing to see them.

As for my health, as I said during your last visit, I am still feeling pains from the swelling and aching of the leg and the tinnitus. For the past ten days, I have been taking the "Listen" tablets you have been talking about, thanks to an arrangement with a doctor here.

Recently, I have been reading Fromm's *To Have or To Be?*, Weber's *Economy and Society, Culture and Rule*, published by the Christian Institute of Social Problems, Kissinger's *White House Years*, and Maurois's, *The History of England*. I am also reading Yi Tongch'ŏl's *Five Widows*. It is a report filled with the author's affectionate but unexaggerated feelings about countless stories we hear about powerless people who are being ridiculed and destroyed in our evil social structure. My heart is imbued with the author's feelings for these people as if I were a companion who shares life and death with them.

Yi Tongch'ŏl is indeed a Christian who takes part in Lord Christ's purpose and can be said to be an outstanding example of conscience in action. When we consider his former life, which was so corrupt, we realize the great possibilities of human beings and find a reason to be hopeful about tomorrow.

In the summer season, everyone in the family should take good care of their health, especially you, because you cannot endure the heat. Health in the post-midlife period requires, more than anything else, avoiding overexertion. I hope you will never overdo as you did last fall when you were knitting socks. You cannot realize how much solace and hope the letters you send every day bring to me. In the more than five hundred letters you have written, you have given me comfort and strength. You have done a truly marvelous thing. How can I express my feelings with simple words of thanks?

I have great expectations of Hong-il. I sincerely hope that he will attain greatness as a person who will serve our country and our people, as I have not been able to do. Once in a while I think to myself that we can hang our hopes on him because of his personality and ability. Incessant efforts for self-development are required in preparation for such a future, and I am hoping from the bottom of my heart that he will not be lazy in his efforts but will persevere with tenacious will and persistence. From his letter I can tell that Jee-young's mother is looking after her husband and children with affection and sincerity.

I can see Jee-young's image is gaining in intelligence each day, and I cannot help but smile when I read about Chung-hwa's profile, sulking and stubborn. When we think of the personalities of the two children, which are in sharp contrast in spite of the same parents and environment, we cannot help but wonder again at the mysteries of human beings.

I received your letter of the 22d only yesterday and learned that Hong-up's application for a passport was moving along. That is lucky, indeed. I cannot contain my happiness and gratitude when I think that this will give him a new beginning and great possibilities for his future. I am very pleased by your efforts and judgment and want to praise Hong-up's agreement to it. Actually, it must have been difficult for him, at his age, to begin studying in an unfamiliar country. I believe that God will bless Hong-up generously for his gentle and beautiful heart.

Candidly, from the instant I heard during the last visit about Hong-up's plan to study in America, I was delighted and yet felt very sad to have to part with my child under these circumstances. We must rise above petty emotions and unfortunate fate, however, and bless the road that leads to our child's future. I feel reassured in knowing all the preparations and guidance for the trip to America will be well taken care of by your experience. If you have a chance, please send my gratitude to the Reverend Crowe, who sent the invitation, and President Laney of Emory University, who helped in securing a visa.

I am very happy that I will get to see Hong-gul the next visit. It will be the first time in nearly half a year. I will see him as a college student, with his hair grown, and in a suit. When I read his letters, I can see a noticeable increase in his inner growth. Even though they were brief postcards, I judge that he is progressing in a very desirable way. I get a glimpse of his attitude when he calmly reflects on himself and things, seeing through problems in a basic and balanced manner. If we could talk enough, I could understand him more deeply, and I feel I could give him really useful advice. But what can I do in these circumstances?

Do give thought to traveling around the country during vacation, as you suggested last time. Tell him to send me the title of the book he read.

I send my regards to the Dae-ui family, the Dae-hyun family, Pil-dong, and all the other relatives and friends. Particularly to those who have suffered on my account and have prayed and worried about me, I extend my limitless gratitude. When will we have a chance to thank them and to pay them back?

I am writing the following for you and the children to refer to. Please examine it to see if my views are consistent with those on the outside.

The Middle Eastern Situation and Israel

I know the facts of the Israeli invasion of Lebanon from the recent letters from you and Hong-il. The Middle Eastern uncertainty and repeated military clashes indeed present a grave situation, and I cannot but feel concerned, because they are serious enough to determine the fate of the free world and our country for reasons I will explain below.

First, let us survey the relationship between Israel and Palestine from a historical point of view. During the prehistoric age, the Palestine area, now occupied by Israel, was inhabited from 3,000 B.C. by the Jacobs and by the Shems. From 1,200 B.C. on, however, Israelis moved in under Moses' leadership. At about the same time, the Palestinians (the blessed according to the Bible) probably came from Crete. They cohabited with the Hebrews, but sometimes drove them into mountainous areas. They survived this period of conquest and settlement, according to the Bible, and were ruled first by the kingdom of Israel, under David, and subsequently by the kingdom of Saul.

After King Solomon, the kingdom of David was divided into Israel and Judah. These two kingdoms were subsequently destroyed by Assyria (722 B.C.) and New Babylonia (587 B.C.), respectively. The Palestinian area meanwhile had entered a period of colonization by foreign enemies which lasted until the middle twentieth century. After New Babylonia, it changed hands—from Persia to Alexandros to Ptolemy of Egypt and Seljuk of Syria—until it finally became a Roman territory from 63 B.C. to A.D. 395. During the time from A.D. 66 to A.D. 70, the famous war of Judah resulted in the expulsion of the Jews, which was completed by the middle second century. For the next 2,000 years, the Jews lived in the Diaspora, while Palestinians alone resided in Palestine. Then the Palestine region fell under the rules of Byzantium, the Saracens, the Crusaders, the Mameluke, and, for 400 years from the sixteenth century, the Ottoman Turks. In 1920, it was placed under British trusteeship.

Meanwhile, the Jews, who were scattered all over Europe, grieved by the destruction of their homeland

and religious persecution, in the late nineteenth century began the Zionist movement, which aimed to rebuild Israel in what had been Palestine. England, which needed Jewish support in World War I, supported the establishment of Israel in the so-called Declaration. But this Declaration resulted in the endorsement of an independent Palestine by the Hussein-MacMillan agreement. Thus, the struggle between the Jewish and Palestinian people intensified. Later, during World War II, Jewish refugees fleeing from Hitler's persecution led to a rapid growth of the Jewish population in England. They expanded their domain by economic force or through the purchase of real estate. In 1947, the United Nations General Assembly adopted a resolution dividing Palestine into two independent states, one Jewish and one Arab. The Jews established Israel in 1948, but the Palestinians opposed it, and the Arab states went to war—the first Middle East war. There were four Middle East wars before 1974, and peace still remains remote.

In the wake of these years, Israel forcibly or through socioeconomic pressure drove out the Palestinians, who were gathered mainly around Lebanon. The number of Lebanese refugees may total about 3 million.

When we judge the Palestinian situation objectively, it seems only natural that Israel should acquire living space in its ancient homeland. Who can object to their demands when 6 million of them were victimized for no reason at all during World War II. Such sacrifices would not have happened if they had had a state of their own. The more we understand the Israeli position, however, the more we are compelled, regretfully, to feel that the Israelis are shifting onto the Palestinians the blame for the destruction of their country and are not making an honest effort to solve the Palestinians' righteous demands. Many sensible persons point this out. Israel should demonstrate that it recognizes the

Palestinians' right to independence, as determined by the United Nations General Assembly in 1947.

Should Israel insist on its current narrow-minded attitude and maintain its position of arbitrarily using force, it will produce very unfortunate results, even for Israel itself. In other words, if Israel, with a population of only 4 million, continues to fight, constantly taking on enormous war expenditures, its strength will be exhausted and its international isolation will increase. As is already becoming apparent, opinion in the free world—even in America, its most dependable ally—will deteriorate. Once that happens, Israel will win a battle but lose the war, or win the war but lose the struggle for existence. Such an outcome seems likely.

When we consider that it is the birthplace of the Christian religion and that Lord Jesus was of the Jewish culture, we cannot treat the fate and misfortune of Israel strictly as someone else's business. We are deeply involved in the Middle East situation because it is a problem directly linked to the survival of the free world and our own country. The Middle East supplies nearly half the oil needed by the free world, including our country, which makes it an economic lifeline and a vital trading zone. The Soviet Union, which has advanced into Afghanistan, Ethiopia, and South Yemen, is attempting to establish military and political dominance in this region by fostering confrontations between Israel and the Arab states, hoping to destroy the free world economically and at the same time divide East and West militarily. For this reason, the Soviet Union is keeping a closer watch on the Middle East than on any other area in the world. Unfortunately, this region is characterized by the great political instabilities of the countries there.

If the free world is to avoid a devastating catastrophe, the Israeli-Arab dispute has to be settled at any cost, and the solidarity between the Arab states and the free world, led by the United States, has to be strengthened again so as to crush Soviet ambitions. Furthermore, even if Israel were to win the war against its neighbors, it cannot survive if the Arab states are pushed by anti-American and pro-Soviet sentiments that might place the entire Middle East under Soviet influence. It is regrettable that Israel is not cooperating with America, its only protector for all practical purposes, instead of frequently putting the United States in a difficult position. Israel needs to exercise long-range judgments and decisions. (Even though it is in the minority, the Labor party holds almost half the seats in the Knesset and seems tobe taking a very sound position.) We cannot overemphasize the significance of the Middle East problem for the whole world.

Love that Gives and Love that Takes

In reading Fromm's *To Have or To Be*? recently, I gained a new understanding about the love that gives and the love that takes, which made me realize again the importance of reading.

Why do a young man and woman appear beautiful and wonderful to each other when they are in love but feel disillusioned after they are married or even, in some severe cases, get divorced? When children are young, parents and children are in loving harmony, but, as children grow, they also grow apart and begin to grumble and criticize each other. Close friends at school become almost strangers after leaving school and friendship cools. Why? We tend to view these things as inevitable and somehow natural. They are not inevitable and natural, however, but can be attributed to mistaken changes in our loving attitude. In premarital relationships, our minds are preoccupied with caring for the lover only. One is preoccupied with giving love and is content with it. There is no ulterior motive or greed. It is only natural that a person with such unselfish and great love would appear beautiful and wonderful. In fact, it is said that people become beautiful when they are in this loving and giving state. Once married, however, the husband's attitude suddenly changes, and he demands that his wife fulfill her duties as a wife. His love has now become the taking love. The wife also becomes demanding, expecting her husband to live up to his responsibilities and obligations to support her. Hers may be less compelling than his, but it too has become the taking love. Therefore, the couple becomes disillusioned and dissatisfied, each feeling the other is a different person from the one they married. So the relationship cools.

As for parents and children, when children are young, parents feel only giving love, and the children respond by loving as if their parents were the only people in the world. Once the children begin to grow up, however, the parents begin to demand that their children do well and live up to their expectations, that they preserve the family reputation and show filial piety. Children begin to look critically at their parents and to compare them with other parents. Both sides start to stress the taking love, and their relationships grow distant and deteriorate. The same sort of thing holds true in peer relationships.

If we are to build a happy married life, we have to maintain the giving love of the premarital period. If we are to maintain a loving and caring relationship between parents and children or if we are to keep peer relationships as lifelong friendships, we must continue our original, giving love. Those who are successful in their marital relationships and their relationships as parents with children or as friends to friends are those who practice the giving love.

We know well that Lord Jesus is the prime example of the love that gives. He befriended and served the troubled and the alienated with unconditional love and, in the end, gave his life for us. He was the perfect expression of giving love. His only demand from us was that we should practice this sort of giving love. "Love each other as I have loved you. . . . If asked for clothes, give even your shirt. . . . If invited to travel five miles together, travel ten together."

King Sejo and Dr. Rhee

When we contemplate King Sejo, the seventh king of the Yi dynasty, and the first president, Syngman Rhee, we see that both committed the same mistakes and left us with the feeling of frustration. Their mistakes were first, the destruction of legitimacy; second, the promotion of a political climate based on expediency and opportunism; and third, misdirection of historical progress.

Let me discuss first the destruction of legitimacy. King Sejo stole the crown from his young nephew, Danjong, and committed regicide, thereby brutally violating loyalty and filial piety, the first principles of the Confucian code, which was the official religion of the Yi dynasty. By killing the king, he was guilty of high treason, and by betraying the wishes of King Sejong, Tanjong's father, who had earnestly requested him to look after his son, he grossly breached filial piety. Trampling on the state doctrines of loyalty and filial piety, he usurped the throne and thus repeatedly violated the legitimacy of the dynasty. Since forcing the abdication of a legitimate king and robbing him of his crown was, judged by the laws of the dynasty, an illegal and improper act, the legitimacy of the dynasty must be considered to have been breached.

Syngman Rhee did not hesitate to protect Japanese sympathizers. There was a moral imperative that once liberated from Japanese colonialism, the government of the Republic of Korea should eliminate pro-Japanese elements and promote the independence movement that had been organized by anti-Japanese activists or at least by those who did not collaborate with Japanese colonialism. Further, there was the legal imperative, according to the preamble of the constitution, that the Republic of Korea was the government to inherit the spirit of the March 1 Movement and the legality of the provisional government of the Republic of Korea. Rhee ignored these imperatives. He used force to prevent the Special Commission to Punish Anti-Nationalists from operating, even though it had been legally established by law, and he also disbanded the commission's police. In such illegal actions, he violated the founding spirit of the nation and annihilated the legitimacy of politics. (Further, even though his complicity is not known, his lieutenants assassinated Kim Ku, the leader of the anti-Japanese struggle and head of the provisional government of the Republic of Korea. This was the most dramatic measure in his destruction of legitimacy.)

Moreover, Rhee repeatedly violated democracy, the founding framework of the Republic of Korea, and stirred up political turmoil. He railroaded a constitutional amendment using the "arithmetic rounding method," he repressed the opposition party and the press, and he committed illegalities in elections.

Rhee's second mistake was the creation of a political climate based on expediency and opportunism. The dynastic government was split into two factions because of Suyang Taegun's disloyal and impious destruction of legitimacy. One was the opposition force, which centered around six officials, including Sŏng San-mun, who were to lose their lives trying to return Tanjong to the throne; the other group was led by Chŏng Inji and Sin Sukju who supported Suyang Taegun. The former group of loyal officials who adhered to conscience and justice were, without exception, overthrown and killed, and the latter group of unprincipled opportunists gained influence and power. So, the men who followed the rules of expediency and opportunism reigned supreme and no one could or was compelled to live righteously.

As a result of Rhee's policy of protecting the pro-Japanese elements, the world became a society dominated by Japanese sympathizers and their children. Those who belonged to the independence movement or rejected the pro-Japanese policies in favor of their own principles had no power. If an anti-Japanese patriot had suffered much hardship, living in a shack until he finally died, people would learn about him only when newspapers reported his death. Rhee's antidemocratic, dictatorial politics persecuted all democratic compatriots and made a mockery of constitutional provisions for human rights and the basic principles of democracy. Honesty, conscience, ideals, and the like were obstacles to career advancement. The only way to succeed was to live expediently and opportunistically, riding the tide of the times. Such a wrong attitude was hammered into the minds of most people. In brief, the destruction of national ethics was brought about.

Rhee's third grave error was the enormous harm his policies wrought in national progress and development. Sejo's sweeping destruction of the Confucian ethics suffocated the spirit of the Yi dynasty for the next 450 years. A traitor instead of a king had to be honored, and any attempt at direct criticism was met with terrifying persecution. A good example of this was the persecution of Muo. A certain Kim Chong-jik, head of the Yŏngnam Confucian school, wrote his own poem, "Mourning Yidi," on a tablet and had it hung at Youngnam Belvedere while he was living in his birthplace, Milyang. This poem was to comfort the soul of Yidi of the Chu dynasty, a victim of regicide by Xiangyu. This was regarded as a satirical criticism of Sejo, and Yŏnsan'gun staged a persecution. Kim Chongjik was dug out of his grave, his coffin was smashed open, and he was decapitated. Countless scholars were either killed or exiled. Freedom of speech was banned, and free discussions of loyalty and filial piety, the founding principles of the nation, were made absolutely impossible. This sort of spiritual atrophy made the intellectual life of the Yi dynasty arid, confined to empty talk. Coupled with the philosophy of expediency and opportunism discussed earlier, this forced the factions of the Yi dynasty into frivolous disputes over manners and was one of the principal reasons that the factionalism of the period was so ugly.

There are some who point out Saejo's accomplishments after his coronation, but these were very minor in import when compared with his wrongdoings in destroying legitimacy, overthrowing the entire state, and corrupting and suffocating the national spirit. Even if his accomplishments had been significant, his use of whatever means necessary to attain his goals (e.g., destroying the legitimacy of succession) cannot be forgiven from the standpoint of the ideals and ethics of politics or long-range interests.

The result of Rhee's protection of pro-Japanese elements was to make a new beginning for Korea, in spiritual and personal terms, impossible. Consequently, the remnants of Japanese colonialism are still deeply rooted and causing harm in many areas. Also, his antidemocratic rule undermined the development of democracy in this country and was a decisive factor in our continuing struggle to institutionalize democracy. He was deaf to the pleas of the people for the triumph of justice and popular rule so as to preserve his own power and permanent rule. Some negligible accomplishments in his life cannot make up for all this, and his errors are not the kind that can be excused.

I have discussed the mistakes of Sejo and Rhee at some length. What, then, is the feeling of frustration mentioned at the outset? The problem is that if these two men had defended the legitimacy of the transfer of power and cared about justice and conscience, their glory in history would have been secure. Above all, they could have left behind a great example of human virtue that our nation could always respect and follow. They had great opportunities to make our national history fertile and glorious, but instead they ruined them and did immeasurable harm.

There is a man who is revered as a saint in the Confucian school; Confucius was so inspired that he said with regret, "I cannot see Zhougong in dream." He was Zhougong Tan, who was the brother of King Wu, the second king of the Zhou dynasty. When his brother died, he helped his young nephew to become king and left a record of great accomplishments in strengthening the nation and caring for the people. He is most highly revered, however, for having served his young nephew and for devoting himself wholly to preserving peace, rest, and a secure life for the people. Zhougong-Tan worked with his brother to bring down the Yin dynasty and became a founding member of the Zhou dynasty, and he had absolute power. During turbulent times, when might was right, it would not have been impossible or strange for him to have pushed his nephew aside and ascended the throne. Nevertheless, he flatly rejected such possibilities for the sake of establishing the legitimacy of the dynasty. Because of this, he became a model of human virtue for the following three thousand years of Chinese history.

If Suyang Taegun had followed this course of action, he would have become the Zhougong of Korea and, like King Sejong, Yi Sunsin, and Chang Monju, a proud example of human virtue. What a tragedy. He usurped the crown from his young nephew, Tanjong, demoted him to Nosan'gun, then to a plebeian status, and finally killed him by denouncing him as a traitor. For two hundred years after his death, Tanjong was ignored, but he was restored to kingship during the reign of the nineteenth king, Sukchong. Popular feelings of resentment toward Sejo's injustice and sympathy for Tanjong persisted, and finally, after two hundred years, put so much pressure on Sukchong, Sejo's descendant, that he was forced to repudiate and humiliate Sejo.

The details of Rhee's career are part of modern history which we still remember vividly. If he had not protected the pro-Japanese elements but had proceeded to form an anti-Japanese government and follow anti-Japanese policies, the legitimacy of his period in office and the national spirit would have been enhanced. The expectations of the people for the triumph of justice, good results for good causes and bad results for bad causes, would have been satisfied, and a climate that sneers at conscience and justice would not be prevailing today.

If Rhee had not played into the hands of the pro-Japanese and had not conducted antidemocratic politics, there would not have been the Pusan Political Turmoil, the constitutional amendment for a third presidential term, and the irregular March 15 election. Had he left office after two terms as a democratic president, he would have become the George Washington of this country and a founding father of the nation. We could have laid the foundation for democratic freedoms and peaceful transfer of power in the beginning phase of our nation and could have avoided many misfortunes which we have experienced thus far. Unlike Sejo, before his death Rhee witnessed complete defeat. How sad and frustrating this whole episode was for him and for us.

Rhee's one saving grace was that when he had to, he showed a respectful attitude toward popular will, perfunctory as his obedience may have been. Both Sejo and Rhee ruined rare opportunities given to them and to the people by heaven. We must learn that the reason for this was their preoccupation with what they were to become and failure to make decisions on the basis of what kind of lives they should live. One more thing to add to Rhee's mistakes is more the fault of the people, who are the masters in a democratic nation. They relinquished their power and responsibilities and avoided taking action to prevent Rhee's wrongdoings.

Thought Fragments

★ When we fall down, we have to rise up again each time and start anew. Life is a traveler on a road that has no end.

★ A mind that is ready to receive God is the place to experience goodness directly. (Pascal)

★ Confirmation of faith comes from being faithful to one's responsibilities in the secular world. Secular responsibilities are serving neighbors and society.

★ Human beings should become neither poor nor excessively affluent. Whether poor or affluent, we become slaves of money. We should live moderately and become free human beings.

★ The universe created by God is not a complete one. That is why there are misfortunes and sins. Humans must join God and participate in God's second creation through perfecting this world. Progress toward this perfection will determine the degree to which misfortunes and sins are overcome; the final perfection will completely eliminate them. That will be the day of the Second Coming of Jesus.

★ Those who love the country and love the people should be lauded and respected. In many cases, however, they are persecuted instead. Therefore, those who intend to live justly should not seek satisfaction in rewards but in the mode of their being. And they should be comforted by the fact that history never fails to give just rewards.

★ The highest form of dialogue is listening.

★ Those who are faithful to their conscience are happy even if they may live in hardship. They are even happier when the world acknowledges the value of that hardship.

* To think that the world is not worth making a sacrifice for is to go against God. God created this world and, out of His love for this world, sent His only son to open the way to salvation. This world has been made sacred and part of God's kingdom by the resurrection of Jesus.

* Not everyone can succeed in life's projects. Everyone, however, can succeed in life. Set the goal on what to become but the objective should be set on how to live.

* God's blessing is not the guarantee of trouble-free life and prosperity. It is to give us the strength to overcome hardship, adversity, and failure no matter what they may be and stand up to new possibilities.

* There is an adage, "Even if the heavens were to crash down, there is a hole through which to rise up, and even if taken in a tiger's teeth, there is a way to survive." This expresses very aptly the wisdom of our ancestors about life. They survived with grasslike tenacity and snakelike cunning amid repeated conflicts and the relentless badgering by a brutal government.

* Experience that has not been scrutinized by logic is chitchat, and logic that has not gone through experience is empty talk.

* It is not true that God bestows evil on us to train us. Evil originates in human egoism that is selfishly disfigured, and it is also inevitable in the imperfection of this universe. Therefore, we have to fight certain evil for immediate correction, while against other evil we should fight expecting its future eradication. We have to accept evil like death, quietly.

* Freedom is an asset only to those who will defend it. Therefore, freedom is not a right but a responsi-

bility. Freedom is neither wild behavior nor rejection of all principles. Freedom is a spontaneous behavior that accepts the restrictions and conditions necessary for human life and individual perfection.

1. *The Life and Thoughts of Nietzsche, The Life and Thoughts of Pascal, The Hundred School of Thoughts, The Origins of Thoughts in Korea* (all published by Pakyŏng).

2. Hans Küng, *On Being a Christian*.

3. *Han'guk k'at'olik chidosŏ* (Kyŏnghyang Chapjisa).

4. Edmund Wilson, *Axel's Castle*.
Kim Yŏlgyu, *Ŏttŏk'e ilkko salgŏsin'ga* (How to Live and Read).
E. H. Carr, Dostoevsky (all published by Hongsŏngsa).

5. Please find out what new books by Father Teilhard de Chardin are published and, if any, let me know.

6. Yi Ŏryŏng, *Shukushō shikō no Nihonjin* (an original Japanese version).

7. Kim Hongsin, *Haebang yŏngjang* (The Liberation Warranty).

Gandhi, the True Disciple of Jesus

July 27, 1982

To you and my beloved children with love and respect:

The rain that has been long awaited has finally come and the Ch'ŏngju area seems to have gotten a little rainfall. This year's heat is truly something we have not experienced before, and even a person like me, who usually does not mind hot weather, felt much discomfort. I thought how difficult it must be for you. It will be hot for another month, and I want you and the family to be careful about your health.

By the end of the month, I will have been here in Ch'ongju Prison for exactly one and a half years. How can I adequately describe my anguish, solitude, and grief during this period? I would get the feeling all over again that this was the most painful period in my life. But when viewed in contrast to my life before this, it may have been a most worthwhile period in terms of faith, intellectual development, and character formation. I am infinitely grateful that in spite of those countless moments of despair, sorrow, and anxieties, I now can see this positive aspect. Looking back, my life has been a life of grief, whose turns have been marked by grief after grief, sorrowing, biting my lips, and surmounting grief to rise again. My life has been a continuum of this. I conclude once more that life is learning in hardship, discovering possibilities, and growing like grass, and such is God's providence. Furthermore, through my life of conflict up to this point, there has not been a single person from whom I would turn away if we met on the street, nor has there been a person whom I hate so much as not to be able to forgive. I am grateful. What is sad is the fact that I have been forced to live a life away from my beloved friends and their situations due to my circumstances.

One of my great joys is that so many people have remembered me and worry and pray for me. How could this not be a great solace?

In Hong-up's letter that I received several days ago, there was mention of your taking care of a flower bed for my sake. He said, "There do not appear to be people who care for one another and think about one another in adversity the way our family does." I agree with that, but reading it made me truly happy. I heard from Jee-Young's mother about her meeting with Hong-gul, dining, going to a movie, and sharing warm conversations with him. From Hong-il, I heard about the visit to a nature farm with the family on Chung-hwa's birthday. Above all, I think about how Jee-young and Chung-hwa are growing up happily. All this leads me to believe that we are blessed amid this ordeal, and I say prayers of gratitude every night. I think about how great your care, sacrifice, and love have been in our journey up to this point.

I learned from your letter several days ago that Mr. Cho Pŏmwŏn has unexpectedly developed cancer and has little hope. It was a great shock. He is such a rare, kind person who has sacrificed himself for justice—quietly, unassumingly, and consistently. If not rewards, why is he given such a misfortune? My heart cannot help but feel the pain when I think about his dignified manner during the trial at Suwŏn for violation of the emergency decrees and about his wife, who has made such magnificent contributions to her husband's life. I am grieved that I have reached today without having in any way reciprocated for my colleague Cho's special friendship and care for me. I want you to comfort and encourage him and his wife as much as you can. I am praying.

These days, I am reading "There is righteous breath in heaven and earth," by Ham Sŏkhŏn. Under this title he interprets the writings of the Tao Zhuang Zi and Mencius with his unique flair and enthusiasm. Ham is a Christian but transcends Christianity. His thoughts range broadly across Eastern and Western philosophies, and although advanced in age, he possesses the vigorous spirit of youth. His sentences are plain and yet filled with the distinctive flair of our language. It is a tragedy that our era has not paid enough attention to such a precious person and learned more from him while he is alive. It would be nice for you and the children to visit and look after him often.

One of the books I have recently read is *Is the Korean Church All Right as It Is?* and I want you to be sure to read it. It is a roundtable discussion moderated by Dr. Han Wansang. People who are professionals in the field examine the whole range of problems which the Korean Protestant church faces today, and this will be a great help to you in your church life and Sunday school teaching. Also, if you can get around to it, make sure to read *The Status and Structure of the Movement for Holy Spirit by the Korean Church*, published by the Christian Academy. This volume contains articles by Han Wansang and by Kim Kwangil, written from a medical standpoint, and they were very helpful to me. A novel about the countryside, entitled *Our Village*, by Yi Mun'gu, describes the big difference between the countryside and farmers we knew before and those of today. It shocks us with its description of the agricultural economy and the consciousness of the peasantry, which are changing and being destroyed in the course of modernization. I wish the children would read these three books.

On Constitution Day, July 17, you wrote about the varied fate of our constitution. I too had deep emotions that day. France has been notorious for its political instability since the 1789 revolution. There have been five republics, alternating between monarchical and republican systems, and the Nazi control during World War II. Frequent as these political changes seem, they total only five in about 200 years. In our case, in only 33 years, since the founding of the nation in 1948 until 1981, we have had five republics. The status of our constitution and our people living under such conditions has been wretched. One of the characteristics of our constitutional history is that we do not pay proper attention to the constitution itself. We seek solutions to problems when the affairs of state are not going very well by tearing up the constitution, and most of the constitutional amendments have been brought about not by the demands of the people but by the needs of the rulers. No matter how good a constitution may be, it cannot demonstrate its value unless it is faithfully observed, and no matter how good the purpose of a constitutional amendment may be, it cannot take root without popular approval expressed by the spontaneous participation and support of the people.

At this time, we have to survey the strange fate of our constitution with a sober mind, a penitent and reflective attitude, and make a resolution.

As you wrote in your letter, during the last year and a half you have visited Ch'ŏngju 146 times and written daily, which means you have written 577 times by the end of this month. Hong-il has written 66 times this year alone, and Hong-up, Jee-young's mother, Hong-gul, and even Jee-young continue to write to encourage me. Dae-hyun, Hong-il, and Hong-up have visited Chung-ju quite a few times. I marvel at how many favors we have received during the course of life—favors from the family, favors from siblings, favors from friends, relatives, and strangers. I wonder if we can return them. When we reflect deeply on life, we realize once again that we can maintain our existence only through favors done for us, for example, God's favors, family favors, society's favors, nature's favors, and history's favors. After all, life is worth living and being thankful for in any kind of hardship.

The Nonviolence of Jesus and Ghandi

Even though Gandhi was a believer in Hinduism, he is often spoken of as a man who most resembles a disciple of Jesus in the twentieth century. Gandhi resembled Jesus in terms of his unselfish love of neighbors, total self-sacrifice, a life-style as austere as that of the masses, magnanimity toward his enemies, and even his assassination at the end by someone of his own race and of the religion he loved. Gandhi's resemblance to Jesus consists in his adherence to strict nonviolence, even though, like Jesus, he did not hesitate to oppose evil vehemently. His resistance against enemies was based on his great wish to rescue them from the sin in which they were mired. Gandhi himself admits to having been greatly inspired by Christ's Sermon on the Mount. The principle of ahimsa on the basis of Satyagraha, which was Gandhi's guiding principle, was the iron law in the anti-British independence struggle. If a struggle showed any hint of violence, he suspended it immediately, in spite of his colleagues' objections and no matter how much time had been spent in preparing it.

There are two important aspects to Gandhi's adherence to nonviolence. While it is true that he stressed nonviolence as a basic principle in his religion and philosophy, he did this because it was the best possible weapon the powerless Indian people could use in their struggle against British rulers armed with modern weaponry. In addition, nonviolence was effective in instilling a sense of righteous wrath in the masses who were watching and in arousing sympathy in world opinion. The latter factor was the reason that such Western-oriented leaders as Nehru at first were discontent with Gandhi's leadership methods. But in the end, they accepted and supported Gandhi.

Gandhi was a saint and a superior strategist. If the people in Judah who advocated independence had followed the path of nonviolent resistance to evil, according to the teaching of Christ, and had resisted the powerful Roman Empire and its puppets Zadok-te and King Herod, the outcome of their struggle would not have been so tragic.

The so-called Judaic War between A.D. 66 and A.D. 70, caused by the Jews led by the zealots, made the Jewish people a race without a state, forced to wander around the world for two thousand years.

Gandhi also condemned inaction against evil as much as he did violence. He once said that he preferred violence to standing idly by in the presence of evil. This by no means implies that he approved of violence, but he made his attitude clear that combating evil had top priority.

In these attitudes of Gandhi's we seem to find a contradiction to the absolute nonviolence of Christ. It is interesting that Tolstoy, who was a Christian, advocated nonviolence and absolute nonresistance, contrary to Gandhi. Tolstoy's belief that the world could be straightened out only by love and nonresistance seems farther from Jesus than from Gandhi.

History and Humanity

When we read history, we are convinced that humans are the products of their times but that the destiny of a state or nation in any era depends on whether there are leaders who can embody and express the contemporary spirit and demands of the time.

The Japanese invasion in Imjin was the greatest crisis since the beginning of our history, but our nation survived, and the country was saved because there were such warriors as Yi Sunsin and Kwŏn Yul, leaders of the volunteer army like Cho Hŏn, Kyŏngmyŏng, Kim Ch'onil, Chŏng Inhong, and Kim Tŏngnyŏng, Buddhist saints like Sŏsan Taesa and Samyŏngdang, and such government officials as Yu Sŏngyong, Yi Tŏkhyŏng, Yi Hangbok, and Chŏng T'ak.

During the latter period of the Yi dynasty, however, there were no outstanding individuals. As a result, several opportunities were lost and national politics could not break loose from the hands of those who were blinded by selfish greed. Therefore, we had to withstand the sorrow of losing our country. The impact of this still troubles us.

When we consider the late Yi dynasty period, it is true that a difficult time to maintain statehood is in the face of onrushing foreign powers. We can point to the following reasons for the lack of progress: lack of spiritual and material readiness for modernization, the period of decay after the long reign of the Yi dynasty, the extreme poverty of the masses, the sweeping corruption of national politics, the reactionary politics of Confucian officials who stubbornly depended on foreign powers, the greed and exploitation by the in-laws of the royal family, and incompetence. It is surprising, however, that no individuals worthy of note appeared, as they did in the time of the Japanese invasion in Imjin.

In the waning days of the Yi dynasty, we can list four people who were able to have decisive influence on the fate of the nation: Taewŏn'gun, Kojong, Queen Min and her family and Kim Okkyun. Taewŏn'gun was a truly outstanding figure in the last years of the Yi dynasty, and the accomplishments during his ten-year rule were substantial. He repudiated the influence of the in-laws of the royal family and the struggle among the four factions. He enacted bold recruitment policies and massive closing of traditional schools as well as reform of finance and taxation, including the elimination of tax evasion by the powerful and the removal of corrupt officials who were giving the nobility hemp and cotton instead of military service, tax reduction, which enabled him to leave the state treasury with a surplus after his ten-year reign, and social reforms such as the suppression of arbitrariness by the nobility, simplification of dress, encouragement of color, and prohibition of extravagance by female entertainers.

Unfortunately, however, Taewŏn'gun lacked any insight into historical trends and domestic and international situations. He thus unleashed brutal and pointless repression of Catholicism and a stubborn isolationist policy, thus ruining the chances of achieving his great goals and making a breakthrough for the new destiny of our nation. The ugly programs he undertook to return to power, such as the 1882 Military Revolt, Kaho Reform, and the Ŭlmi Incident, were events that destroyed even his integrity.

Thinking about Kojong, we realize that it is a great crime for a leader to be incompetent, no matter how gentle he or she is. Kojong appears to have been a kind and well-meaning person, but he was too incompetent and cowardly. It was a time when a most courageous, able, and insightful ruler was needed to face the most complex international situations since the beginning of our history and the foreign powers that were closing in like a pack of wolves. Instead, our country had a king who was the exact opposite.

The thirty years between Kojong's coronation and the Ch'ing-Japanese War of 1894 offered a golden opportunity. Japan did not dare think of annexing Korea but was hoping that the Korean peninsula would at least stay neutral vis-à-vis Ch'ing or Russia. This was also the hope of England, America, Germany, and France. If we had been able to manage our own affairs adequately, we could have played the four great powers off against each other and preserved our independence as a neutral buffer state, à la Thailand. The Kojong government was corrupt and inept, however, and seeing this, Japan began to entertain ambitions. England and America were concerned about the southward advance of Russia, so they approved and supported Japan's domination. In a way, the collapse of the Yi dynasty was caused by human weakness, by the self-destructive rule of the king and ruling class.

As for Queen Min, she and her family have to take most of the blame for the fall of the state. She was queen for thirty years, except for the ten years of Taewŏn'gun's reign; for all practical purposes, her rule lasted twenty years. Until the very last day, she thought of nothing but maintaining her power and the influence of her family. There is no trace of any efforts to improve the situation of the country and the people. She did not hesitate to take cruel and unrelenting revenge against her political enemies, such as Taewŏn'-gun and Kim Okkyun, to attain her goals. She perpetrated all sorts of corrupt and bizarre acts, and her eyes were blood-shot with the effort to retain power. For example, she distributed a stupendous sum of money to bribe the influential circles of the Ch'ing government to have Sunjong designated as heir to the crown. She drained the national treasury hiring witches and diviners to pray for good forture. Further, she placed one sok of white rice, one pil of fur, and a great sum of money on each of the 12,000 peaks of Kŭmgang the Diamond Mountains and wasted 800,000 ryang in one day for the April 8th festivities. Meanwhile, there was widespread sale of government positions, the people were hurled into absolute distress, and the treasury left by Daewonkun was so empty that for several months the soldiers could not be paid their salaries. Moreover, Queen Min did not hesitate to rely on foreign powers such as Russia and ask for their active intervention.

It is true that we rate Kim Okkyun highly as a precursor of modernization. Politics, however, is a science of action that implements ideas, and politicians accordingly are assessed not by their ideas but by their accomplishments. Kim Okkyun's claim to fame is the Kapsin Chŏngbyŏn 1884 Political Incident, which we know failed after lasting only three days. We have to criticize Kim Okkyun sternly, however, not because of the failure of the Kapsin Chongbyŏn but because he organized and promoted it. Briefly, he deserves reproach for his inadequate thinking and careless handling of things. We know this from the memoirs written later by Pak Yŏnghyo, Kim's intimate colleague. In the memoirs he characterized Kim Okkyun as talented and skillful in diplomacy but lacking in virtue and prudence.

I regret Pak Yŏnghyo's attitude in criticizing his

deceased colleague so harshly, but it appears true. The proof is a series of actions which Kim Okkyun undertook during the 1884 Political Incident.

First, the class that stood to benefit most from Kim Okkyun's modern reforms was the general public, but he had absolutely no intention of organizing or enlightening the masses, for whom he allegedly cared. If he had shifted his attention and striven for a mass organization like the Tonghak Movement or the Movement of the Council for Democracy, his modern reforms would have succeeded.

Second, he was so tactless and reckless that he confronted the 2,000 man Ch'ing army, which was powerful enough to prevail over Japan, trusting in the words of a Japanese envoy and the power of only 200 workers. Although reputed at home to be most knowledgeable about international situations, he judged Ch'ing-Japanese relations too hastily.

Third, he was thoroughly dependent on foreign powers. Even so, why did he have to be so partial to Japan, which was most hated and distrusted by our people and which was arbitrarily exploiting Korea after it descended like a pack of wolves following the opening of the ports? What made him believe so much in Japan? He trusted the Japanese envoy and foreign minister, who only a year before had deceived and betrayed him in loan negotiations. In addition, during the three days of Jungbyun, he made a series of mistakes such as invading the Department of Postal Service and preparing weapons for the protection of the king. He failed to justify the revolution and thus did not command the support of the masses, who showered rocks on him.

Therefore, the reform movement failed, which was a misfortune for him and his supporters. In reaction, the conservative forces led by the Min family came into power, and the entire reformist wing was driven out of politics. After that, no one could even raise the subject of modernization until the Ch'ing-Japanese War. The failure of his reckless revolution brought irreversible misfortune to our country.

Although there are several reasons for the fall of the Yi dynasty, it would not have disintegrated so easily if leaders such as Japan had before and after the Meiji Restoration and the United States had during the War of Independence had emerged. We produced a few outstanding leaders outside the government, such as Chŏn Pongjun and Sŏ Chaep'il, but they were eliminated by corrupt conservative forces as soon as they appeared on the scene and never had an opportunity for success.

The kind of individuals we need must, first, formulate the path our nation is to follow with incisive awareness of history and intelligent insight; second, not only respect popular will as the will of heaven but also help the people work out their own destiny by actively promoting their participation in all fields; third, reconcile conflicting opinions and interests with magnanimity, self-restraint, and persistence; fourth, carry out responsibilities with diligence, sincerity, and devotion; and, fifth, instill hope, aspiration, and participatory awareness in the youth.

If we are to overcome this overwhelming challenge of our age and successfully preserve our existence against the threat of communism, we have to search for and find capable people and foster them. National efforts are necessary to outgrow the unfortunate practice of eliminating all opposition by framing it, as was done in the struggle among the four factions in the Yi dynasty. These should be the lessons we learn from the collapse of the Yi dynasty.

In recent letters from you and Hong-up, there have been occasional references to the possibility of Taiwan's approaching the Soviet Union. Can this be possible? Naturally, any country can rise above old animosities or ideology for the sake of its national interest and ally itself with other countries. This is commonplace in international politics. But for the following reasons, it seems to me it would be difficult for Taiwan and the Soviet Union to cooperate, even if both might want it. If this should happen, however, it would constitute a problem with significant bearing on our country, for reasons listed later.

The first reason that I see Taiwan might approach the Soviet Union is that it was first to recognize the Communist regime in China, after its establishment in 1949, and has continuously insisted on Communist China's territorial rights over Taiwan at the United Nations and elsewhere. The Soviet Union has not changed its position at all. How can it make an about-face now and step forward to support and defend Taiwan? How can it rationalize such a clear-cut violation of international law?

Second, from the standpoint of interests, Communist China is likely to resort to military intervention if the Soviet Union should adopt such a position, which would inevitably lead to a full-scale war between China and Russia. Is there any reason why the Soviet Union should support Taiwan at such a risk? Moveover, at this point Taiwan's usefulness to the Soviet Union, which now has a naval base at Danang in Vietnam, has greatly dwindled.

Third, if Taiwan is brought under the influence of the Soviet Union, Korea and Japan run the risk of having the lifeline in the transportation route to the oil-producing countries of the Middle East cut off, and their trade with Southeast Asia, Africa, the Middle East, and Europe would be in great danger. In the meantime, the security of the immediately adjacent Philippines would be directly threatened. In such a situation, not only these three countries but also the United States, which has alliances with them, could not stand idle. Can the Soviet Union really do such a thing in spite of the threat of World War III?

For these reasons, even if Taiwan should want such a reconciliation, the Soviet Union cannot accept it, nor does it have any need to. Please let me know what views you hear on the outside.

The Threat of the Soviet Union and Measures Against It

The phrase "Threat of Communism," which has constantly alarmed the free world since World War II, seems to have been replaced by the phrase, "The Threat of the Soviet Union." Apparently this is the result of the Sino-Soviet rift. At any rate, according to present trends, which are likely to endure for a while, it is the fate of Communist China to have to confront the Soviet Union, and so it must ally itself with the Western world for help. The Western world also will try to use Communist China in its anti-Soviet strategy. Therefore, the new threats seem to converge on the Soviet Union.

The threat of the Soviet Union is a very real and important issue so long as the North Korean Communists are standing between China and the Soviet Union, using both sides to their own advantage. How serious is the threat of the Soviet Union? There are differences of opinion, but from a military standpoint, the United States and the Soviet Union are evenly matched in terms of nuclear capabilities, air force, and navy, though not army. Possibly the United States is slightly superior to the Soviet Union. When we take the military capabilities of the Western nations and Communist China into consideration, the United States, from an overall military standpoint, is substantially or maybe slightly superior.

The Soviet Union's GNP is about half that of the United States and is showing a trend that will soon make it even with that of Japan. Communist states, however, can concentrate their economy on a single goal, even at the expense of the livelihood of the people, so we cannot judge national strength solely in terms of the aggregate GNP. We have to be careful in our judgment, but there is no reason to be afraid of confrontation with the Soviet Union when it comes to productive capacity. The suppression of hostilities or the maintenance of peace, therefore, appears probable.

The problem is that the Soviet Union continues to exploit our internal weaknesses, while the Western world has not come up with effective countermeasures. First, the threat of Soviet nuclear attack creates strong resistance to the installation of American nuclear weapons in American-held territories in the Western nations and Japan.

Second, as evidenced by the recent dispute between the United States and the Western nations over the gas pipeline incident, there is a tendency in the West and in Japan not to even hesitate to contribute to the strengthening of Soviet military power if it will gain an economic foothold in the Soviet Union and East European countries.

Third, although it is almost forty years since the end of World War II, the Western world has not succeeded in helping the non-Communist countries under their influence to overcome their internal weaknesses. They are thus providing an ideal stage for Communist infiltration and propaganda. Countries in Central America, Southeast Asia, the Middle East, and Africa are, almost without exception, suffering from the chronic ailment of dictatorship, corruption, and the severe gap between rich and poor and so have become targets of intense Communist subversion.

Fourth, the Western nations have been reticent or have failed to give effective assistance in the development of the Third World countries. As a result, anti-neocolonialist feelings have arisen in these countries which are being aggressively exploited by the Soviet Union and Cuba.

Fifth, the West has suffered a series of setbacks because of the problems of Israel and Iran in the Middle East, which has military and economic control of the entire West. Its position vis-à-vis these countries has been made very shaky.

Sixth, what is more important than anything mentioned heretofore is that the leading nations of the free world, like the United States, have failed to understand clearly the ideological and political nature of their struggle and confrontation with the Soviet Union and thus have failed to take a confident ideological and political counteroffensive.

In light of our weaknesses, the way for us to overcome the threat of the Soviet Union and rescue the world from Communist domination is quite evident. The leading nations of the free world must reconfirm a belief in democracy, encourage its realization in the entire non-Communist part of the world, and supply the peoples there with clear reasons to oppose communism by realizing freedom and justice. By energetically and effectively aiding the economic growth of the Third World countries, their desire to become part of the free world camp will be strengthened.

The disputes between Israel and the PLO must be resolved quickly and fairly and the reconciliation and unity with the Middle East Islamic nations, including Iran, must be pursued with restraint and sincerity.

The Western great powers should adjust their economic policies toward the Communist camp fundamentally and rationally to prevent internal dissent or subversive actions favoring the enemy. In view of their experience with Hitler, they should remember how dangerous it is to adopt a conciliatory or submissive position when dealing with the threats of dictators.

On the basis of these programs, we can confront the threat of the Soviet Union with confidence. We can triumphantly take the political and ideological offensive and rescue the world from destruction and the catastrophe of enslavement.

The Modern Way of Filial Piety

When we observe animals, we see that mothers will risk their lives for their cubs. But when the cubs are grown, they go their own ways and do nothing for their mothers in return. It is instinctual and natural for human parents to love their children, but it requires effort for the children to take care of their parents. Filial piety is a regulatory norm of human life which has been developed, consciously or unconsciously, to meet the needs of patriarchy, the extended family system for agricultural management, and the maintenance of feudal order.

Filial piety is the proudest of all systems of ethics achieved by human beings, if we can eliminate the undesirable side effect of coerciveness. It should be particularly valued as a great characteristic of Korean society. Filial piety should be strongly encouraged not only from an ethical standpoint of reciprocity but also from a social standpoint since it provides care and protection for the aged and weak.

There seems to be a great deal of conflict over the problem of filial piety in our society today. While the traditional filial piety demands that obedience and self-sacrifice be emphasized and praised, there are, nevertheless, many instances of children turning their backs on their parents. Now is the time for us to refer this problem to a national debate in order to mobilize our national wisdom to find a modern form of filial piety. For the healthy maintenance of filial piety is the proudest virtue of Korean society.

I have no expert views on this problem, of course, but the rational and realistic maintenance and development of filial piety seem to require the following improvements. (1) The concept of filial piety should be expanded into a humane one based on mutual respect and understanding between parents and children instead of the traditional idea of one-sided obedience and sacrifice. (2) Filial piety should be reinforced not as an ethic that applies only to relations between parents and children but as a social ethic as well. In this regard, the state should provide financial support to indigent children for their parents and develop a rational system of support that is stable and permanent for childless parents. (3) A system should be encouraged whereby all children assume the expense of supporting aged parents, instead of the feudal custom of having the first son alone carry the burden. (4) There should be development and encouragement of exemplary and rational relations between parents and children, especially between mothers-in-law and daughters-in-law. (5) I have been thinking about developing and recommending new interior layouts applicable to various life-styles for the purpose of providing privacy for parents and children who share the same home. I am not going to list examples in detail because of lack of space, but if we think about these problems, many ideas will occur to us.

We should never praise and encourage as filial piety certain common situations such as a young widowed daughter-in-law never remarrying but sacrificing her life for the sake of parents-in-law and her children, or a young woman sacrificing herself by entering the entertainment business to support her poor parents and the education of her siblings. Although these situations are common and may seem praiseworthy, they are too inhuman and antidemocratic for society to approve.

Thought Fragments

⋆ The crux of democracy is the people. A democracy cannot exist without sufficient and free participation of the people, no matter how much their well-being is promoted.

⋆ It is a mistake to urge perseverance during times of hardship for the sake of waiting for times of happiness. Happy days may not come, and even if they do, one must be unhappy until their arrival. We have to make the period of hardship itself happy. So the goal of life should be how to live rather than what to become. (This is very difficult. Recently I have been endeavoring to attain this.)

* We must always accept everything critically and with independent minds. Any authoritative theories or truths must be acknowledged only after one's own intellectual scrutiny. When we enjoy drama, music, or literature, for example, we must evaluate it according to the way we feel. This is ten times better than parroting the words of critics as if they were our own, even though our own evaluation may be unsophisticated.

* Courage is the power to work and struggle for what is right. It is the highest of all virtues. Courage alone can dispel fear, temptation, and laziness.

* Religion originated from a guilt complex and has its ultimate objective in freedom from sin. Many religions, however, are very strict about individual sins, to the extent that a microscopic scrutiny is used to detect them. But when it comes to social sins, these religions look the other way: preaching against killing, individual murders are punished but nothing is said against genocides such as Hitler committed; asserting everyone to be God's children, religions supported slavery and colonialism; warning against stealing, they tacitly allow unfair profits by businesses and unjust exploitation of workers. This kind of religious person says, "When everyone becomes a Christian, social sins will automatically disappear." In the first place, it is extremely unlikely that everyone will become Christian, but even then, such a society is not necessarily just. How much sin has been perpetrated in and out of European societies, which are uniformly Christian?

If Christianity is to become a genuine religion of

Jesus, it must fight against both individual and social sins. Only then will it become congruent with the will of Jesus, according to which He delivered the gospel to the poor, gave freedom to the chained, restored the sight of the blind, liberated the oppressed, and declared the year of Lord Jesus' grace.

⋆ The life of a Christian means offering one's entire life twenty-four hours a day to God through worship and prayer. Why, then, do we have to go to church, and why is church necessary? It is necessary in order that we may praise God together and socialize with each other to form a community. It is difficult today, however, to find such a collective consciousness and love in established churches. The body may attend the assembly in church, but the mind remains lonely. This must be a major reason why new religions are popular today.

⋆ For modern parents, educating chidren is a problem that causes total confusion and considerable anguish. Whether tolerant or stern, there is a problem. The way to educate children truly is for parents to establish authority through continuing to develop and integrate their own personalities, no matter what occupation or status they hold, and demonstrate strength to them.

When children are attracted to parents for personality reasons, either the Spartan way or the liberal way will do.

The other day, I received a letter from Hong-eun's mother, and yesterday one from Hwe-young. In Hwe-young's letter I could feel her innocence and genuine love for her uncle. I was very happy to have seen Hyung-joo and Hong-min had grown so much. It was very sad that I did not get to see Yun-soo and Yun-hak. I am always wishing health for the younger brother's wife. In Hong-up's letter there was mention of a vacation, and I want you to see to it, as I wrote in my last letter, that the children spend their summer vacation happily and meaningfully. Do not hesitate to do so on my account, for doing so is also a way to help me.

Please send my thanks to Song Chwabin for having come here to visit me from Taejon.

Request for books:

1. Min Kyŏngbae, *Han'guk kidokyohŏesa* (A History of Christianity in Korea) (Taegisŏhŏe).

2. Sato Tomo, Dodaibatsu.

3. Hwang Sŏkyŏng, *Tŏaeji kkum* (A Pig's Dream).

4. Sigmund Freud, *An Introduction to Psychoanalysis* (Pŏmu-sa).

5. *Chamkkan pogo on sahu-ŭi Segye* (The World after Death Seen Briefly) (Chŏngu-sa).

6. No Myongsik, *Hyŏndae yŏksa sasang* (Modern Historical Studies).

7. Pak Hyŏmjae, *Minjung kwa kyŏngje* (People and Economy).

8. Kanoi, *Education and Cultural Colonialism* (Hangil-sa).

9. Mircea Eliade, *Cosmos and History* (Hyŏndai Sasang Chongsŏ).

10. Yu Tongsik, *Minsok Chonggyo wa Han'guk munhwa* (Korean Culture and Folk Religion).

11. Cho Sŭnghyŏk, *Tosi sanŏp sŏn'gyo ŭi insik* (The Popular Image of the Urban Industrial Missions).

12. An English Bible (Catholic).

The Origins of the Masses and the Nobility

August 25, 1982

To you and my beloved children with love and respect:

From your letter dated the 16th, I know that you were very concerned about my attitude toward the results of August 15th. In fact, for several reasons, I was expecting some measures this time that would relieve this sort of life. I spent the night of the 14th, however, in an unexpectedly calm mood. This was probably because the expectations that were not fulfilled concerned the fate of others, not my own. As I said during our last visit, I am going to make up my mind again to make sincere efforts toward a new, worthwhile life. As you wrote in your letter, I want you and the children to turn over a new leaf. Each of you must strive patiently for your own goals and growth. Candidly speaking, I am always concerned as to whether the family and relatives outside are making efforts to learn and grow in adversity by living through these hard times faithfully.

As I always say, others can harass me, but it is up to me whether I succumb to pain or use it as an opportunity for growth. I shared your feelings on the thirty-seventh anniversary of the August 15th independence.

It is true that the overwhelming exultation and burgeoning expectations on the day of liberation have given way to feelings of despair and frustration. It is with these feelings that we greet this day. There must be many reasons, but the most basic of them all is that we could not attain independence by dint of our own power, and even if liberation had been given us by others, we lacked the national consciousness and dedication to manage its inner substance through our own sacrifices and efforts.

The outlook for the future is not necessarily pessimistic. You wrote in your letter that the trees in the yard have grown quite a bit. I am particularly curious about whether the two gingko trees are doing all right. After we had them moved, one was withering away. I will be very happy if both are growing well, and I wonder if the gingko nuts matured this year. When you write about the dogs, there is always mention of Smarty but not about Captain, Jindol, and Jinsook. It would be good if you would write about all of them.

As I said during the visit, it would be good if you

and the children could tell me in your letters about our area in as great detail as possible. These days I feel very anxious about the delay in Hong-up's admission papers. I hope that you keep pressing the issue, but you will know what to do. I am delighted beyond words that Jee-young and Chung-hwa are growing up to be so kind and bright, that Jee-young is playing the role of big sister so well, helping Chung-hwa in her studies, and that she is praying morning and night for me and helping Chung-hwa to pray too. It is a sheer wonder that Chung-hwa has become so pretty. Actually, when she was just born, I was somewhat worried. Chung-hwa resembles her mother more and more as she grows up. Hwe-young writes frequently these days. Among the nephews and nieces, she is really the one I have had the least opportunity to meet, but she seems to think a great deal of her uncle. Even though she is only in elementary school, the content of her letters is very logical and contains quite persuasive statements about religion. I want you to encourage them on my behalf.

Often these days I think about the following while praying and meditating.

Let us offer our entire life, twenty-four hours a day, to God. Let us always listen to the words of God and respond sincerely and responsibly.

Let us open our minds to accept God and neighbors.

Let us find our selves and happiness in giving love rather than taking it.

Let us follow Lord Jesus with the cross on our back.

Let us actively participate in God's purpose to improve and perfect this world.

Let us calmly accept the inevitable woes (e.g., death, illness, hardship) with faith and hope. This is the way to peace of mind.

Let us critically reflect, repeat, and strive to find out if we are growing daily, spiritually, morally, intellectually, and healthily. Growth without repentance and repentance without growth are equally inadequate.

Let us always remember to become one with the family, friends, nation, and the motherland.

Let us work to be able to love everyone in this world as we love our own people.

The History of the Masses

In recent writings, there are frequent mentions of the word "masses." For your and the children's reference, I am putting down my thoughts on the subject.

In a secular sense, the "masses" has the same meaning as the "ordinary people." They form the base of social classes and comprise the overwhelming majority of society which is the principal production force in any age, but they are dominated, suppressed, and exploited.

In ancient days of slavery, slaves were such a class. And serfs and apprentices in the feudal period in the West; peasants, artisans, and servants in Asia; and workers, poor peasants, and other groups of ordinary people in the capitalist era belonged to such classes.

Today, in advanced countries where there is industrial democracy, the masses have freed themselves by their own power from the traditional exploited status and have acquired a solid position of equality with the capitalists in such fields as politics, economy, and culture. A clear example of this popular phenomenon is seen in the fact that labor parties and social democratic parties in many countries are now in power.

The twentieth century is a monumental century in terms of the history of the masses, or even the history of mankind. Some scholars use the term "masses" to refer to people in industrial countries, and I am following this definition.

What kinds of influence have the masses left in the history of Korea? Simply, it may be called a history of hardship and grief, but at the same time, it reveals a tremendous will to live rather like grass that keeps rising even when it has been trampled on over and over again.

When the history of the Korean masses is seen from a static viewpoint, it is one that makes us feel infinitely sad and despondent, but when viewed in the dynamic terms of its undercurrents, we cannot help but feel reverence for our ancestors. It has been a history in which they looked for a hole through which to arise, even though heaven might crash down and violently shake their bodies. It is the history of finding ways to survive even when held in the jaws of a tiger.

Concomitant with the development of agricultural productivity, classes unrelated to production emerged, such as rulers, warriors, priests, and officials who are responsible for maintaining social order, defending against foreign enemies, and handling religious rites. This led to the formation of the ruling class while peasants and slaves became the masses under their domination. The masses in our country date much further back than the era of the Three Dynasties.

It was in the latter period of Silla, however, that the masses began to show their power as the moving force in history.

1. At the beginning of the Silla era, internal chaos and struggle within the ruling class was at its peak. Contradictions, corruption, and exclusive privilege based on the bone-rank system sharply alienated the populace. Those officials of the head-rank sect whose career advancement had been blocked, the priests of the Sŏnjong sect who were discontent about the Kyojong sect, which was supported by royal power, and powerful families in various localities either controlled or allied themselves with the agitated masses and rose up against the royal government.

The emergence of local power blocs was concentrated in Kungye and Kyŏnwŏn, which formed the period after the Three Dynasties. Wanggŏn, who could have called himself a local power, unified the country and established the Koryŏ. He remembered the contributions of the masses to his triumph and implemented a historic reform in taxation, that is, the rate of one-tenth replaced the harsh exploitation of the Silla era and also established and reinforced a relief system for refugees. The resistance of the masses thus won benefits.

2. When Koryŏ settled down and its royal power had become stabilized, the nobility began to agitate again in sinful greed, thus restoring the brutal exploitation of the masses. The contradictory policies of the nobility resulted in the alienation of the populace, which emboldened the warriors to seize power by removing the servants of Wanggŏn and slaughtering the nobility. Among them was Chŏng Chungbu, who was of poor origin. Many warrior officials, like Yi Ŭimin, were of lower-class origin. This did not mean that their attitudes favored the masses, but their fantastic rise to power made the peasants and servants throughout the nation aware of their rights. Initially this stimulated a surge of power on the part of the masses. Typical of this was the uprising led by Ch'oe Ch'unghŏn's servant, Manjŏk. This was not merely a slave uprising; they had well-defined ambitions for power, which puts this uprising in a unique place in the history of mass resistance in our country.

The awareness and resistance of the masses, which began to swell, manifested itself as an amazing power in the anti-Mongol struggle after the Mongol invasion in 1231. While the ruling class retreated to Kanghwa Island and enjoyed a comfortable life, the peasants and slaves throughout the country united to resist the Mongol invasion on six occasions over a thirty-year period. The resistance by the Koryo masses was a major factor in forcing the Mongols to accept Koryo as only a tributary state when it brought China, Central Asia, Russia, and Iraq under its rule.

When national politics became chaotic during the latter period of Koryŏ and the exploitation of the masses intensified (i.e., the ownership of land by those in power), the populace became alienated. The Sadaebu (the literati), who began to rise at the time, received the support of the masses. They were the offspring of local officials or impoverished nobles, and they adhered to Confucianism but rejected Buddhism. They were the intelligentsia who, like the masses, were engaged in agriculture. The masses pinned their hopes on them, while the Sadaebu acted with the aid of the masses. Together, they helped Yi Sŏnggye overthrow Koryŏ.

3. The Yi dynasty was also aware of the power of the masses, to some extent, and worked hard to formulate policies to please them. We can cite as an example the implementation of a system of land distribution to officials. This system, which was an improvement on Koryŏ's, the invention of hunmin chŏngŭm, an alphabet for the masses, publication and distribution of a variety of books for the improvement of agricultural techniques, and large-scale adoption of a system of relief, including medical care for the poor, were some of the measures taken to please the masses. From the middle period of the Yi dynasty, which was blinded by factional struggles, politics for the masses increasingly gave way to harsh exploitation and arbitrariness, and the populace began to be alienated. In the midst of all this, the Japanese invasion in Imjin took place. Although the masses set fire to the much-hated royal palace and threw stones at the fleeing king and high officials, they rallied throughout the nation as volunteers to defend their lives and the land from the invading Japanese army. We already know how brilliant their contributions were during Imjin.

Even after the turmoils in Imjin and Pyŏngja, politics continued to deteriorate and the greedy exploitation of the people became even harsher. With their backs against the wall, the masses began to resist by force, as in the turmoil of 1811 and the turmoil in the thirteenth year of Ch'ŏlchong (i.e., the outbreak of the popular uprising at Chinju in 1862). The former centered around the P'yŏngnam and Buk regions, while the latter took place in the Kyŏngsang, Chŏlla, and Ch'ungch'ŏng areas and then spread to Kyŏnggi, Hwanghae, and Hamgyŏng provinces. Even though they were put down, they shook the foundation of the dynasty.

In this period, the masses became more sophisticated as they were made aware by Catholicism of the equality of all people, the equality between sexes, and the way of scientific thought, represented in particular by Ch'oe cheu, a brilliant ideologist and leader. They established the Tonghak which became a great antigovernment revolutionary force by immediately securing the support and involvement of the masses. Finally, it staged the Tonghak Revolution under the great leadership of Chŏn Pongjun, whose reputation shines brightly in the world annals of mass resistance.

4. Since then, when the invasion by Japanese forces reached its height, our masses have fought as volunteer armies or by joining hands with the nobility. They also cooperated with the forces advocating modernization and independence as part of the Association for Independence Movement of All People. After the collapse of the dynasty, they died as nameless soldiers in the armed anti-Japanese struggle in the mountains and fields of foreign countries such as Manchuria and Siberia.

We know that at the time of the March 1 Movement under Japanese colonialism the masses forged ahead with such an unprecedented large-scale movement of their own that cowardly leaders shirked leading the masses. From the time of the March 1

Movement until the defeat of Japanese colonialism, the power of the masses to resist declined markedly, and it was in adversity and inertia that we gained liberation. This might have been a transitional phenomenon that is all too common.

5. It was when we were invaded by the Communists on June 25 that the power of the masses became stronger than it had been since the liberation. The masses, who rose to defend freedom from Communist dictatorship, which they knew from experience, succeeded in repelling the Communist aggression. The power of the masses also crushed the tenacious North Korean Communists' attempt to take over the south.

We can see the aspiration for democracy that the masses have consistently demonstrated since their enthusiastic support of the April 19 Student Revolution and the energy they have shown in economic reconstruction. We can also point out several problems and concerns. It may not be a grave mistake, however, to judge that the energy of our populace is increasing and moving forward.

As we have seen thus far, the masses have consistently been the motivating force in history. We have survived because of their vision, their yearning for what is right and just which, though flickering, is not yet extinguished.

When we consider the rise and fall of the Silla, Koryŏ, and Yi dynasties, no matter who played the clown, only those who had the support of the masses, who were squirming in the gutters of society and seemingly powerless and ignorant, were the ones to prosper. Those who did not have the support of the masses fell. From a long-range perspective, the mind of the masses was the mind of heaven. But although it was the masses who have moved history, their rewards have always been meager.

From a political and social standpoint, the twentieth century might be deemed the beginning of the era of the masses. If we are to overcome the greatest crises in our history, that is, the division of our fatherland and the threat of communism, and attain genuine security, economic growth, and unification, the masses must be seen as the major force of destiny and must be treated as the master. They must rise to the challenge of controlling their own destiny.

We know the weaknesses of the masses and the limits of their abilities. But there, the only way for them to become the masters of their own fates is through their direct participation. Our Lord Jesus was born a poor man in the house of a carpenter, Joseph. He lived His life with the masses and was nailed to a cross for the sake of their salvation. The way of Jesus was the way of the masses.

The Origin of the Nobility

The manner of the development of the ruling strata of our country since unified Silla has been quite varied. The Silla era was an age of the bone-rank system, in which the sacred bone and the true bone reigned. Even a person of such prominence as Ch'oe Ch'iwŏn could not advance beyond the head-rank six.

In Koryŏ, the politics of the nobility was dominant until the eighteenth king, Ŭijong, was driven out in a coup by the warriors. For about a hundred years after the coup (1170–1258), the military reigned. This was followed by rule by the aristocracy. Finally, in the latter period, Koryŏ was ruled by the newly prominent Confucian officials or military officers.

In the Yi dynasty, aristocracy, on the one hand, and scholars and generals, on the other, competed and fought each other in the early period, and power changed hands between them. In the middle period, scholars and generals controlled the stage by themselves. It is this period that is referred to as the period of nobility politics.

From the time of Sunjo in the final period, the Kims of Andong, or sometimes the Chos of P'yŏngyang, monopolized national politics through their influence as the royal in-laws. During Kojong's reign, except for the first ten years when Taewŏn'gun was regent, politics was also dominated by the royal in-laws, headed by Minbee.

Yangban is an expression that originated in the Koryŏ period. It referred to a part of the scholarly and military classes, or the Eastern and Western sections. Yangban was simply an official title. The Yangban, a social class that left a great impact on the political and social history of our country, was formed in the middle period of the Yi dynasty. I would like to survey the origins of the Yangban briefly, because I think this is indispensable to understanding our history and also to grasping the reasons for our nation's collapse.

1. Entering the final period of Koryŏ, Neo-Confucianism, which was founded by Chŏng Ich'ŏn of the Sung period, began to be popularized in our country, producing such eminent individuals as Chŏng Mong-ju, Yi Saek, Kil Chae, Chŏng Tojŏn, and Cho Chun, who were renowned for their erudition. As discussed in the previous section, the Sadaebu of various localities accepted this scholarship. They helped establish Chosŏn by supporting Yi Sŏnggye, and Neo-Confucianism became the National Academy.

   Neo-Confucianism is the old Confucianism taught by Confucius and Mencius but made metaphysical by incorporating the thoughts of Buddhism and Taoism. In our country it reached its peak in the middle part of the Yi dynasty by Yi T'oegye and Yi Yulgok.

2. The Sadaebu, who, in the early period of the Yi dynasty, subscribed to Neo-Confucianism and up-

held the way of justice that would be in line with great duty and obligation, were engaged in fierce theoretical disputes and power struggles with the nobility. At the same time, they promoted the movements for Sach'ang, Yuhyangso, and Hyangyak for the peasants with whom they lived, together with a view to securing their support in confronting the nobility. In the course of this, they met resistance from the nobility and suffered massive casualties in repeated massacres of scholars during the years of Kapcha, Muo, Kimyo, and Ŭlsa.

These people had three strong points at the time: they were intellectually superior to the nobility; they had the support of the populace; and they owned all the land in the countryside and could return to their villages upon resigning from government posts and still have the material base for continuing the struggle.

3. At the beginning of the middle period of the Yi dynasty, they won a complete victory, and power fell into their hands. No sooner had they seized power but the positive dimension that they initially possessed disappeared and negative aspects began to surface.

First, they fought in opposition to the privileges of the nobility, but once the aristocratic class was overthrown, they established themselves as the new aristocracy. They solidified the Yangban as a new title of hereditary status, which, up to that point, had been nothing more than an official title for civilian and military bureaucrats. This is the meaning of Yangban as we speak of it today.

Second, as soon as the nobility against which they fought had collapsed, the Yangban immediately began internal struggles and became divided, first into Eastern and Western groups, and then into Old Theory and New Theory factions. Fragmented in all conceivable ways, they engaged in factional conflict and the dark and shameful struggle of vendetta, wiping blood with blood. Especially after the Japanese invasion in Imjin, the strife became worse because the Yangban share of the pie had diminished as a result of the drastic reduction of national revenue and the impoverishment of the people.

Third, they forget about practicality, the spirit of opposition, and the humanity of Confucianism, and they also lost the spirit of justice according to which one lived and died after having performed the great duty and obligation. Instead, they staked their lives on trivial matters and turned away completely from reform of national politics or the well-being of the populace.

Fourth, they became divided into the T'oegye faction and the Yulgok faction and into the Yŏngnam faction and the Kiho faction, thus drawing new battle lines based on human connections and regional ties. During the reign of Yŏngjo, however, the Old Theory faction finally gained power and displayed thorough exclusiveness in making the government the private domain of the Yulgok faction, which, at the same time, was the Kiho faction. (Here, even though they addressed themselves as the T'oegye faction and Yulgok faction, both were diametrically opposed to the will of these two people. It was only that the various factions took advantage of their intellectual prominence after their deaths.)

4. Yangban politics, which lasted two hundred years, produced intense internal disputes and division, the corruption of Confucian scholarship, the intensification of exclusiveness, and the loss of popular support and thus lost the vitality to lead the country.

A new brand of nobility politics, called the politics of influence, began in the latter period of the Yi dynasty. As stated earlier, it began in 1800 when the 23rd king, Sunjo, was enthroned by the Kims of Andong. The Kims of Andong were naturally Yangban, as were the Chos and Mins after them. They always proudly referred to themselves as the Yangban class, and the original Yangban themselves were recruited for government posts on the basis of their close ties with the influential. In a way, this may be called a perverted version of Yangban politics.

From the opening of harbors in 1876 until the Political Turmoil in Kapsin in 1884, there was a tense confrontation between the Modern Reform faction and the Traditional faction. Due to the failure of the Political Turmoil in Kapsin, the pro-Ch'ing conservative faction had the stage all to itself. Following the Ch'ing-Japanese War of 1894, they were, in turn, divided into pro-Japanese and pro-Russian factions, which were heavily dependent on foreign powers while madly trying to repress the Tonghak Revolution of the Independence Club movement, which sought independence and liberation. In 1905, when Japan emerged victorious from the Russo-Japanese War, however, the pro-Japanese Yangban threatened the king and repressed independence-minded compatriots and anti-Japanese masses in order to have the Protectorate Treaty and the Korea-Japan Annexation Treaty ratified. Thus they delivered our country to the Japanese colonialists.

They not only presented our nation with the bitterness of losing the country for the first time in our nation's history but also ravaged the political climate. This has been a major reason for our troubles today. In other words, as mentioned earlier, our problems are the result of factionalism, regionalism, and intense vengefulness that brooks no dialogue with, or magnanimity toward, political opposition.

We have to realize that these bad habits are not a unique characteristic of our nation, as some argue, but the products of the Yangban politics since the middle period of the Yi dynasty. We must recognize that the vestiges of evil, such as that political climate was, still persist to a large extent among us, and we must strive boldly to be rid of them.

Loving Others' Children

I read in the newspapers published in prison last month about people who were adopted abroad when young and returned as adults to the motherland to visit, either alone or with stepparents. I could not but feel touched and shamed as well when I thought about the fact that although their homeland abandoned them, they came to this land again.

One American stepmother said that she had two sons and three daughters of her own but decided on adoption out of sympathy when she read about Korean orphans. When I was in the United States, I visited Professor Reischauer in his home. He said that his son had adopted a Korean child even though he had his own child and wants to adopt yet another one. I remember that when I heard this I realized many things.

We Koreans dearly love our children, of whom we are very proud. This is the simple fact and may be considered one unique characteristic of Korean society. It is a common phenomenon, however, that as dearly as we love our own children, we have surprisingly and shamefully little or no idea of loving other people's children. This can be called a shortcoming of our national character which we should regret. Furthermore, are we not a nation that treats coldly and discriminates against stepchildren who belong to husbands or wives? Such stories as Changhwa Hongnyŏn abound in our folklore, and this kind of bad custom persists even today so that we often witness instances where widowers and widows with children are reluctant to remarry. In the case of women, in particular, the handicap is even more serious. Even now, men rarely want to accept widows with children as their spouses.

Some time ago, I read a tale about the former president of the United States, Gerald Ford. President Ford's mother remarried and he and his stepfather got along so well that President Ford finally dropped his real surname and changed it to his stepfather's—Ford.

Recently it has become more frequent to boast about our country. I hope that this is genuine pride instead of mere pretension and that we recognize the disgraceful shortcomings of our nation and try to correct them. I hear that four thousand children every year are being adopted abroad, even now. With the economy having grown so much, how can we rationalize abandoning our children to foreign countries?

This problem is a completely different issue from that of immigration. If we are to truly adopt love of children as a meritorious aspect of our national character, we must be able to extend our concern and love to other people's children, who are frolicking on the streets as if they were our own, and we must be fully loving and responsible toward stepchildren or adopted children. Improvement in this respect is a serious and urgent issue.

The Islamic Hemisphere and Our Fate

I learned from your letter that the Lebanon situation has been resolved finally and that for now the PLO is in the process of withdrawal. It is good that hostilities have ended. I think, however, that this resolution has not solved the problem, much less served as a clue to the real nature of the conflict. The issue here is that the Palestinian refugees should be able to return to their homeland and establish their own state, and at the same time, the Arab states should recognize the legitimacy of Israel. A way must be found for peaceful and friendly coexistence between Israel and the newly founded Palestinian state.

The fate of our free world is bound to be influenced greatly by which way the Middle Eastern Islamic hemisphere turns, and this makes it imperative for us to establish friendly relations with it. The first step is to solve the Palestinian problem. Unless we do this, friendly relations with the Islamic hemisphere are inconceivable. Even though I alluded to these points briefly in my letter of last month, I am going to touch on this subject again in view of the change in the Lebanon situation since I wrote and especially because Hong-il wrote that he wanted to hear my opinions. In fact, this is an important problem that deserves our attention.

First, the importance of the Middle East Islamic hemisphere is that it is rich in oil reserves, as everyone knows. For Asian and European countries and the United States, which are heavily dependent on Middle East oil, the secure supply of Middle East oil is a problem on which their survival and even the fate of the free world depends.

Second, the Middle East Islamic states occupy a strategic location. Look at the map! The Soviet Union is surrounded on all sides, like a giant monster wrapped under a net. The Soviet boundary is hemmed in by the following lands, from east to west: Alaska, the Japanese archipelago, South Korea, the Chinese mainland, Pakistan, Iran, Turkey, Greece, and the Western European countries.

The Soviet Union has naval bases on the Baltic Sea, the Black Sea, and in Vladivostok. It would take only a few ships to be sunk to contain the Baltic fleet in the Straits of Jutland in Denmark, the Straits of Dardanelles in Turkey, and the Straits of Bosporus, like a rat trapped in a pot. As for the fleet in Vladivostok, the Korean Straits and Hokkaido in Japan serve as defense posts against any attack in this region. Thus the Soviet Union is completely locked in, surrounded on all sides from the land, sea, and air. This is the situation today.

Since the Iranian situation developed, however, the net surrounding the Soviet Union has begun to unravel. The menacing power of the Soviet Union has grown in the Middle East region and has become even greater with the Afghanistan invasion. If the Soviet Union pushes down to Pakistan through Afghanistan, it will come to control the Indian Ocean, the Persian Gulf, and the Arabian Ocean. If the situation reached this point, there is a possibility that East Africa would fall under Soviet domination.

We have to establish cooperative relations with the entire Islamic hemisphere, at any cost. In coming to terms with the Islamic world, it is critical to recognize its importance. In the Islamic world, unlike in other religious areas, the power of religion is overwhelming, and its devoutness is something to behold. It is reminiscent of the medieval European Christian states. Since Islamic doctrines originated in Judaism and Christianity, in a way Islam has a blood relationship to the Western Christian world.

Relations between Islam and Christianity have been turbulent ever since the birth of Islam in the seventh century. Hatred of domination and exploitation by the Western nations has become intense. However, the profoundly religious faith of Islam prompts great caution and reaction against atheistic communism. Only the age-old prejudices against the West and the Palestinian problem have stirred immediate interests that prevent Islam from taking a definitive stand against communism. Solving the problem of Israel, therefore, is a top priority. Without resolution of the Israeli problem, conciliation and cooperation with the Islamic world are absolutely impossible.

Once this problem is resolved, however, the Western nations will be able to form harmonious relationships with the Islamic nations, as countries which share monotheistic beliefs. Practical and economic dependence will further facilitate this.

I have repeatedly stressed the importance of the Palestinian problem, not only because the danger is too great if things do not turn out well but also because the potential gains are equally great if things do go well.

If a genuine cooperative relationship is established with the Islamic world, it will bring great contributions in economic terms and in anti-Soviet strategy and will stabilize international relations to keep world peace. (In the Soviet Union there are 40 to 50 million people of Islamic faith.)

The Problem of Japanese Textbooks

The textbook case, which has aroused great controversy recently at home and abroad, seems to be a very important problem. It appears that the lack of critical reflection on the past and nostalgic feelings that are deeply ingrained in the Japanese, especially in the top echelons of their leadership, have found their way into schoolbooks.

Several years ago, I read a war chronicle. It was a multivolume work by a Japanese author entitled *The Pacific War.* The author became famous with *Tokugawa Ieyasu*, and I was astounded when I read *The Pacific War.* Instead of critically reflecting on the Japanese invasion, the book asserts its inevitability and justifiability throughout its pages and consistently glorifies the war of invasion.

We know well from the Mishima Yukio incident that such an attitude is not his alone. This portrayal of Japan is in sharp contrast to the exhaustively reflective picture of Germany, which was also an invading power. In German textbooks, the crime Germany inflicted on humanity is critically examined, and the younger generation is encouraged to know and learn from it. We know that when the Germans locate those guilty of massacring the Jews, they still punish them.

Japan not only lacks a critical appraisal of its past but also has displayed an incomprehensible attitude toward a neighbor that it harmed. At the time of normalization of state relations with China, it expressed apology, but when it was a question of normalizing relations with our country, which was so long and brutally invaded, there was never a public apology.

I am afraid that in the end, in the process of correcting this textbook problem, China and our country will be treated differently. At any rate, it is absolutely necessary to resolve this problem correctly to restructure Korean-Japanese relations and to be genuinely friendly. If we put up with humiliation again, the skewed Korean-Japanese relations will be frozen in their present form.

We believe that correction is necessary not only for the integrity and dignity of our nation but also for the true spiritual rebirth of Japan. We want to point out that there are a great many ordinary people as well as leading figures who oppose such a wrong attitude that stems from the past. The leading force in the textbook case is the right-wing element of the Jiminto with whom we have been in contact. In Japan, however, there are many people in various strata, in opposition parties and the Jiminto, who oppose such an insensitive attitude. Realizing this, we should expand our contacts in the future.

It would not be appropriate to regard the textbook problem from the perspective of fear that Japan may reemerge as an aggressive country if it is allowed to follow its own course. The era of territorial invasion is over. Invasion is no longer necessary and is only remotely possible. Lack of critical reflection and arrogance of the kind revealed in the Japanese textbook case are allowing everything to run wild at the moment, including trade problems, the issue of Korean residents in Japan, the problem of tourists, investment, and economic loans. This is a new version of imperialism.

We should not be harshly critical only of others but should also be stern in examining ourselves. In my last letter, I pointed out that our responsibility for the collapse of the Yi dynasty was great. In the process of normalizing relations, or even since then, haven't we encouraged Japan's arrogance or accepted it as natural? Have we maintained an attitude that deserves the respect, support, and cooperation of enlightened people in Japan? There should be a sweeping critical examination of these questions.

The Crisis in England at the Beginning of the Nineteenth Century and Its Resolution

From the Glorious Revolution of 1688 until the early nineteenth century, England strengthened its national power by undertaking three great reforms: takeover of the executive function by Parliament, the system of giving responsibility to an endogenous cabinet, and peaceful changes of power. England was thus able to forestall the hegemonic control by Louis XIV and Napoleon on the Continent, and during this process went ahead of France in foreign competition to emerge as a great colonial power. This was the way England appeared when it triumphed in the Napoleonic War in 1815. In reality, however, England was on the brink of an explosive crisis at home. That is, the peasants who lost their land in the Industrial Revolution flocked to the cities and aggravated the restless urban situation.

City dwellers gave vent to their discontent over the monopoly of voting rights by aristocrats and capitalists, while the workers revolted against terrible working conditions. When England stood at the crossroads of a great internal revolution, or even worse, catastrophe, there were four categories of people who rescued England from crisis and opened the path to glory for the radiant Victorian age in the nineteenth century. The first was the Methodist church, founded by Wesley. Following Wesley's teachings, it stood on the side of the workers and the ordinary people, reassuring and defending those whom the Anglican church had abandoned and leading them out of discontent to solace and hope. The second group was the newsmen who reflected the legitimate demands of the citizenry and the workers. They could let the world know their intents without having to resort to violence. Third was the legal profession, which made it possible for those who had grievances to rely on the court for protection of their rights as a last resort. Fourth was the Whigs (later the Liberal party), founded in the eighteenth century, who strove for reform in the liberal spirit of Fox, who opposed the government's American (colonial) policy, urged liberation of the Catholic church, promoted emancipation of the slaves, supported the French Revolution, and opposed repressive policies against the masses.

Efforts by these groups overcame the persistent opposition by the Tories (the Conservative party), the aristocracy, and the king and endowed the general public with the right to vote by enacting the first reform of the election law in 1832. Thus, the first stage of the crisis was hurdled.

The results were modest, almost to the point of being nonreformist, contrary to the intent of the Conservative party. Feeling confident now, the Conservatives took the initiative in the second reform of 1867. They proposed and passed legislation giving the workers the right to vote. Disraeli was the principal figure in this reform.

We can see that no matter how discontented the masses are, disruption will not come about if they have spokespersons, outlets, and supporters. Through the lessons learned from nineteenth-century England we know that under these circumstances alone, we can expect stability and unity.

Development of the Five Greatest Trading Nations in Asia and the Confucian Hemisphere

In Hong-il's letter, there was mention of the five greatest trading nations: Japan, Taiwan, Hong Kong,

Communist China, and Korea. From a quick glance, we can tell that these five nations belong to the Confucian hemisphere. As I said when I was outside, the countries that emerged as the middle-tier nations in the 1970s, including Singapore, are all nations in the Confucian hemisphere. I read the same statement in a book by Herman Kahn which I read after I came here.

I have wondered why the Confucian countries are developing faster than countries in other religious hemispheres.

First, it seems to me that the rationalism, practicality, and secularity of Confucianism have formed a spiritual basis for accepting the modern industrial system and techniques without pain or resistance.

Second, the highly hierarchical consciousness and system of Confucianism blend with modern industry, which demands militarylike discipline and order for the sake of productivity.

Third, the high degree of ethics and the system of extended families, which are salient features of Confucianism, may have translated into conscientious cooperation and familylike solidarity within enterprises.

Fourth, what is most important is the fact that Confucianism is a philosophy and body of knowledge that purports to rule the world rightly. Such knowledge was spread even more widely by the civil service examination. The high level of educational attainment must have been a reason that Western civilization and the industrial system were effectively assimilated.

Confucianism is not necessarily perfect, however. It has many problematic areas, such as holding government in esteem and the masses in contempt, bureaucratic complexity and corruption, discrimination on the basis of status, disrespect for labor, indolence (the Yangban system), and a repressive patriarchal system. One may question all this by pointing to Japan, which, in spite of these shortcomings, succeeded in becoming an advanced industrial nation. There are, however, considerable differences between Japan, on the one hand, and our country and China, on the other. Japan cannot be considered a purely Confucian nation.

For nearly seven hundred years, from the Kamakura Bakufu in 1192 until the Meiji Restoration in 1868, Japan was ruled by the military. Confucianism was acquired after the Tokugawa Bakufu because of the need for enlightenment of the military officers and administration. It did not prevail in the entire domain of Japanese life. In addition, there were various other influences on the Japanese spirit, society, economy, and other fields. Bushido, Shinto, Buddhism, and Western scholarship came to Japan through Nagasaki.

I think that this is the time to investigate fully the influence of the Confucian tradition on the modernization and industrialization of our country.

1. *Maengja* (Mencius).

2. *Changja* (Chuang-tzu).

3. *Shigyŏng* (Shih-ching: Book of Poetry); the books above are included in The Classics of the East series I have at home.

4. Matthew Bunker Ridgway, *Korean War* (Chŏngu-sa).

5. Song Kŏnho, Sŏ Chaep'il kwa Yi Sŭngman (Sŏ Chae Pil and Syngman Rhee) (Chŏngu-sa).

6. Chu Sŏkkyun, *Nongmin ŭl wihayŏ* (For the Farmers) (Chŏngu-sa).

7. *Introducing Korea* (Chŏngu-sa).

8. *Sakharov's Voice* (Sammin-sa).

9. Yi Sunyŏl, *Ŭmagŭl ch'ajasŏ* (Seeking Music) (Sammin-sa).

10. *Jaspers ŭi saengae wa sasang* (The Life and Thoughts of Karl Jaspers) (Pakyŏng Mungo).

11. *Nietzsche ŭi saengae wa sasang* (The Life and Thoughts of Friedrich Nietzsche) (Pakyŏng Mungho).

12. *Chŏng Tasan ŭi saengae wa sasang* (The Life and Thoughts of Chŏng Tasan) (Pakyŏng Mungo).

13. *Schweitzer ŭi saengae wa sasang* (The Life and Thoughts of Albert Schweitzer).

14. Albert Camus, *The Exile and the Kingdom* (Pakyŏng Mungo).

15. Immanuel Kant, *Foundations of the Metaphysics of Morals* (Pakyŏng Mungo).

16. Johann W. von Goethe, *Die Leiden des Jungen Werthers.*

Father's Sorrow

September 23, 1982

To you and my beloved children with love and respect:

Today is the autumnal equinox when night and day are of equal length. From now on, the beautiful autumnal sky will make us feel enchanted, even though it will not last long. Ch'usŏk is only eight days away, and I am writing this letter earlier than in other months, hoping this may be my Ch'usŏk present.

I sincerely hope that you will greet the Ch'usŏk festival happily, without despairing because of my absence, and that it will be a happy festival for Jee-young and Chung-hwa.

Judging from the last two visits, your face looks more haggard. I wonder if hay fever is over with now. I hope that you will always take care of your health.

The rejection of Hong-up's passport this time really jolted me. I had not been at all worried that a passport would not be issued, considering the circumstances surrounding the passport application and the humanitarian aspects. This is truly an agonizing outcome. As I said during the visit, on the night of the 15th, when I learned about the passport being turned down, I could not contain my sad feelings and violent thoughts. The pain I have felt over the innumerable adversities that our children, siblings, and friends have had to suffer on my account has always been greater than the pain of my own hardship. The case of Hong-up is just too tragic.

How can it not be a great sorrow when a 32-year-old child has not been given a job or could not be married? While praying that night, in tears I asked to be enabled to provide spiritual freedom, if possible, through the teaching and practice of morals and discipline, even though I might have to endure the pain of being cut off for the rest of our lives from the preordained relationship with my children and siblings. As you have said, I am hoping for a blessing by turning the present misfortune into good luck, according to God's will, and praying for a special blessing for all those who are in trouble because of me.

When I read in your and Hong-il's letters that your calligraphy, presented at a bazaar given by the Association of Christian Presbyterian Women, was sold out, I was very happy and could not help but feel grateful to those who purchased your work. I often think I would like to practice calligraphy here but have given up the idea because it does not seem at all feasible. I hope that you will continue to work on it.

I read in your letter how disappointed you are that the flowers have wilted early this year. The reason may be this year's unusual heat. I water the flower beds that I tend here and have cared for them in a variety of ways, but it is not like last year. My heart is really bitter that particularly the flowers that are weak are withering in the heat in spite of special care. When I see, however, that many of the flowers in the beds I tend have blossomed beautifully in spite of this year's scorching heat, I feel rewarded and delighted.

One psychologist has remarked that to love a human being, an animal, or a plant is to give life. To give life probably means facilitating the genuine growth of the recipient of care. When I am caring for the flowers I frequently recall that statement. Actually, flowers or agricultural products are not like mechanical products in a factory. They are critically influenced by the attitude of those who care for them. Probably this is because horticulture is a creative project based on sincere effort and love, like a mother rearing a child. I think this explains a major reason for the failure of agriculture under communism—the work is imposed by external will.

On the 21st, you came unexpectedly and sent in purchased items and books that I was happy to receive. I realized why you came on that day and felt very content.

Some day, a harmonious and peaceful life will come to us as it does to others.

Congratulations on Your Birthday!

I sincerely congratulate you on your birthday and earnestly pray that God will bestow special blessings on you in light of your hardship and devotion up to this point.

Last year, Hong-il wrote in a letter that "when we tried to prepare a birthday party on mother's birthday, she retorted, 'What birthday, when father is in that kind of situation?' so we arranged a lunch at home for her, and when she was served, she clasped her two hands and prayed for a long time, which brought tears to our eyes." I recall this vividly, but it was a year ago already. These days I think about your birthday, remember you in many ways, and pray for you.

To Hong-il and Jee-young's mother:

I know that both of you suffered a great heartbreak over Hong-up's passport case. I appreciate the thoughts behind what Hong-il said to console me during his visit. I sincerely hope that whatever you two brothers plan will turn out well so that you can live with vigor.

Both of you are dependable, but whenever I think about you, I still earnestly want you always to work for self-growth. A life that has no outer and inner growth is an old life approaching its end, even though it may reside in a youthful body. How many young men squander away their youth and regret it in their old age! This is a criticism of myself, too. I do not want you to repeat this sort of mistake. Always be strict with yourselves! I want you to strive persistently for self-improvement, remembering how important and difficult it is to control oneself and to integrate one's emotional self and willful self.

When I was reading Jee-young's letter, I was surprised that her penmanship was so good. Some parts, however, were very loose and uneven, which was probably because she was not concentrating. I smiled to myself when I thought that. I am illiterate about music but want to hear her play the piano. In her letter, she boasted that she could play up to No. 60 of the second volume of her lessons. She also said that piano lessons were a lot of fun. It is very good that she keeps at it with interest and pleasure.

Not knowing music, I should not sermonize about it, but I have seen so many bad habits around us, I want to put in a word of advice regarding piano lessons. Those who teach music to city children should instruct them not only in simple techniques but also help them love and understand music as well as the creative spirit.

All that many people want from their music instructors is to gain mastery of techniques or the satisfaction of their vanity by seeing their children win prizes in contests. Such parental attitudes misguide and contaminate the sensitive minds of children. You must have seen many such cases. Think about this.

I was very surprised to learn during a visit that Jee-young was wondering why our people prefer sons to daughters. Considering that she is only six, she is very bright and precocious. The brighter children are, the more parents and the people around them must be careful of their own words and behavior. Actually, we must eradicate from our consciousness the feudal attitude of discriminating between daughters and sons. I want you to tell Jee-young that I said our family considers daughters and sons equally and that it is wrong thinking to be partial to sons.

I hear Chung-hwa is also learning to write, and I hope she gets good enough at it to be able to write her grandfather soon. I found it absolutely hilarious when Jee-young said in her letter, "Chung-hwa is copying me and playing like a monkey." I am sure you will be instrumental in their education, but what else could you call it but a great blessing that the two sisters get along so well?

Any time I think about your family, I am happy. In my earlier letter, I wrote that our people were very particular about loving their own children but had a shortcoming in not knowing how to love other people's children. I want you to be especially mindful of this point. Both spiritually and in practice, you must set examples for the children. When you have good food, have their friends come and share it, and encourage them to play with lonely children who have no friends. In doing so, you should make sure that the Biblical passage "Love thy neighbor as yourself" should not become only mere words used in sermons or in church. The greatest corruption and sin for the human spirit are egoism and greed. Such attitudes are contagious when parents love only their own children when they are young and ignore other people's children. Think about this.

To Hong-up:

I have no comforting words for you concerning the passport case, and I do not know how to describe my feelings when I think about your sacrifices on my account; I have no face left as a father. Nevertheless, on the 11th, the night of the same day your passport was turned down, you wrote a long comforting letter, concerned about your father. As your father was reading that letter I was thankful and proud, even though my emotions were quite mixed.

When I was thinking about how much you understand and care for your father, I suddenly remembered something you did when you came home on leave from the military service. This was when I returned by abduction from Japan. At that time you said, crying, "Father is not solely responsible for the affairs of this nation. Why do you try to shoulder all the troubles by yourself?" Well, you are now sharing the suffering with me.

No one enjoys suffering, but it is unavoidable when one lives according to one's conscience. This is an inevitable fate due to the sinful and imperfect nature of this world.

As I have often said, however, suffering in itself is not misfortune, and whether it becomes misfortune or not depends on one's attitude toward it. Furthermore, the genuine inner growth of human beings is possible only through hardship. The prophets and saints who attained the highest spiritual summits in the history of mankind are the ones who, when confronted by outer and inner challenges, daringly rose up, responded, and overcame.

Not only in the cases of these great spiritual mentors but also in human civilizations, nations, and individuals, there has not been a single example of success without challenge. We are experiencing hardship because God does not work for us on things human beings have to solve for themselves. He also is ready to prove that our lives can become meaningful.

I do not know how much solace these words will bring you as you are going through this trouble, but your father is sharing the agony and pain with great love and understanding for you. As your mother always writes, God will surely bless your life, if for no other reason than your kind mind. Actually, while working with you for a year and a half between 1979 and 1980, I realized that your power of judgment and ability to handle things are quite substantial. That also must be an asset acquired and refined in adversity.

Your father's unchanging resolve is how to live meaningfully in this world—from an immediate standpoint, how to become a father who sets good examples for his children. These thoughts seem to have sustained me, at least up to this point. Judging from my experience, opportunities never fail to arise. As you are demonstrating these days, one must work persistently with hope and belief in order to build up ability. If you stand ready with ability, opportunities will surely come for you to make a leap, recovering in one stride the ground you have lost before.

When I think about you here, I feel remorseful and ashamed that I have not done much for your school years. I hope from the bottom of my heart that my strengths and weaknesses, all together, can become useful for your living successful lives. I hope that what you are planning with your older brother turns out well.

To Hong-gul:

The greatest joy for our family this year is your entrance into the university of your choice, as we all had been hoping. Further, whenever I read your recent letters, your father gets the impression that you are handling with aplomb this period in your life which is full of dreams and changes. It also seems that you are moving into a fast-paced process of intellectual awakening and growth.

This proud state you are in is a result of the fact (so I want to believe) that you have overcome such difficult and shocking adversity, just as your brothers have, and this is now energizing you. This assessment makes me proud of you and your older brothers. This is attributable to your wonderful attitude, but I wonder if you realize the influence, visible and invisible, of your mother who, with faith and great determination, has stood up to all sorts of adversities. At any rate, I have high expectations for your future. I believe you will attain your goals because of your unique tenacity, intellectual curiosity, conviction, and judgment. This is what I am earnestly hoping.

You asked for words of advice in your latest letter, and I am putting down a few opinions for your use.

First, it will be well for you to concentrate on the school curriculum during your first and second years. Being a student, it will be advisable for you to focus mainly on your schoolwork and make your outside reading relevant to it. Schoolwork is not only the basis for one's specialty, human beings must have an attitude toward life which is faithful to primary tasks.

Second, you must get the highest grades of all in French and English because you are a student in the French Department. If your grade point average goes up because your grades are higher in courses other than languages, your academic life cannot be a success. Language studies are important not only for the sake of academic performance but because language has become an indispensable means of adequately understanding others and having others adequately understand us, of living as world citizens in this incredibly internationalized society. It will become necessary to learn not only English and French but also Japanese and Chinese, even if not right away, not to mention German, which is a necessity for studying philosophy.

Third, in addition to course work, it would be good to read materials over again carefully rather than skimming through a lot of books. You will do well to select truly basic books and read them carefully until you have completely assimilated them.

As you said, always live with intellectual curiosity, but I hope this curiosity develops into a systematic and purposeful concern and also into research that delves into the essence of things with a firm objective. At any rate, it is advisable to concentrate on forming a solid basis, whether in course work or in outside reading.

Fourth, it is good that you seem to be working on relationships with your schoolmates. In my earlier letter, I once made brief mention of it but will add a few words here.

1. Be especially careful in choosing friends in school more than anything else.

2. Always listen to others and try to find points of agreement rather than differences of opinion between your arguments and the other person's. In the end, no matter who wins or loses the argument, strive to gain productive results through the dialogue and share them. Never monopolize conversations, and avoid destructive ways of discussion which raise and emphasize differences.

3. Try to understand others, even if it does not please you. Understanding others is made easier by two different processes, the one of becoming the other person and the one of putting oneself in the other's shoes.

4. Once you have done something for your friends, don't expect any compensation or returns. To live thoroughly in giving love rather than in taking love

is the way to become one with your friends and the way to ensure a schoolmate will not disappoint.

5. You may have developed a thoroughly defensive psychological process, whereby you have secluded yourself in a little enclave of self and firmly shut off your mind toward others so as to protect yourself from despair in this harsh adversity. This is how it looks to me, but it could have been predictable at a young age. You have grown considerably, however, in spiritual and intellectual terms and hopefully will make a conscious effort to break and free yourself from such a withdrawal.

6. What is most important is endeavoring to perfect your character. It is not philosophers who have reached the summit of learning who are respected and emulated. Rather, it is the saintly characters who loved their neighbors and devoted themselves to, and worked for, humankind. Among schoolmates also we know that those who are leaders and succeed are not academically outstanding types but rather the ones with moral repute. Keep this in mind.

P.S. No. 3 above: The ways to understand others do not seem to have been explained fully enough. For example, in understanding General Yi Sunsin, you, Kim Hong-gul, will have to be General Yi Sun-sin for once, and experience the history that he experienced. At another time, you, Kim Hong-gul, retain your thoughts and experiences and try to experience the Japanese invasion in Imjin from his position.

The letters I sent right after you started college are my overall and basic opinions, and I hope you will always consult them.

Missionary Work Concerning God

The church has performed two kinds of missions: evangelical and missionary. These missions are manifested in social work, such as schools and hospitals and missionary activities outside the church. Those whom they address are not necessarily believers. They are simply services for society, based solely on God's love. Evangelical works are projects to attract people to the church, that is, their aim is the spread of Christianity. The former mission will mean social salvation and the latter individual salvation.

The church has long been negligent in its mission of social salvation but even so has entertained the arrogant thought that social salvation can be achieved only through the church. Twentieth-century theologians and church leaders have been surprised to learn that God has been consistently engaged in missionary works, regardless of the church. For example, when the church was indifferent to slavery and even supported it, advocates of enlightenment, humanists, and democrats dedicated themselves to the abolition of slavery based on the inalienable rights of all people in this world since they are all equally God's children. They finally attained their goal and this great success led to the dismantling of slavery throughout the world, whether Christian or not.

When the church was looking the other way during the brutal exploitation of workers in the West by the capitalists of the nineteenth and early twentieth century, many reformists joined the fight against the exploitation of humans by humans. They upheld the spirit of Jesus, who fought all his life on the side of the poor and powerless and struggled for the improvement of working conditions. The same was true for racial discrimination and opposition to war.

God never depends only on the church, and when the church is lackadaisical about the missions He assigned, He Himself recruits the necessary individuals and organizations for His projects to realize His kingdom on this earth and to bring about His freedom, justice, and peace.

Since the latter part of the twentieth century, the church has awakened from its long sleep and has begun to participate actively in the missionary works of God. This can be seen in the changes in the Catholic church after the Second Vatican Assembly in 1965 and the attitude of the Protestant church, led by the World Council of Churches, after the 1966 Geneva Conference. Absurd as it may sound, only since we entered the twentieth century has the church begun to uphold the will of Lord Jesus and the example of the original church. Therefore, we are truly happy to be living in this age, when we can witness the true image of the church and lead a religious life.

The awakening of the church, however, is limited to its leadership and a few clergypersons and believers with a cause. The majority of people still turn their backs on God's missionary works and the lambs (non-Christian as well as Christian) who are persecuted by hardship and the Satan of temptation.

Is not our bitter experience here at Chung-ju one such example? Lord Jesus said that people in prison should be looked up to. Instead of looking up, however, even those who visited from this side were shabbily treated. Actually, that incident shocked and grieved me greatly. My sorrow and irritation were not for me but for the church, or really for Lord Jesus who was nailed to the cross. No matter how hard the pope works and no matter how diligently the cardinal and a few others try, what can be done if the church as a whole does not move?

As I wrote earlier, God is not constrained by the cooperation of the church. God will not stop in His mission until the last day of the Second Coming of Jesus, when this society has matured and been made perfect. He did not yesterday, He does not today, He will not tomorrow. Thus, freedom, justice, and peace in God's love will be realized day by day in this world. When we look at life from moment to moment, there are frequent cases when evil triumphs, but when viewed from the perspective of the flow of history, we see that God has continuously won and will continue to do so.

We have to participate actively in God's missionary works, with faith and hope. I sincerely hope that my life today and our family's hardship today will become a small part of such participation.

The Future of China and Our Fate

Information about the Twelfth Party Congress of Communist China reaches me only in occasional fragments in the letters from home. Not having any detailed or systematic information, it is almost impossible for me to judge what is happening. But as this problem is significantly related to the fate of the world and especially to our fate, I have decided to write this, at the risk of being suspected of bravado. I hope this may be of use to you and the children and want you to correct any mistakes.

First, Deng Xiaoping seems to have gained a substantial victory in this congress. He seems to have solidified a new decisive triumph, judging from the content of the party constitution that was adopted and from the elimination of the glorification of Mao Zedong, a firm decision in favor of modernization. It is difficult to say one way or the other, without knowing the facts, whether the retention of Hua Guo Feng as a member of the Central Committee and the reinstatement of other party members should be considered as a tie to Mao's forces or their co-optation. Even if all this is viewed as a vestige of Mao's forces, the aforementioned accomplishments suggest that this is not sufficient to shake the decisive coordinates.

Second, the political path of Communist China seems to have been fixed at the congress to proceed in the following direction: abandoning permanent revolution at home; self-restraint in the export of revolution abroad for the purpose of world revolution; promotion of the Four Great Modernizations with the cooperation of Western economic powers; slight liberalization at home, and opening China to the outside world for the sake of advancing these purposes. If Communist China, even for the sake of expediency, should go the way of liberalization and open up to the outside world, its impact will be great, especially on North Korea.

Third, even though Communist China's goal of modernization is to join the ranks of economically advanced nations by the end of the twentieth century, its real intent must be to move ahead of America and the Soviet Union, becoming literally the Great Middle Kingdom of prosperity. This can be easily surmised in light of China's history and the structure of Chinese consciousness. The Chinese are trying to accomplish modernization by relying mainly, or almost exclusively, on Western industrial nations. The fact is that there are no alternatives for them. Japan alone has a GNP that matches the Soviet Union's. It is thus rather obvious which side Communist China will join.

Communist China will have to undertake certain measures to put itself in a position to receive economic aid from the West. This will include finding concrete ways of repayment, opening its doors to the Western world, and a series of liberalizing acts to import capital from the West. Economic cooperation with the West will be determined by these factors, and more than anything else, the nature of Sino-soviet relations will have a great impact.

Fourth, what is most noteworthy and worrisome for us is the prospect of future Sino-Soviet relations. With certain reservations, we can assume the fundamental rapprochement between China and the Soviet Union will not materialize. The reasons are many and varied.

1. There is the historical conflict of interests between China and the Soviet Union. China and the Soviet

Union face each other as enemies over nearly half their extended boundaries, and China has the bitter historical wound of the Russian invasion. Even today, Communist China reserves the latent right to demand the return of the north of Amuri, which Russia took by virtue of the Aigun Treaty of 1858, as well as the territory lost in the maritime provinces as the result of the 1860 Beijing Treaty. At any rate, the mutual fear and antagonism between China and the Soviet Union, who share territorial boundaries, are deeply rooted.

2. There is the problem of hegemony in the Communist movement. According to Communist dogma, capitalist countries will soon collapse. China and the Soviet Union are arguing over who is going to grab global hegemony when this happens. For us, this is an absurd thought, but they treat it as an article of faith. Viewed in this light, the animosity between China and the Soviet Union is like a hatred between close relatives—a very malignant emotional conflict.

3. However, even if China were to realize modernization by relying on the Soviet Union, the Soviet Union today is not capable of extending sufficient assistance on the basis of its current economic and technological capability. Furthermore, if Communist China were to choose modernization by relying on the Soviet Union, it would have to accept two conditions: an overall subjugation to the Soviet Union and abandonment of future competition for world hegemony. These are terms China can never accept.

4. Therefore, as long as the need for economic cooperation with the West remains as it is now, there will be a natural limit to exploring the improvement of relations with the Soviet Union since there will be no basic approaches. It is self-evident that if a fundamental change took place, economic cooperation be-

tween Communist China and the West would become very difficult. It may be that Communist China's gesture toward the Soviet Union is motivated by a desire to relieve the heavy military pressure of the Soviet Union and to counteract or check the Reagan administration's Taiwan policy.

5. The only reservations concerning what I have said above have to do with the situation if the opposition came to power because of the failure of the modernization program undertaken by Deng Xiaoping's forces and in the event that the West avoided economic cooperation. The chances for the first possibility are unknown, while the latter is not likely to happen for the time being.

When we examine the relationship between China and the Western world, especially the United States, it appears that relations have deteriorated under the Reagan administration, but this may not be a fundamental change. At any rate, Communist China seems to be moving in the direction of managing its economic cooperative relationship within the context of a balanced and competitive relationship with America, Japan, and the West, rather than with America as the dominating power. United States refusal of a proposal for a united front against the Soviet Union, arms sales to Taiwan, and weakening political and economic leadership in the Western world have cooled off Communist China's attitude toward the United States considerably and might lead it to adopt a conciliatory approach to the Soviet Union.

6. There is the problem of Communist China's future direction and our fate. This is an issue we should be greatly concerned about not only now but in the future as well. Basically, insofar as Communist China promotes modernization, relying on the West, it clearly will not want another outbreak of hostili-

ties on the Korean peninsula. This is because of the possibility that if a conflict occurs again, China might get caught up in it, directly or indirectly. In such a situation, smooth economic cooperation with the West would be impossible.

The other night there was an exchange of visits by the top leaders of Communist China and North Korea, and Kim Il Sung appears to have received a warm welcome in Beijing. This could be interpreted as North Korea approaching Communist China. As long as North Korean Communists hold the ambition of forcibly unifying the south, there has to be a limit to Communist China's influence on North Korea. Communist China does not have the capability, at the present time, to provide sufficient arms and economic assistance to North Korea in the Soviet Union's stead.

In conclusion, it is true that Communist China does not want another war on the Korean peninsula, but it seems to lack decisive influence on North Korea. North Korea appears to be somewhat sympathetic to Communist China but does not seem likely to chill its relations with the Soviet Union. As to what direction Communist China will take in the post-Twelfth Congress period, we have to keep in mind the reality of our bitter experience during the Korean War and Communist China's representation, even today, at the Panmunjum military conferences. We have to consider a variety of possibilities and establish wise and insightful measures.

Modernization and Democracy

Theoretically, it may be said that modernization does not in principle have to be accompanied by democracy. The combining of these two systems is the product of the geniuslike ability of the British people. When we study the British experience, we find that each system influenced the development of the other. Many countries learned about the development in England but were divided into two types. That is, America and France incorporated both modernization and democracy, while Prussia, Japan, and Imperial Russia accepted modernization but rejected democracy. As a result, everyone succeeded in modernizing, and even the Soviet Union is in the process of succeeding.

As for the fates of these countries, America and France have maintained national unity on the whole throughout a variety of difficulties and have sustained national development without great danger. The countries that rejected democracy, however, suppressed their people harshly at home and continually engaged in aggressive wars. In the end, Russia became Communist and Germany and Japan came to taste bitter defeat. When we examine the reasons for all this, they become all too evident.

First, the democratic countries of England, America, and France have ready systematic methods for solving contradictions in the modernization process, especially workers' or citizens' discontent. They systematically resolve problems that are expressed from time to time in the free press or in the political process, and thus they succeed in overcoming crises very effectively, as we have seen in their histories.

Countries such as Russia, Germany, and Japan, which rejected democracy, did not have freedom of the press and thus blocked the way for popular discontent to develop into and become reflected in public opinion. The people could not participate in politics either, and thus there was no systematic way to correct mistakes. The capitalist economy has inherent strengths as well as shortcomings, and unequal distribution of wealth is an inevitable phenomenon. As long as ways to remedy problems through public opinion and orderly channels are blocked, popular discontent and concentration of wealth are destined to become even more pronounced.

The countries that were solely concerned with modernization trumpeted patriotism at home and the theme of making the country wealthy and powerful so as to repress popular resistance. Outwardly, they diverted popular dissatisfaction onto the outside world by talking loudly about national crises and the right to exist. Russia, which was the most backward among them in terms of modernization, collapsed early before the upsurge of communism; Germany went through World Wars I and II and lost both; and Japan drove itself through the Japan-Ch'ing War, Russo-Japanese War, Sino-Japanese War, and the Pacific War before finally being destroyed.

Japan and Germany justified foreign invasion by calling up the specter of communism after the Russian Revolution, but their anticommunism without democracy brought about nothing but Communist regimes in East European countries, the Chinese mainland, and North Korea. In the wake of their complete destruction in World War II, Japan and Germany were forced to accept democracy. They lost all their colonies and occupied territories, and Germany even had its own land divided in half. Under democracy, however, their economies recorded one brilliant success after another, and Japan and Germany have both reached the peak of modernization, with Japan holding the status of the world's second greatest economy and Germany recognized as the foremost giant in the West. This is an ironic and telling fact. Moreover, the anticommunism they had talked about so loudly has finally begun to show results. For example, in West Germany, the Communist party used to make large gains in parliamentary seats after World War I, but today it is unable to secure even a single seat. In Japan, the Communist party has not been able to outgrow its minor status as the fourth or fifth party.

When we analyze the economic reconstruction and success of anticommunism in Japan and Germany, they may be considered as natural developments. First, freedom of the press and other basic freedoms of the people have been guaranteed, and popular participation in politics has been implemented. As a result, popular discontent or demands are freely converted into public opinion, which, in turn, can be politically resolved through orderly channels.

Second, as an inevitable consequence, fair distribution of wealth and the ideals of a welfare state have been realized.

Third, fair distribution of wealth contributes effectively not only to the perspectives on social justice but to the formation of a strong market, as distributed wealth means purchasing power. In this way, the expansion of production, which is the key to capitalist economic development, is ensured.

Therefore, the inevitable causes for the demise of capitalism which Marx pointed out, for example, a breakdown in the effective accumulation of capital due to an imbalance between production and consumption, falling profit because of intense competition, and outbreak of revolution as a result of the continuing impoverishment of the workers, have become mere fiction. It is an undeniable fact that the workers and the general populace in countries where it is possible to enjoy both freedom and sufficient bread reject communism fundamentally.

We now have to learn a passive historical lesson from the failures of Imperial Russia, Germany, and Japan but, at the same time, a positive lesson from the present successes of Japan and Germany. If we learn these lessons properly, we will be able to look ahead to a triumphant future based on the happiness of the people and a secure, strong state. Otherwise, there is great danger that we will not be able to avoid following the path that leads to misfortune.

When we scan the contemporary non-Communist

world, we find that too many countries have not learned these lessons. The fact is a number of countries in Central America, Asia, and Africa are looking away from the historical lesson that is right in front of them. What is even more worrisome is that the United States is less than enthusiastic in defending its own history of exemplary success in the achievement of modernization. Whatever else we do, we who are confronting the Communists in a divided land must pave the road to victory by mastering these very real historical lessons.

Thought Fragments

⋆ Living faithfully according to one's conscience is the only way to a successful life. Following one's conscience guarantees the true value of success and, even in failures, ensures that one's life is made meaningful. This is because such a life has God's blessing whether it succeeds or fails in practical terms.

⋆ Selfishness and greed are the greatest sins; selfishness idolizes self; greed idolizes its object.

⋆ Nationalism should be democratic. Only then can there be division between independence from and coexistence with the outside world and the parallel existence of integration and diversity at home. Nationalism without democracy is prone to become chauvinism and an instrument for repressing the people.

⋆ Poverty is not to be feared. What is most fearful is that the poor think themselves undeserving of poverty. No matter how much material growth is recorded, such a society cannot be called healthy.

⋆ History always asks the questions, Where do you stand? What have you learned from the past, and what are you contributing now? What are you going to leave behind for your children?

⋆ In some ways, all human beings are hypocrites. When we perform a good deed, it is rarely because it has become a habit of ours or because it is emotionally pleasing. Instead, in spite of everything, we act with reason and will. This sort of hypocrisy is commendable, however, because it stems from an altruistic motive rather than a selfish one.

⋆ Even though the world looks sinful, why does it never collapse? It is because the aspiration for truth and justice is consciously or unconsciously lodged in the minds of all human beings. This is the very will of heaven. Such an inner aspiration explodes into an unbreakable popular desire when it meets an opportunity and time, and it crushes the domination of evil. Many of our creative precursors waged lonely and seemingly hopeless struggles. They knew well that their efforts might not bear fruit in their lifetime. They knew equally well that the people could be capricious, gullible, selfish, and cowardly. They also knew, however, that the people could not ignore for long the voice of truth and justice that rang out from their writings. The reason for the continued existence of the world is twofold: the principled efforts and sacrifices of our forerunners and the ulimate following of truth and justice by the populace.

Resolution of a Difficult Situation

Confrontation between rulers and the ruled is possible in states, in organizations, or in any society. Such a confrontation occurs when rulers have lost the creative and progressive capacity for leadership that they had demonstrated originally. There are three ways to resolve this difficulty.

The best method is to find a unified solution secured by an agreement between the rulers and the ruled which is arrived at through dialogue. There are no victors or losers, and the only issue is what is best. If this kind of agreement is reached, society recovers its vitality and moves forward. Second, the rulers conquer the ruled by force and pave the way for a future direction.

The situation is very fluid in this case, and the possibility of establishing a new beginning for development is uncertain. Third, both sides are engulfed in endless confrontations, unable to resolve the situation in either of the above ways. This can result in the eventual destruction of that society. We can see examples of the first way to resolve problems in England and America, of the second in the revolutions in France and Russia, and of the third in prewar Germany and Japan.

Economic Development and Human Resources

In Hong-up's letter some time ago, I read that Mexico, thinking it had struck oil, was swaggering in its extravagance but that it has now reached the brink of bankruptcy, with its foreign debts totaling over $80 billion. He referred to this as nonsense, as laughable, and said that one should not jump for joy simply because there is oil. Also, from recent letters from you and Hong-il, I can tell that Venezuela, a similar oil-producing country, is in the same situation and Brazil, richly endowed with a variety of resources, is in an economic crisis. We are witnessing here that economic success cannot be accomplished, no matter how abundant the natural resources, without the human resources to manage them properly.

The equation between economic growth and human and natural resources is very informative. First, it is a lesson of history that regardless of how richly they may be endowed with natural resources, nations cannot accomplish successful economic growth if they have not developed human resources capable of effectively managing them and competent, honest governments. We can see countless examples in Central American countries, Asia (Southeast Asia), and Africa.

Second, even if they lack natural resources, those countries with an abundance of well-developed human resources can record astounding accomplishments.

Very impressive examples are the Western nations, Japan, and the nations that are now emerging as new industrial countries, such as Korea, Taiwan, Singapore, and Hong Kong.

Third, there is the example of America and the Soviet Union, which possess both natural and human resources. And Communist China is outdoing itself to join them. (Seen in this light, the competition between America and the Soviet Union for global hegemony may be the result of this richness.) We can reconfirm that the future course for our country ultimately is to devote greater efforts to securing even more highly developed human resources.

I send my regards to brothers, relatives, and all our friends. I extend my gratitude to those who worry about me and pray for me.

Please find the following books written by Father Teilhard de Chardin, either in English or in Japanese. English versions are published by Harper and Row in New York.

1. *The Divine Milieu* (1960).
2. *Letters from a Traveler* (1962).
3. *The Future of Man* (1964).
4. *Hymn of the Universe* (1965).
5. *The Phenomenon of Man* (1959).
6. *The Appearance of Man* (1965).
7. *The Making of a Mind* (1965).
8. *Man's Place in Nature* (1966).
9. *The Vision of the Past* (1967).
10. *Writings in Time of War* (1968).

What Is This Called My Life?

November 2, 1985

To you and my beloved children with love and respect:

Now winter seems to be approaching, step-by-step. I am already worried because it is said this coming winter is very likely to be the severest in this century. The 25th was one day after the first frost, and the temperature dipped quite a bit.

It was heartbreaking when I went out to the flower beds and saw that all the flowers except the chrysanthemums had vanished. Petunias, globe amaranths, hollyhocks, yellow cosmos, and cockscombs—I grew them with all the care I could give and kept them going for more than a month longer than the ones in the other flower beds. One good frost, and they were gone in one morning. When I saw the miserable shapes of the flowers, I was overcome by feelings of sadness and emptiness, as if I were watching a loved one on a deathbed. Human beings are bound to be attracted to something, and once attracted, they have to taste the sorrow of parting sometime. This is what I felt all over again.

As I briefly mentioned yesterday during the visit, I had a severe case of indigestion from the night of the 22nd and was in great pain for two or three days. I was groaning in pain because the front and back of my chest felt as if they were pulling each other. Fortunately, the prison authorities brought in a specialist from outside and provided medical care. Although I am still eating only porridge, I have become more comfortable. This is why I am now getting to the October letter.

While I was physically ailing, I got so homesick I

was constantly thinking all I wanted was you at my side, taking care of me.

Lying on my sickbed, with a needle in my arm for the injection of Ringer's solution, I spent the hours of boredom in sundry thoughts about my life, asking myself questions and then answering them.

> ⋆ And what is this called my life? Throughout my life there has been one adversity after another, and I have reached this age without once having lived happily—free of all worry, with my family—like other people. Can we still say that this is living?
>
> ⋆ This does not mean, however, that living comfortably is the only road to happiness, does it? Among the people we know who live such lives, how many are there who can confidently say they have been happy? When they reflect on life, they will regret that they have spent their lives meaninglessly, in pursuit of comfort.
>
> ⋆ Nonetheless, this is also a matter of degree. If one's life is spent in poverty and pain and in a continuum of death and adversity, such as mine has been, how can one not doubt the meaning of life?
>
> ⋆ Does this mean, then, that I am having second thoughts about the life I have lived? Do I regret the life that I have tried to live sincerely for my people and conscience, the life that tries not to bequeath to posterity the sorrowful times we have endured?
>
> ⋆ I am not going to say I have second thoughts. As Hong-up said some time ago, however, it is too much to say that I alone must live this kind of ordeal. Furthermore, it has not been only my personal ordeal. My family and so many of my brothers, relatives, and friends have been sacrificed on my account. I cannot describe how my heart aches whenever I think about them. There is nothing in this world more anguishing than idly watching other

people suffer on my account. This is not all! Throughout my life, how many favors have I received from so many people. My heart is distraught because I have not repaid any of these favors—favors from individuals, favors from my election districts in Inje and Mokp'o, and favors from my people.

While living this life of adversity, I have unwittingly inflicted injuries on others and have not been able to return the favors of others. Moreover, I have not had a single opportunity to realize my small ambitions. From these standpoints, I wonder about the meaning of my life.

* Actually, we frequently become skeptical about life. After all, what does adversity mean? Is it a punishment for one's sin? If so, how is it that we observe innumerable instances of bad people prospering while good ones are crushed?

Si Maxian, who may be considered the father of history, at least in the Orient, raised the issue of "a way of heaven" formally in his historical biographies. He earned the ire of the Han dynasty's Mu emperor when he presented a justifiable defense for a friend. For this he was castrated, which for a man is a worse punishment than dying. When we think of him as exemplary of a good man suffering, his outcry over whether there is or is not a way of heaven affects us even more deeply.

* I have given this problem a lot of thought. Actually, why good men suffer and bad ones prosper is a long-standing puzzle; indeed, it has not been solved in the history of human religion and ethics. What is clear, however, is that this problem can never be solved by using the logic that adversity is a punishment, whereas success is a reward for good deeds. There are two opinions that may be useful here. One was advanced by Dostoevsky. In *Brothers Karamazov*, Dmitri Karamazov received a guilty verdict he did

not deserve after being falsely accused of having murdered his father. He came to a certain understanding at that time by overcoming many psychological conflicts, anguish, and anger.

Dmitri's perception was: I do not deserve this. Why, then, do I have to suffer the ordeal of being exiled to Siberia? I am shouldering my countless sins of the past, all sorts of vulgar sins of my father, and the sin of the Russian people. A human being's adversity cannot, and should not, be avoided because as a member of a group, it stems not only from one's own sins but also from the sins of those who make up the community. Thus, he gladly endures the guilty verdict when he realizes its meaning, and it is because of this realization that he is saved.

★ Dostoevsky's thought seems like a great awakening. Just look at ourselves. Let us not even talk about the remote past. How can we avoid the sin of those who led this nation to destruction when the Yi dynasty was losing to the Japanese aggressors or the sin of our ancestors who lent cowardly cooperation by simply looking on? Let us remind ourselves that liberation from Japanese colonialism was not attained by our own strength and that there were many pro-Japanese elements at that time. After liberation, did our national spirit stand on solid ground, cleansing itself of pro-Japanese elements and pushing the patriots to the fore? The sin of this kind of betrayal of the legitimacy of our nation has since become the karma that suppresses all the regions of this country. It has made empty slogans of conscience, justice, and patriotism and has made the country a playground for those who would use any means to attain their ends, those motivated by devilish and selfish intents. How can we escape punishment for these sins? We should gladly accept it. At any rate, we have held up as well as we have because our young people paid the price of sacrificing themselves for freedom and justice during the Korean Conflict and the April 19th Revolution.

What, then, is the other opinion I alluded to earlier? It is Father Teilhard de Chardin's view, which I will summarize as follows: The sins and the human predicament in this world are inevitable phenomena that stem from the world's imperfect nature. Since the birth of the earth several billion years ago, the world continually evolved toward increasing complexity and consciousness and continues to do so. As the center of the evolutionary process, Jesus came, and it is because of his presence that the world moves toward consummate perfection. We are progressing, therefore, from imperfection to perfection and from a world with the possibility of sin and hardship to the kingdom of heaven where sin and hardship will be no more. Our endeavoring to perfect this world in spite of difficulties has great significance, which is that we are participating in God's momentous project.

From a broader perspective, it is true that the history of mankind is moving forward in the direction of a better and more just life, although there still remain many sins and troubles. Therefore, there is little reason for us to doubt that, judging from the past, this evolution will occur both spiritually and materially. This is not simply a theological argument but rests on clear scientific evidence. We thus have to accept, and at the same time try to overcome, all sorts of sins and adversities with a calm and peaceful mind and in faith and hope. Even when we are beset with difficulties, God will always open up the possibility of salvation for us, should we seek it.

I believe that I have found an understanding of salvation through Father Teilhard de Chardin's thought. When we note the following facts, we can believe not only on the basis of faith but also on a scientific basis in the presence of God, in His projects and His tireless work. During the several billion years of the earth's existence, vegetation developed out of simple organisms, then came marine life, some forms of which moved onto land, and, finally, humans appeared about two million years ago. When we think of the continuing evolution of human beings and all things in the world, both organic and inorganic; when we observe the gradual liberation from countless sins and from slavery, racial discrimination, and human exploitation, which have persisted throughout history; when we observe the continuing emphasis on human rights; and when we face the extermination of great epidemics or their noticeable reduction and the conquest of starvation and disease, we can believe in God and His projects.

* Those who feel their calling should accept as part of the inevitable and necessary process their belief in the bright future that will shine on the future of mankind and the meaning of the forward march of which they are a part.

* After all the questions have been asked and all the analyses have been undertaken, a genuinely happy individual is one who can face his conscience with pride and believe that his life has been meaningful for society and history.

* In the last analysis, until the final day of perfection, there is bound to be sin in this world, as Jesus once said. We have to comply with the dictates of our conscience, however, and fight against sin, always with God's help. Those who feel the calling to improve this world and help it progress should repudiate completely their egoistic selves and strive to contribute to progress by combating sin. Have we not seen many prominent people who became the light of our nation through self-denial? The six dead officials, Yi Sunsin, Chŏn Pongjun—these are our

models, and we can be proud of them, no matter who they are compared to.

It goes without saying that it is Jesus Christ who attained the most brilliant and complete self-abnegation. If adversity is the inevitable fate of human beings and if accepting and overcoming it is the genuine path for contributing to history and making oneself visible, anyone who wants a meaningful life should not try to avoid the storms of adversity.

The Four Great Powers and Peace in the Korean Peninsula

In a recent letter from home, there was mention of a high-ranking Soviet official who visited our country. I have become very interested in him. It is too early to pass judgment, but opening the channels for dialogue between our country and the Soviet Union would be a noteworthy event that should be positively evaluated.

Judging from the international situation or south-north relations, our complete unification seems very remote. As a precondition for unification and also to allay the heavy burden and tragedy of fratricide, peaceful coexistence and mutual cooperation between south and north should be aggressively sought.

As one government official responsible for foreign policy reportedly said in London the other day, peace in the Korean peninsula and a trouble-free solution of the south-north problem have as prerequisites of equal import sincerity on the part of both south and north and cooperation among the four great powers. In this sense, we have to hope patiently for the opening of channels with China and the Soviet Union, with whom our relations are strained, and we must strive toward that end from many different angles.

In the final analysis, the objectives of the first stage should be the establishment of a firm peace between south and north, mutual recognition of south and north by the four great powers, and membership of south and north in the United Nations. South Korea must develop a solid democracy and national economy, which will make North Korea, China, and the Soviet Union realize there is no other alternative to peaceful coexistence. It cannot be too strongly emphasized that a genuine unity and prosperity in the south is the road to peace and the way to eliminate the possibility of a war.

Taking these conditions as indispensable, I believe we must consider the problem of promoting peaceful cooperation among the four great powers in the following manner. First, Japan and especially America should be consulted on every project to be promoted. We have to rid ourselves of any nationalistic bias, and at the same time, we must realize clearly that close cooperation with America and Japan is required in the interests of our nation.

Second, depending on the progress of various situations, we have to consistently maintain the basic position of treating China and the Soviet Union equally, although one may be contacted before the other or there may be differences in the substance of athletic and scholarly exchanges with them. We should make every effort not to be misunderstood on this point, for if we are, there will be no gains for our security or interests, and we may suffer great losses.

Third, we have to work hard to secure the support of not only the four great powers, who are directly concerned, but also influential allies and neutral countries, such as the European nations, in promoting relations with the four powers. It is my judgment that world opinion is in favor of the peaceful coexistence between south and north, the simultaneous establishment of diplomatic relations between south and north and with the countries of the world, and the membership of south and north in the United Nations.

It appears to me, however, that North Korea is unable to give up its mistaken yearning for the possible takeover of South Korea, which is holding China and the Soviet Union at bay. Because of this, things may not work out well. I want to stress once again the extreme importance of national conciliation and democratic unity within the Republic of Korea.

It is our fate to take seriously relations with the four great powers because we are divided into south and north, with the north allied with China and the Soviet Union and the south engaged in an alliance, or quasi-alliance, with Japan and the United States. Above all, it is because the Korean peninsula is surrounded by the four great powers and, from a geopolitical and historical standpoint, is an area where their interests converge. Further, although in terms of population South Korea is among the twenty largest of the world's 150 nations, it has not been able to join the United Nations and has diplomatic relations with only a small number of countries. This kind of irrationality can never be corrected unless solutions are worked out first in the four-power relations.

Of course, cooperation among the four great powers is an indispensable condition for south-north unification, which is our nation's aspiration. We must always remember that, whether we like it or not, the fate of our nation is inextricably bound to the four great powers.

When I emphasized the promotion of peaceful cooperation by the four great powers in 1971, I was criticized for a way of thinking in which our security is entrusted to others. When I stressed simultaneous membership of the south and north in the United Nations and simultaneous diplomacy right after the July 4, 1972, joint communiqué, I was rebuffed by the government for talking nonsense. We all know, however, that subsequent events proved consistent with the directions I had emphasized.

For our existence and security to be assured, these problems should receive the serious attention of our nation and should be worked at continuously, and our national policy should be adjusted and strengthened for its realization.

Fond Remembrance of a Certain Individual

Fundamentally, people are the products of history and cannot sway its axis. Great people, however, can leave an indelible imprint on history, decisively influencing the fate of many. Those who greet the people with understanding and affection, keeping pace with the course of history, become highly respected and adored by everyone, regardless of historical period.

Zishan of the Zheng dynasty, who is discussed below, is one such person. He was of the Confucian period about 2,500 years ago and is highly regarded by the historians of the East and the West not only as a great man of the past but also as a great man in the modern sense. Toynbee also rates him highly. Zishan was a finance minister of Zheng, a small country that existed during the mid-sixth century B.C. When Confucius visited Zheng, they related to each other as affectionate friends, and Confucius praised him afterward.

As finance minister, Zishan checked with able diplomacy Jin in the north and Chu in the south, which harassed Zheng as if doing so were an annual activity, and fortified the basis of peace by making Zheng a buffer zone for the Zhou royalty. He did not simply use diplomacy to check these two great powers which were preying on smaller powers. As a foundation for such diplomacy, there was a solid domestic government, and he showed successful statecraft at home, which earned the spontaneous support of the people.

He sought to stabilize the political scene by mediating confrontational disputes between aristocrats. Further, he implemented reforms of national policies by establishing a fair rule by law and by improving the position of the people, who were struggling against the aristocrats and corrupt and greedy government officials, through reforms in taxation and the land system. His politics and ethics consisted of respecting human relations and establishing justice, and it is noteworthy that he exhibited an attitude that absolutely rejected superstition. Politics for the people, rational reform of the system, rule by law, pursuit of justice, and rejection of superstition—it is difficult to imagine that such a politician lived 2,500 years ago. The story is this.

In Zheng during Zishan's time, there were school buildings in the villages where peasants congregated at night after their agricultural work to discuss various topics, occasionally criticizing the government. One of Zishan's subordinates told him the people should not be allowed to use the school buildings because they would get together to criticize the government for no constructive purpose, which might lead to social unrest. This was the shallow thinking of a small-minded person with a bureaucratic distrust of people, the kind of thinking that can be found in any historical period. Zishan responded, however, that preventing people from expressing themselves was not a way to forestall social instability but rather a way of inciting it and that when people spoke openly about their concerns, their dissatisfactions would not build up. If the chance to express their discontent were blocked, it would accumulate and finally explode, setting off great turmoil. Therefore, when people are dissatisfied, it is good to let them speak out promptly. Furthermore, it would be helpful for the government to hear their complaints. If we listened to what they freely said, we could know accurately what their complaints and demands were. Would this not make governing easier? If the people's freedom of speech were stopped, the government would become deaf and they would be angry and restless and watch for an opportunity to rebel. People should never be prevented from meeting in the school buildings, he said.

Zishan's attitude toward free speech cannot be considered an enunciation of the democratic ideal, which holds freedom of expression as a basic right of the people. Nevertheless, in a time when people were treated as domesticated animals and agricultural management based on slavery was the order of the day, this sort of thinking may be especially noteworthy. Even today there are many rulers in all countries of the world whose thinking about freedom of expression does not measure up to Zishan's. If he had appeared in this country as finance minister in the final period of the Yi dynasty, his policies and attitude toward expression would have earned him popular regard as a most enlightened, distinguished finance minister. Greedy, brutal, and reactionary rulers crisscross the chapters of history. When we run into leaders like Zishan, who pursued justice and progress for the people in his time, the freshness of their thoughts, which leap across the gap of time and space, strikes a responsive chord. We feel anew the worth of life and understand one reason that mankind has persisted.

Perspectives on Economic Problems

Our economy seems unable to shake off the residual effects of the mistakes in the policy decisions and implementation of the 1970s. The most important rule in formulating new economic policy is to adhere to the basic principle of a free economy. Unique situations in countries may produce great differences in the means, but the principle cannot be undermined.

The mistakes of these economic policies lay in ignoring this principle, seeking excessive growth, and concentrating on trade, thereby weakening the entrepreneurial structure and making it dependent on special power. As in geometry, there is no king's way in economy. It should be realized that safe and consistent development depends on perseverance.

I believe the principles we must pursue with firm resolve today are as follows.

Economy with Balance among Three Elements

More than anything else, the policy to be pursued has to ensure a balance in growth, stability, and distribution. During the 1970s, policies that sacrificed the latter two elements for the sake of growth continued, and today they are even jeopardizing growth itself. Because these three conflict with one another, they are referred to as a devil's triangle. For sound economic development, they have to be balanced and mutally complementary.

Stability of price is an absolute necessity for sustained growth. The workers' incentive to produce has to be encouraged through just distribution, and their purchasing power has to be increased. Stability is not possible without appropriate production and supply of goods, and prices can be prevented from falling excessively when distribution is right and just. Improvement in distribution can be expected only in a growing economy. Without price stabilization, hard-earned income falls prey to inflation. High growth rates of the GNP are not desirable as an end in themselves but are important for the sound development of national economy only within the context of a balance in growth, stability, and distribution.

The Ethics of Businessmen

The economic history of advanced countries has amply proven the indispensability of a high code of business ethics for the maintenance and development of free economy.

Not long ago, a deceased owner of the Yuhan Yanghang bequeathed all his assets to society, for which he was lauded as an entrepreneur par excellence. His action can be commended as an expression of his lofty individual spirit, but as a model for business ethics, it presents a problem.

True ethics of businessmen are nothing but economic ethics, not personal ethics. The ethics of businessmen in a free economy are as follows.

First, a businessman must have pride and a sense of mission as a defender of free economy. He must believe in it and must strive to form a human image brimming with enthusiasm, creativity, and adventurism.

Second, a businessman must recognize his absolute responsibility to produce and distribute high-quality goods at low cost.

Third, he must accept his obligation to pay fair wages, commensurate with the increase in productivity.

Fourth, profits from an enterprise should be reinvested in toto for its expansion, with a view to contributing to the creation of new employment and increased production.

Fifth, the life of business management depends on the improvement of productivity. This should be the top priority of businesses. All kinds of efforts must be made to rationalize management, reform technology, and improve the rate of capital outlay for labor equipment. Entrepreneurs should be unequivocal in their conviction that the improvement of productivity alone must be the source of business growth and profit increase.

Sixth, as Schumpeter pointed out, it is not necessarily bad and is an inevitable phenomenon in the development of free economy for enterprises to monopolize the market by supplying inexpensive, good-quality products by improving productivity. The problem, however, is that a noncompetitive monopoly may abuse its political and financial clout to absorb weak enterprises and dominate the market, forcing consumers to purchase low-grade goods at high prices. Businesses should sternly reject such a temptation.

Seventh, as a result of technological improvements and the global expansion of the market, businesses are becoming so enormous that they are turning into social institutions rather than private businesses. Businessmen, therefore, must be determined to assume the social responsibilities of business in the rise and decline of national economy, stabilization of prices, maintenance of employment, prevention of environmental pollution, and preservation of natural resources.

These considerations, I think, may define the boundaries of the ethics entrepreneurs must observe. In a country like ours, half of whose territory is ruled by a Communist system that is the antithesis of free enterprise, there is little reason to doubt that the mission of businessmen and the importance of business ethics are much greater than in other countries.

What would happen if the code of business ethics were as follows? First, suppose businessmen transformed themselves from standard-bearers of free economy to pursuers of selfish interests, regardless of methods. Second, what if they made a habit of exporting high-quality goods that command high prices and leaving domestic consumers with inferior goods instead of serving them? Third, what if they refused fair distribution to the workers and refused to pay workers even subsistence wages? Fourth, what if they used their income on luxury and wastefulness and smuggled their assets abroad instead of reinvesting? Fifth, what if they schemed to expand their businesses not through improvement of productivity but through alliance with political power and hoarding profits accrued from inflation? Sixth, what if the national economy were monopolized by a few businessmen not as a result of improved productivity but because of noncompetitive and unnatural methods and then they drove small- and middle-sized businesses into bankruptcy at the cost of the consumers? Seventh, what if businesses neglected their social obligations but did not hesitate to ravage the land and pollute the environment?

Businesses would become targets of criticism instead of earning the confidence of the people. Would they not be blamed for proving the validity of communism and inviting the unintended consequence of guaranteeing its victory instead of becoming champions in demonstrating the superiority of a free economy?

People conduct politics in the same way they manage the economy. The master of free economy is business. We do not ask businessmen to become philanthropists. Instead, we are emphatically urging them to become absolute believers in the ethics of free economy.

Creativity and Improvement of Productivity

The greatest mistake of the economic policy of the 1970s was its disregard of creativity and improvement of productivity. In the 1960s, we demonstrated substantial economic growth. This was not due to the immanent strength of our economy, however. It amounted to no more than the setting up of a simple economy and exporting its surplus, making use of cheap and limitless labor just as oil-producing countries tap underground oil and export it. At that time, we had an enormous number of unemployed, and human resources were a kind of unbounded, free-floating material, like air or water. Moreover, educated human resources represented a double blessing. This is how we were able to rely on loans to bring in machinery, or materials, or half-finished goods and employ abundant labor at cheap cost so as to export consumer goods to the international market. This situation continued until the first half of the 1970s.

But such easy moneymaking could not last for long. After a while, labor becomes scarce, which pushes up wages. Internationally, we soon were challenged intensely by other middle-tier countries.

Government and business should have aimed to build with great creativity and effort an industrial structure that would be appropriate for our situation and also to promote the simultaneous international development of a competitive, heavy chemical industry and light industry by improving productivity. The government, however, judged the situation very optimistically and made no such preparations but raced down the road of one-sided development in the heavy chemical industry. But with no plans for managing the modern heavy chemical industry in an internationally competitive way, there could not possibly have been success. Most of all, businesses should have been developed on the basis of available natural resources. Also, there should have been concerted efforts to stabilize prices and attract foreign money by continually stressing domestic demand and export-related light industry. Instead, these were neglected while 80 percent of invested capital went into heavy chemical industry. As a result, prices soared and exports slowed.

In the meantime, the deluge of construction projects for heavy chemical industry, which did not have the basis to improve productivity through rational and effective management in such areas as government, business, finance, and education, caused an enormous waste of resources and myriad futile enterprises. Huge sums of money were spent to bail them out, thus creating more waste.

So today we are groping in the wrong direction for economic growth for which there was a golden opportunity in the 1970s. Today, our business community is in an extremely precarious condition, with a high debt ratio (i.e., 82 percent of total assets) and a very low profit margin. Another chance for development may come when the government understands the principle of free economy, which rewards the superior and defeats the inferior in fair competition and leads the way for government, business, finance, and related fields to dedicate themselves fully to creativity and improvement of productivity. Above all, the entrepreneurial practice of growing rich through extraeconomic methods, even though the businesses fail, should be completely eliminated.

Strengthening a Self-Sufficient Economic System

First, for the sound development of our economy, we have to concentrate on making it self-sufficient as well as on solving the problems mentioned above. This requires evaluating agriculture from an economic standpoint. Today, we are importing more than 40 percent of our food, which makes agriculture an important industry to replace imports.

Agriculture has an additional high value because the ratio of materials, energy, machinery, and equipment is very small. Agriculture provides an important market for business. In addition, the rebuilding of the agricultural economy is important for a balanced management of our national lands, prevention of overurbanization, and social stability.

Second, we have to stress the value of small- and middle-sized businesses and home industries. These enterprises still enjoy strong competitive power and offer the advantages of a high-rate employment market and low reliance on imports. Until now, the small and middle-sized businesses have consistently been the sacrificial lambs for economic growth. From the standpoint of exports, however, they have to be boosted because of their still relatively cheap labor costs and the edge they have in the international competition in labor-intensive products.

Third, it is indispensable for the healthy development of our economy to endeavor to attain balanced growth in the relationship between big, small, and middle-sized businesses, between city and rural economy, between regional interests, and between export and domestic industries.

Fourth, fair distribution is often the Achilles heel of our economy. This is an urgent problem not only for the unity of our people and for social stability but for providing a stable domestic market.

Fifth, we have to conserve and cultivate invisible, indirect capital. According to Weber's *The Protestant Ethic and the Spirit of Capitalism*, in the developmental process of modern economy, a dynamic role was played by the spirit of Protestantism, the spirit that claimed that business success based on conscience, diligence, and frugality is proof of God's salvation.

The long-term, sound growth of our economy must have, as important preconditions, the aforementioned ethics of business, the creation of an economic climate that is congruent with our social customs, popular mentality, and ethos, and one in which honest and diligent people can succeed.

Liberalization of Finance

I have learned from letters from home that the financial conglomerates' monopoly of the five largest banks in the city, after their return to civilian management, has created controversies in the National Assembly and is being closely watched by the people. The most crucial problem inherent in finance is the realization and guarantee of its liberalization. My opinions on this issue are as follows.

First, it should be noted that placing banks under civilian management should not be equated with liberalizing finance. Even under civilian control, the government still has the legal and substantive power to violate or interfere with the autonomy of financial institutions at will, either directly or through the supervisors of the Bank of Korea. However, banks may be owned by the state and yet not liberalize finance.

Second, liberalizing finance means that, under the government's basic principles of financial management, banks can freely determine the amount of loans and interest rates and that they are not subject to any interference in personnel or other areas of management. So long as the government can intervene arbitrarily, as in the past, finance can neither be autonomous nor can it be expected to develop. It is due to such interference that our banking business lags so far behind. It is absolutely necessary to minimize government intervention and guarantee the autonomy of the banking business for it to grow and catch up. Even with the guarantee of autonomy, however, supervision and monitoring by government agencies would still be in order, since the banks hold the valuable assets of the people in trust and can do great damage to the national economy if their loans are not proper or are excessively increased so that they cause inflation.

The development of finance can be expected only when, within the above-mentioned limits of personnel management and operation, the banks can freely determine the interest, develop a variety of saving plans, and, most of all, are guaranteed autonomous decision making and rights.

Without the development of banking, it is difficult to expect a noninflationary economic development through maximum mobilization of private capital.

Third, as the city banks have fallen into the hands of the financial conglomerates, our country's financial groups are no longer simple industrial conglomerates but have become financial combines, assuming the role of financial conglomerates. As mentioned earlier, what is necessary is to make finance autonomous and not place it in civilian hands. Autonomous finance is possible even under state ownership, as long as the government wants it. In some ways, state ownership appears more desirable. In such a case, we will have to watch closely, and its consequences must be our concern.

If things go wrong, financial groups instead of the

government will wield the power to decide the bank's management personnel as well as credit operations, making the bank the private safe of these financial groups. Is this not something to worry about? Considering that there were tendencies in this direction even under state ownership, this possibility cannot be dismissed as an unwarranted anxiety.

If, miraculously, the banks are guaranteed autonomous management, however, they can achieve the necessary expansion and efficiency and perhaps make contributions to our economic growth—the contributions banks are supposed to make.

Superstition Concerning Indexing the Economy

Both the government and the people are too sensitive to economic indexes. Indexes cannot be dismissed, of course, but they have no meaning unless their substantive contents are scrutinized. (This is true even if an index itself is accurate.)

It is a taboo to be overly optimistic or pessimistic about economic conditions solely on the basis of economic indexes. No matter how much the GNP has grown, a growth accompanied by inflation is extremely dangerous. Without looking into the contents of indexes, there should not be joy or gloom simply on the basis of indexes. For example, it must be taken into account whether growth is balanced or is accompanied by marked imbalance among primary, secondary, and tertiary sectors; and whether the growing sectors are sound or the growth of an abnormal expansion of recreation- and entertainment-related luxury businesses.

Second, no matter how much per capita income has risen, if the distribution of wealth is inequitable, the danger indicator must be viewed as being as high as the growth indicator.

Third, in the case of money in circulation, the volume does not necessarily induce inflation, just as low volume does not indicate stability.

Even if the rate of expansion is high, if the money in circulation is directly tied to production, it is anti-inflationary. Even if the rate of expansion is low, if it is not directly related to production, it can be a catalyst for inflation.

Fourth, speaking of price index, even though the consumer index may be stable in index terms, the cost of living may show a high rate of increase. This is because a variety of nonessential items get averaged in, which may make the consumer index appear stable.

As for wholesale prices, it is not simply their indexes but the trends in the prices of basic materials such as steel and fuel or energy which have bearing on the whole economy.

Fifth, the index for the volume of export became a matter of neurotic concern in the previous regime. We have to think carefully about how much we overexerted ourselves to reach the target in the past and how great were its side effects and the sacrifices by the people. We have to ask whether there is any advantage to exports when their margin of profit is so low, or when they lose money, or when people have to make up for the trade deficit by paying high prices at home. Furthermore, exports cannot be the driving force for economic growth unless there is cheap labor to be bought and sold, as in the 1960s.

It is when an economy develops by virtue of creativity and improved productivity that it can deal with international competition, the same objective as that for economic growth, which can be achieved by exports. This is the way it should happen. The history of economic development in advanced countries testifies to this.

Even in the case of Japan, the paragon of trading nations, a product is sufficiently tested on the home market before it makes an appearance in the international market. The objective of economic development always is to improve the economic life of the people, and exports are needed only to attract foreign capital. If exports are pushed even when they are losing money and are based on the sacrifices of the people, everything is turned upside down.

Even though export targets are established, they should be discarded when there is likelihood of losses. If target indexes have been filled, regardless of their real substance, that year's exports are considered a success, while if target indexes are not filled, no matter how substantive the contents of exports might have been, they are considered a failure. Such an attitude on the part of the government and public opinion should be changed.

Indexes are simply for setting directions and are not absolute behests or the criteria for judging the success or failure of economic policies. We have to shed the superstition about indexing the economy. The time has come, I think, for us to monitor and manage the economy with an even-keeled, mature attitude.

Where I Once Used to Live

November 26, 1982

To you and my beloved children with respect and love:

The weather has turned very cold. I worried about how uncomfortable it must be for those who do not have heating facilities as I do. As things stand now anyway, I think it is fortunate that many have been moved to the places they originally came from. I am praying everyone will be with their loving families as soon as possible.

When I read your letters, I can sense that you have made great strides recently in your faith. This has often been helpful to me. I hope, however, that with the difficulty you have had with your hand you will not make the letters you write every day too long.

The other day I was taken aback when I saw Chunghwa's drawing. It was not like that of a four-and-a-half-year-old child. Jee-young's handwriting also seems to have made remarkable progress. It looks as if she will do very well when she goes to grade school next year.

As I read letters from the children, I reminisced about my childhood days for the first time in a long while. As you know, I seldom dwell on the past, which may be the reason I have rarely talked to you or the children about it. So today I am going to write a few tales about my childhood days.

I was born in a village called Hugwangni, in Hawimyŏn, Shinan County. It was a very difficult delivery. They say I was in a state of unconsciousness when I was born. In a village where there were no doctors or midwives, it was miraculous that I held onto life.

I was extremely fond of animals when I was young. I remember following our family's ox around and getting kicked by its hind foot. When villagers were slaughtering and eating a dog we raised at home, I wailed and caused quite a commotion. In the end, I remember being offered dog meat and eating it.

In front of the house where I was born there was a stream and sea water flowed into it through a water-gate. I used to fish and float toy boats on that stream. On a boat that my father carved for me, I used to set up a mast and sail and play, letting it speed away.

One day, as my father was about to go out, I stubbornly insisted that he carve a boat for me. I still vividly remember him taking off his overcoat and making it.

Father was very kind. He was also very good at traditional singing and dancing. He might have been a big success had he chosen to make a career of them.

At the time, ours was the best of about fifty or sixty

households in all of Hugwangni. Only our family had a phonograph, a real rarity fifty years ago. Thus, when we played records of the then-famous singers such as Im Pangul or Yihwa Chungsŏn, villagers filled the yard to listen. A lot of people used to wonder if a person was crouched inside the phonograph, doing magic, singing. My current interest in traditional singing probably reflects the influence of those days.

When I was young, I liked boiled mixed cereals, as I do now. I used to take a bowl of boiled rice that I was given at home and go around the neighborhood, exchanging it with the boys for boiled rice mixed with millet. When I was little, my best playmate was my brother Dae-ui, who was two years younger. There was a big age difference with Dae-hyun, who was incredibly handsome when he was young. I tended to be well-behaved and rarely argued with others.

I was a real coward and very frightened of ghosts. Houses in rural villages have rest rooms in the yard across from the house, and I was so scared that I could not go to the rest room at night unless someone came with me.

Recently, I read in *Reader's Digest* that Houdini, the famous American magician, often used to cry when he was little, for fear of what would happen if his mother died. I remember doing the same thing. I remember often sobbing at night, thinking about it.

I think it was when I was about five years old that a rice-jelly peddler came to the village with rice-jellies and a variety of other items. He was in a drunken stupor, lying on the road. Older children began to steal his things, and they gave me a pipe that I took home to give to father. I remember being scolded by mother and going to the peddler with her to return it.

What was most fun in rural life was playing in the water in oceanside streams and fishing during the summer. In fall, it was going to the mountains with friends, pulled by an ox, then leaving the ox alone to graze, picking beans in the field, and roasting and eating them.

When I was about seven or eight years old, I attended a private school to study Chinese classics for one year. The school was run by a learned scholar of Chinese classics who was a member of the family. It was probably there that I learned etiquette. The paper I submitted at the end received the top mark. According to custom, the family prepared a lavish amount of rice cakes and food, which mother took over to school to treat the teacher and all my classmates. It was really exciting.

Later, I attended a private tutoring school for a little while. When I was about ten years old, a four-year grade school was established for the first time on our island. I went there with my father when Dae-ui was admitted, and after an unexpected meeting between father and the district chief, I was admitted to the second grade. The admission at that time was a turning point in my life. If I had not been admitted then, I would have been stuck in the countryside and buried there.

The distance to the school was over 10 kilometers for a round trip from home, and it was really difficult when it rained or during the winter. This taught me a discipline that seems to have helped me in later years.

I was a very good student and was especially interested in history. From early in my school days I paid a great deal of attention to everyday affairs, to the extent that I checked the front page of the newspaper each day.

What was very awkward when I was little was the fact that I was high up in the family pedigree. In Daeri, where the tutorial office was located, most of the people were Kims of Kimhae, and even old people were mostly below me in terms of family pedigree. So they would address me as "uncle" or the first in the clan, using honorifics I could not use at all. Mr. Ki-bae, who died some years ago and whom you knew well, was my nephew, according to the family genealogy, but he was the chief tutor. He used to come to our house often to visit father, who was the district chief of Hugwangni, and he used to refer to me as "Uncle Dae-jung." When such an imposing figure as the chief tutor addressed me like that and used honorifics, I was so flustered that I used to hide.

Our village did not have much of a scenic landscape, but it had an excellent view of the ocean. I am extremely fond of the view of the sea in front of Taebandong in Mokp'o, probably because it is like the one from the mountain in back of Hugwangni. Speaking of scenic views, the three best I have seen are the views in front of Taebandong in Mokp'o, the view of the shoreline on Hansan Island, and the ocean along the east coast.

I do not get too excited by the view of mountains. Thus, my only wish even now is to build a house with a Korean-style tiled roof where there is a view of the ocean or at least a river and live there. It appears that I really fell in love with the lines of Korean-style tiles, the grandeur of ridges, and the walls that connect the lines of Korean-style tiles on a Korean-style tile-roofed house.

At any rate, my dreamy and happy childhood took on a wholly new character when I was transferred to Mokpo when I was in the fourth grade. Memory of home makes anyone nostalgic, and for me, Hugwangni village in a corner of a small, almost unknown island called Hawi is the birthplace I remember. Whenever I think about it, I cannot but be overcome with yearning and remembrances. You know very well that it is the reason for my pen name, Hugwang.

Thought Fragments

1. According to Nietzsche, those who fight a monster must take care that they themselves do not be-

come monsters, and when you look into an abyss for too long, it is as if you are looking into your soul.

Those who fight to gain gold must not be eaten by gold; those who are obsessed with power must not be enslaved by power; those who work to capture criminals must not become evil like criminals; and what we have to remember is that we should never imitate the methods of the Communist party while claiming to be fighting it.

2. Those who have received God's calling must become the light and salt of the earth. The light must fight the power of darkness, and the salt, the power of corruption. Therefore, to become the light and salt means to live a life of danger and adversity.

3. Democracy is government by the people. It is the politics of participation. The politics of participation is the politics in which the people become their own masters, determine their own destiny, and enthusiastically build and defend their nation. It is the politics in which the people grow.

4. The essence of loving a nation is people. The people must love the nation, and the nation must be loved for the sake of the people. A few people should not manipulate patriotism, and patriotism should not be for the few. For this reason, the people must become intelligent and strong.

5. This is the century of the greatest changes in history, and Korea is the country undergoing the greatest change. In the middle of all this, one danger that confronts us is becoming a colonial culture, and the other is the danger of becoming a nationalistic culture. The culture that we have built is a culture that combined our nationalistic salience and universality.

6. "If winter comes, can spring be far behind?" This is always a truism. The problem is that nature's spring comes like clockwork but life's spring has a

very irregular rhythm. Sometimes it comes sooner, sometimes it seems as if it will never come.

During the era of Japanese colonialism, a great many independence fighters could not endure the late arrival of spring and gave up waiting. Spring, however, came as abruptly as a thief.

7. There are dimensions to modernization. One is industrialism, which makes possible abundant life by improving technology and production. The second is nationalism, which determines how a nation-state is formed and maintains its independence. The third is democracy, which improves the freedom, equality, and welfare of the people through peaceful cooperation with all countries.

All three are indispensable for the attainment of modernization. Among them, however, democracy is of primary importance and is a prerequisite for industrialism to be able to serve the happiness of the many and also for nationalism to be able to respect the equal rights of other nations.

8. In scholarship or learning, authority should not be accepted blindly. Even if there is respect, a critical eye has to be maintained. All knowledge must be accepted only after it is sifted through one's own criteria. For even if it is not refined or if there may be a mistake, this is the only way to live one's own intellectual life.

9. From the old days there is a saying, "Son-in-law should be looked up to, while daughter-in-law should be looked down upon." Our ancestors found a lot of meaning in this idea.

A society with national unity can be built on the basis of exchange of experience and the interchange of healthy blood through the change of status brought about by marriages between high and low classes. At home also, a daughter-in-law or a wife must manage the household soundly and become a genuine companion to her husband.

These days, however, our society is immersed in forming a class through marriage connections with an upstart upper class. From the standpoint of society or family, this is lamentable.

10. In a democratic state, the media and the judiciary hold the key to the fate of democracy. No dictatorship or corruption can last forever as long as there is a free press. So long as the officers of the court are faithful to their duties, people can be rescued from irrational judgments or human rights violations. When these two institutions do not function properly, however, the country may be called hopeless. Therefore, those who love democracy should not be lax in their supervision and encouragement of these two institutions.

Freedom of speech is more important than the officers of the court. The press represents a citizenry armed with awareness of its rights and obligations and full of determination to become the masters of their destiny, even at the risk of personal sacrifice. The existence of this citizen class is the alpha and omega of democracy and the force that can overcome communism.

11. I have kept in mind that I should never forget the favors of those who extended sympathy when my tears were dropping on my sleeves. Circumstance has not permitted me to respond. I am earnestly hoping that my children will help reciprocate these favors since I have not been able to.

12. It takes scores of years for an individual to grow big enough to be recognized by society. It takes only an instant, however, to destroy a person. It caused great heartache to see those whom our people respected and had faith in destroy themselves by suc-

cumbing to pressure and temptation. How can we help but feel sorry when we see these turncoats behaving arrogantly as if they were still leaders, with the mistaken notion that people still see them as they were?

13. In his teachings, Buddha described the difficulty of being born a human being. It is like a blind turtle being swept away on an endless ocean, encountering a piece of rotten wood, grabbing it, and then finding a hole in it and finally crawling inside. How appropriate this description is as an explanation of the predicament of being born human.

When we watch other animals, we know what a great blessing and what a lucky thing it is to be born a human being. No matter how painful life is, just to be born as a human animal and not some other kind should be sufficient to make us feel eager to face life's pain and adversity and survive.

14. Since the French Revolution, a variety of ideologies such as monarchism, democracy, communism, and nazism have emerged, but it has been nationalism that has been the principal motivating force in the world.

All the countries and ideologies acted according to their own national interest, regardless of what social theory they represented. Without question, World War II was a war between imperialist countries and had little to do with ideologies. It was a war against the Fascist states of Japan, Germany, and Italy. The fight was not because they were Fascists, however, but because they were aggressors against whom national interests had to be defended. England and France were preoccupied with the policy of conciliation until Hitler invaded Austria and Czechoslovakia, and the United States did not rise up to stop the Japanese invasion of Manchuria and China until Pearl Harbor. Moreover, the Soviet Union concluded the

Russo-German nonaggression pact and shared the division of Poland with Germany, and it signed a neutrality pact with Japan, drawing attention away from its aggression.

England, France, the United States, and the Soviet Union could have been united, as they actually were on the basis of ideology. Furthermore, the United States and the Soviet Union formed a pact to crush fascism even though they were diametrically opposed in ideological terms, and then, when the mission was accomplished, they began the cold war. They joined hands because of common interests, and when those interests were fulfilled, they returned to a state of hostility.

Although China and the Soviet Union are allies and share the same ideology, in the 1960s China called loudly for antirevisionism, claiming to have a different ideology, and then opposed Soviet hegemony and socialist imperialism in the 1970s. This reveals the fact that the true cause of the Sino-Soviet rift was not ideological but an issue of national interests.

Recently, there have been signs of Sino-Soviet rapprochement. As its condition, China is not demanding that the Soviet Union abandon revisionism. Rather, it is asking the Soviet Union to abandon its designs for hegemony and remove the threats along the Sino-Soviet border.

All these facts demonstrate that, no matter who is right or wrong, we are still in the high tide of nationalism. Although the United States is our ally and Japan is our quasi-ally, we have to see through the interests that motivate them to join hands with us.

Fortunately for South Korea, there is a congruence between interests and ideology. Korea is a country that is divided between south and north because of different ideologies. The south-north confrontation is an ideological confrontation between communism and democracy. Accordingly, the common interest shared by Korea, the United States, and Japan in resisting communism is possible only when democracy makes steady progress in South Korea and stabilizes the political scene, demonstrating with the support and unity of the people the superiority of democracy over communism.

When we see that the realization of democracy in South Korea is in the interest of South Korea, the United States, and Japan, arguments that democracy at this stage of fighting communism is premature are simply not right. This is beyond question.

Philosophers and Their Political Perspectives

For several days I have hesitated to write about the political views of the four philosophers Plato, Aristotle, Rousseau, and Nietzsche. I was wondering whether it would be appropriate for a layman like myself to express a critical opinion of these masters, although my comments would not touch on metaphysical, epistemological, or theoretical philosophy and although a substantial part of it would be based on criticisms by authoritative philosophers.

As you will see from reading what follows, many people in our society today respect such distinguished authority as these philosophers represent to such an extent that there is a strong tendency to evade present reality. Thus, I took up the pen to express my thoughts only so that they might be of help to you and the children.

After you have read this, I believe you will realize the importance of critically examining scholarship or knowledge, as discussed at the beginning of this letter.

Plato (427–347 B.C.)

Plato's life and works Plato was born to a prominent Athenian family and was taught by Socrates from the age of 20 to the age of 28. Greatly shocked by his mentor's terrible death, he was decisively influenced to hate the democratic politics of Athens.

Subsequently, he studied in the Euclidean and Pythagorean schools of thought. On the island of Sicily, south of Italy, he encountered some considerable political difficulties. He was ultimately sold into slavery and barely escaped to return to Athens.

He set up an academy (a kind of university) in the suburbs of Athens and dedicated himself to education for forty or more years until he died at the age of 80. He is the greatest philosopher Greece ever produced, and as the leading exponent of idealism, his influence on the history of philosophy is indelible.

His thought influenced the theology of the medieval period, including that of Augustine, whose *The Divine Kingdom* is said to be based on Plato's philosophy. He left thirty-five anthologies of dialogues and other collections of letters. It is his well-known *Republic* that will be reviewed here.

The nexus of Plato's philosophical thought is the theory of idea, according to which the world we experience is a semblance. The world of idea is the true world and the prototype of all things and is a more valuable world than the empirical world. For understanding the concept of idea, there is the theory of recollection and of admiration, which will be omitted here. We will survey his political views.

Plato's political views Plato's theory of the state deals with utopia, the first of its kind in history. He advanced the idea of rule by a philosopher-king.

The goal of politics is the realization of justice. His justice is not a concept predicated on equality in the sense we talk about it today. Rather, it refers to a situation in which the three classes, referred to later, exclusively address their respective roles and do not interfere with the work of other classes. Also, he presupposes that nobody will be overly busy.

Plato divided the citizenry into three classes: the ruling class, which is engaged in governing; the warrior class, which is responsible for defense; and the plebeian class, which takes care of the production of food and other necessities. The ruling class is hereditary in nature. Extremely inferior members of this class are demoted, while those with superior ability in the lower classes are promoted. This is an exception rather than a norm. For the ruling class, there are special privileges in areas such as education, economics, family relations, and religion.

Plato's view of education The goal of education is to nurture dignity, manners, and courage. In literature, the works of Homer, for example, would be banned because, first of all, they portray gods in an unfavorable light; thus, they are potentially a bad influence. Second, the description of the fear of death may undermine courage. Third, the scene in which the gods laugh loudly is contrary to the virtue of moderation. Fourth, the image of gods indulging in banquets and passion conflicts with the idea of self-restraint.

Because bad characters appear in plays, they should not be shown to children. Tales about heroes who were born to renowned families are exceptions.

In music, that which expresses courage and moderation would be acceptable, while that which is tragic or erotic would be disallowed.

For health, fish and beef could be eaten if cooked, but seasoning and sweets would not be allowed.

In childhood, those of the ruling class should be protected from ugliness. When a little older, they should be exposed to temptation so as to develop strong will. Emotional situations should be avoided, and finally, before reaching adulthood, they should witness an actual scene of combat.

Women should be educated in the same way as men (athletics and war skills included). They would be used according to aptitude and ability.

This kind of education is Spartan in nature, and Plato valued that highly. It has a number of strengths, but it tends to mold people to fit the needs of the state.

Plato's economic policies The ruling class lives a simple, communal life. Luxury and wealth are altogether disapproved. Wealth and poverty are equally bad, and no class should be dominated by material desires. All classes must be equally kind. The production of food and other necessities is the responsibility of the plebeian class and slaves. (Plato pursued a kind of communist policy in economics. This is evident not only in his economic theories but also in his idea of family relations.)

Family relations Some men and women will live together because it is the order of the lawmaker; they must accept the state's decision. Those who live together form a family. Women are wives shared by all men and children are the children of all. Parents and children are managed without their being aware of it, and all children form sibling relations with those of their own age group. The sick and the retarded are isolated in some unknown place.

To become a father, a man must be between 25 and 55 years old, and to become a mother, a woman should be between the ages of 20 and 40. A child born to someone not within these age ranges is judged unsound and must be aborted or killed immediately after birth. (This is a really wretched plan and is a consequence of the idea of communal ownership of wives and children, which is much more far-reaching than the Spartan concept. Plato seems to have intended to reduce the individual, possessive instinct and advance a more communal life-style.)

Religion For Plato, religion meant a kind of mysticism that the government imposed on the people. Just as a doctor deceives a patient, it was the government's right to deceive the people. A kind of lie is necessary for the ruled and the rulers alike. People should be educated to accept state decisions and arrange their family lives in accordance with the will of the state. The most important belief is that God created human beings of three different kinds: gold, silver, and brass. The gold are those who are to rule, the silver are the warriors, and the brass (or iron) form the plebeian class. (Philosophy is a field of inquiry that is completely dedicated to the search for knowledge. It is a shock that such a great philosopher as Plato should invent this kind of religious argument, so contrary to reason.)

How could Plato have thought this imaginary state would be viable? He seems to have believed it would be. Some parts of his plan were already in practice in Sparta, and the idea of rule by a philosopher-king was already conceived by Pythagoras and his disciples. Also, many of the Greek city-states called on philosophers to advise them in legislation. Plato himself participated in the political reforms in Syracuse, although not successfully.

Taking into consideration what has already been said, I will write a few opinions on Plato's ideal state.

Plato's proposal of a totalitarian state, based on such antidemocratic thought, is said to reflect his aristocratic origin and the corrupt nature of democracy in Athens. In the final analysis, his ideal state is nothing more than a plan to secure the kitchen and food. This may simply reflect the situation in Athens, which was suffering from a food shortage after having lost the war with Sparta.

Plato praised Sparta, the victor, and the ideal state he delineated embodied and even exaggerated many of the Spartan virtues. This seems to have stemmed from his idea that the defeat of Athens was not entirely due to the strength of Sparta but to the weakness of Athens and the alienation of its populace. The citizenry of Athens was discontent with the aristocratic rule of privilege and with the disorder and corruption of the democratic system as well as the international isolation because Athens had lost the support of its allies during the war with Persia.

The goal of Plato's ideal state was to enrich and strengthen the state. The first task for the Greek city-states at that time was to unite and for Greece to prepare itself for confrontation with Persia in the east and Macedonia to the north and with Rome and Carthage on the west to gain control of the Mediterranean. The fate of Greece depended on this, although even Plato did not foresee it.

I have already pointed out the inhuman and irrational nature of his ideal state.

Aristotle (384–322 B.C.)

His life and works Aristotle was born in Stugira, Macedonia. His father was a court physician, but Aristotle was orphaned at an early age and raised by relatives. He came to Athens when he was 17 and studied under Plato for the next twenty years. After Plato's death, Aristotle became the head of the academy. In 342 B.C., when Philip IX of Macedonia invaded Greece, Aristotle became tutor for Prince Alexander who was then 13 years old, but he left the post when Alexander was crowned at the age of 16. In 335 B.C., Aristotle returned to Athens and set up a school (lyceum) where he taught and became very popular. He and his students used to stroll under the shade trees while Aristotle taught, so they were called Peripatetics.

After Alexander's death, anti-Macedonian movements emerged in Athens, and Aristotle was accused of being a subversive. Unlike Socrates, he fled, saying he would not give the Athenians an opportunity to make a mockery of his philosophy. He died the next year, at the age of 63.

Aristotle's writings covered all fields—logic, natural science, ethics, and aesthetics. His works on politics filled eight volumes, and they became known and accepted everywhere, from East Rome to Europe, where they were introduced by the Saracens when they invaded Spain. Most of his work is extant. Aristotle had a great influence on medieval thought, theology, politics, and on the Renaissance. He is considered to be a complete genius, as rare as Michelangelo.

View of the state The state occupies the highest place, and its purpose is to bring about the greatest good for the people and guarantee the happiness and dignity of the general public. Plato's idea of the state is unreasonable for the following reasons: (1) it necessitates too much control, (2) no one would look after the children if they were communally shared sons, (3) communal married life would encourage adultery, (4) in a communal living arrangement, nobody would take responsibility, and (5) communism would foster disputes among neighbors. Under a system of private ownership, people should be trained to share and live together in a generous spirit. (Aristotle's theory of state puts the state ahead of the individual. His criticism of Plato seems not to have been based on humanitarian concerns but his viewpoint is thoroughly utilitarian.

Economic views Money-making, such as commercial enterprises or moneylending, is corrupt unless it is based on the products of the land. Moneylending is evil, even if it is not deliberately taking advantage of someone else. Citizens should not be engaged in commerce, agriculture, or technical jobs. (Greek philosophers were said to have been landlords or dependent on landlords whose interests they represented.) Aristotle's argument against moneylending influenced the medieval church, as a result of which Christians were not allowed to lend money until the changes brought about by the Reformation. Of course, disdain for moneylending was also associated with anti-Semitism and the prejudice against the church and feudal lords.

Kinds and sizes of states The good types of government were kingship, aristocracy, and polity. The bad types were timocracy, oligarchy, and democracy. Of these, the best state was kingship and the worst was timocracy. In Aristotle's view, timocracy was a perverted form of royalty, oligarchy was a perverted form of aristocracy, and democracy was a perverted form of polity. Therefore, those who consider Aristotle an advocate of polity or democracy, as against kingship, will have difficulties. Elections or legislation could be carried out effectively only when citizens know one another well. The size of the territory should be only big enough to be surveyed from the top of a hill. Finally, a state should be self-sufficient.

Qualifications of a citizen Merchants and laborers are not qualified to vote. Because they have to work for a living, they are neither honorable nor virtuous. Slaves must perform the work of farmers, but Greeks are not suited to be slaves because they have spirit. Other people, especially southerners, can be slaves because they are docile. Inferior people become slaves, and the judgment as to inferiority or superiority is decided in war.

Just as domesticated animals are happy under their masters, inferior people are happy living under theirs. Human beings are fated to be rulers or slaves from the moment of birth. The inferior status of women is as natural as that of slaves. (Such a discriminatory attitude represents the Greek view of occupation, slavery, and womanhood.)

Aristotle's political views It is surprising that Aristotle drew up a plan for a kind of city-state that had already been discarded. The inadequacy of the city-state had already been proven by the Macedonian invasion from the north and its conquest of the Greek peninsula. This was a period of dramatic change: Aristotle's pupil, Alexander the Great, had opened the age of imperialism with his conquests, and the Hellenistic era had started with the mixing of Greek and Eastern cultures.

The negative effect of Aristotle's casual regard for labor was felt for many years, even until the medieval period. He did not seem to have realized that the unhealthy customs of Athens were a result of the contemptuous treatment of labor and an economy based on slavery.

He asserted that the Greeks, especially the Athenians, were superior people. But using his argument that those who were defeated in war were proved to be inferior and thus deserved to be slaves, it could be said that Athenians deserved to be enslaved because they were defeated in the Peloponnesian War. It goes without saying that it is wrong to call human beings superior or inferior on the basis of military victory or defeat.

As I said before, Aristotle was Alexander's mentor, but he did not mention him in any of his writings. If Aristotle had paid serious attention to Alexander's career, he would certainly have seen the historical transformation that was taking place, and his theory of politics would have altered.

Incidentally, Aristotle's views of occupation, women, and slavery, which contradicted the concept of equality, make us aware of the difference between Greek philosophy and Hebrew thought, which we know from the Bible.

Rousseau (1712–1778)

Rousseau's life and thought Rousseau was the son of a watchmaker in Geneva, Switzerland. His parents died when he was still in early childhood. After leaving school at the age of 12, he spent his youth in poverty, moving from one job to another. Originally, Rousseau was a Calvinist, but when he was twelve, he was converted to Catholicism to improve his earning opportunities. After he became established, he returned to Calvinism.

Around 1745, Rousseau began living with Theresa, a maid from Paris who was under his guardianship. They had five children, all of whom were given to an orphanage. Theresa was an ugly woman who was illiterate and stupid, but her mother was sly and intent on getting Rousseau's money. Rousseau apparently had no affection for Theresa, although he lived what was in effect a married life with her. It has been said this was because of his protective attitude toward weak people and also his submission to her strong will.

Rousseau became well known in Europe with his essay, "The Theory of Science and Arts," which was written in 1750 and won a prize. His argument was that science and the arts have not benefited mankind. His novel, *Emile*, which embodied his theories of education, was written in 1762 and earned him the ire of French authorities. Subsequently, in exile, he moved to Geneva, then Prussia, and England. When he finally returned to France, his prolonged anxiety overwhelmed him. He was committed to several institutions for treatment but died in sorrow and adversity.

Rousseau wrote a number of books in addition to those mentioned above, and he had a great influence on philosophy, literature, arts, politics, and the humanistic approach to life. He recorded his wealth in great detail.

Rousseau was the founder of the romantic movement, and he was the first to formulate a system of thought that focused on the importance of human emotions. His political views were well known. He was not an extreme advocate of democracy. His thought represented more a combination of democratic and dictatorial leanings. It is clear, however, that he firmly opposed traditional despotism. He called for a return to nature and asserted that human beings were inherently good, as is shown by savages who live peacefully and happily with nature and their own kind.

Rousseau's influence on theology was great. Since the time of Plato, the existence of God was commonly demonstrated by intellectual arguments such as cosmology, teleology, and essential and moralistic proofs. Rousseau advanced a theory of God that was based, for the first time, on certain elements of human emotions, such as a reverent mind, a mystical mind, and concepts of good and evil. Today this is commonplace, but in Rousseau's time, it was revolutionary.

Rousseau's view of the state Rousseau's *Social Contract*, in which he expressed his political views, was, unlike his other works, intellectual in approach. He paid lip service to democracy but showed a strong tendency toward totalitarian politics. The ideas that inspired both the French Revolution and Hitler can be traced to Rousseau. He argued that democracy (direct democracy as in Greece) was suited for small states, aristocratic politics for middle-sized ones, and monarchical systems for big states. Although he favored liberty, he put equality above it. He wanted a one-class society in which there would be no gap between rich and poor and everyone would own the same amount of land. What we call representative democracy today was dubbed elective aristocracy by Rousseau. He considered this to be an ideal state but one not suitable for all countries. According to him, for it to be suitable, the climate would have to be mild and production so abundant that people would not become corrupt.

Rousseau's theory of the social contract The contract simply meant that everyone would cede all rights and concessions to the community, and the concessions would have to be total. Community will would be absolute. Everyone would be subject to the law; if they did not obey, they could be coerced.

Community will, or the general will, would not be the will of the public or of the people but the will of the state as a collective personality. In the end, this becomes the will of the leader who formed the collectivity. The sovereignty that exercises the general will is untransferable, indivisible, infallible, and absolute.

A partial society that can obstruct the expression of general will should not exist. Therefore, a variety of religious groups (except state religion), political associations, and social groups is inadmissible. Rousseau's civil contract is close to Hobbes's but different from Locke's.

According to Hobbes, people enter a contract to protect their natural rights. The power of the sovereign is absolute, and people who have entered into the contract must obey him absolutely. Also, for Hobbes, the sovereign means, in effect, an absolute monarch; this is what distinguishes Rousseau's theory of social contract from democracy.

Although Locke, like Hobbes, began with natural rights, he argued that people form a pact so as to protect nature more completely. Through the contract, they select the most powerful and entrust him with the power. The power of the ruler, who is a party to the contract, is justified as long as he protects the people's natural rights. The people reserve the right to resist if the ruler should default on the contract. Locke's theory is considerably different from Rousseau's, which gives the ruler unqualified power and recognizes absolute obedience to him as well as his infallibility and absoluteness. This is why scholars refer to Rousseau as Hitler's ancestor while Locke was the predecessor of Roosevelt and Churchill.

Several opinions on Rousseau's political views Rousseau strongly opposed feudal kingdoms and tradition, and he was sympathetic to the poor. But, clearly, his political thought contained elements that could give birth to a new form of dictatorship. In fact, Rousseau's political thought was used by Hegel to rationalize despotism in Prussia. It is said to have created the movement that led to Byron or Carlyle's heroism, Goethe's statism, and finally Hitler's nazism. Rousseau's *Social Contract* was a bible for the French Revolution because it not only protested fiercely against the divine right of the king and traditional morals but also contained many elements of democracy. Nonetheless, such a bloodthirsty dictator as Robespierre emerged in the French Revolution as Rousseau's disciple. Rousseau's thought may thus be likened to a double-edged sword.

The most problematic aspect of Rousseau's theory of the social contract is that it presents the danger that the people surrender all their rights, with no exception, and become absolutely obedient to the state. Thus it becomes difficult to argue for freedom and human rights, and resistance is impossible. Rousseau did add a few reservations, of course, but they were not enough to prevent abuses of his social contract theory by dictators.

Democracy is truly a democracy when the people are politically sovereign and can give or take away power. There is nothing like this in Rousseau's thinking. Romanticism was not based on reality but was anachronistic and glorified the medieval period. Sometimes, however, it was its own opposite and was futuristic and illusory, characterized by hero worship, exclusive nationalism, and deification of the nation and purity of blood, which stirred up the emotions of some people.

Human beings have emotions, so anyone can be a romanticist and hero-worshiper or dream of being a superhuman ruler.[1] We should always be alert to this.

Request for Books

1. Flavius Josephus, *The Jewish War*.
2. E. H. Carr, *What Is History?* (Pŏmu-sa).
3. Bertrand Russell et al., *What Is Life?* (Pŏmu-sa).

1. This is where Nietzsche comes in. I will write about him next month because there is not enough space here.

4. Gerhard Konzelmann, *The Theology of the New Testament* (Korean Theological Institute).

5. Yu Inho, *Nongŏp kyŏngje ŭi silsang kwa hŏsang* (True and False Images of Agrarian Economy) (Pyŏngmin-sa).

6. Ch'a Insŏk, *Hyŏndae chŏngch'i wa ch'ŏlhak* (Modern Politics and Philosophy) (Pyŏngmin-sa).

7. Chang Ŭlbyŏng, *Chŏngch'i ŭi p'aradoksŭ* (The Paradox in Politics) (*Pyŏngmin-sa*).

8. Jawaharlal Nehru, *The Emerging World* (Sŏktap Publishing Co.).

9. Pak Hyŏnjae, *Minjung kwa kyŏngje* (People and Economy).

As I was wrapping up this letter, I received more drawings by Jee-young and Chung-hwa. They are supposed to be drawings of their father. Tell them I also received the photographs.

These days, my weight has improved a lot and I can now eat boiled rice. Do not be worried. The pains in my leg persist, and the ringing sounds in my ears are not getting better. But, as you suggested, I have been diligently doing deep breathing. I am not bothered by the cold weather, so do not worry too much.

Your letter, which got here today, had stories about Christmas cards. As I look forward to the month of December, I have very mixed feelings. The Christmases I used to spend with the family seem like a dream. I miss them.

I wish you all good health under Jesus' blessing. This means you, Hong-il, Jee-young's mother, Hong-up, Hong-gul, Jee-young, and Chung-hwa.

I send my greetings to all our relatives, friends, and those who are living with us.

*A Prayer that I Offer to Lord Jesus**

Dear Jesus Christ, Our Lord!

Today is the day of Our Lord's holy birth. This is the day God sent Our Lord to this world as the true God and as the true human being.

Through Our Lord's incarnation, this world became sacred and entered into a wholly new epoch in God's Gospels. The purpose of Our Lord's incarnation was not for the powerful and the rich but rather to tell those who were chained about their liberation, to make the blind see, to give freedom to the oppressed, and to declare the year of Our Lord's blessings.

To deliver the Gospels, God sent His only son, had Him nailed to the cross to save us from sin, and had Him resurrected from the dead to assure us of eternal life. How can there be another message and grace so joyous? How can there be a greater joy than the incarnation of Our Lord, which is to give us happiness today and hope for tomorrow as we groan in sin and despair?

Our Lord came to this world and announced that the God we feared was a loving God. He transformed the image of a punishing God into a forgiving God, freed us from our sin, sealed the gates to hell, and showed us resurrection by triumphing over the power of death.

Our Lord has liberated human beings from the oppression of all powers except the power of God's truth. He freed us from unjust rulers and freed sons from fathers, daughters-in-law from mothers-in-law.

Our Lord repudiated the powerful and the wealthy

*On the night this letter was written, the author was informed that he would be transferred to Seoul National University Hospital. On the morning of that day, the azalea that was moved to a flower vase in the fall and placed near the stove in the hall, bloomed.

and defended the oppressed and the poor. Although Our Lord's declaration of such freedom and justice may seem like a prejudiced love only for the oppressed and the poor, we know that Our Lord's real purpose was founded on universal love, trying to save even the powerful and wealthy from their sins through the realization of freedom and justice.

Our Lord also brought down the thick walls of Jewish consciousness of being the chosen race and staged a great revolution of spreading God's love toward the whole world. The proofs of the universality of Our Lord's salvation are the tale of the hardship of a traveler to Jericho who saw the Samaritans as kind neighbors; the tale of Jesus at a well in Samaria and His delivery of the gospel to the Samaritans; the tale of the saving of the child of a Phoenician woman; the tale in chapter 25 of the Gospel According to Matthew which speaks of the promise of reward or punishment for everyone in this world according to their deeds when Jesus should return to this world; and the tale of Jesus after His resurrection, ordering his disciples to spread the gospel to the end of the earth and choosing Paul as His messenger to foreign lands.

The unlimited, universal character of Our Lord's salvation has long been obstructed by the mistakes of the church. The church has interpreted salvation narrowly, and only through Jesus Christ. Finally, however, the church has realized its error and has come to say that according to God's revelation, even those of other faiths may believe in the promise of salvation by Jesus, as he died for all men and women.

We take pride in our membership in the church of Jesus Christ and firmly believe it to be the best way of following in the footsteps of Our Lord. Such faith, however, can never interfere with the way Our Lord does his work of salvation. This is even truer when you consider that the church has absolutely no possibility of including everyone in the world in its congregation.

The church has accomplished a tremendous amount in relieving the persecuted and those in adversity, relying solely on faith in Our Lord and His love. Catholicism during the last one hundred years of the Yi dynasty constitutes such a chapter in the history of the church. It is also true, however, that the church made many theological and human mistakes: doctrinairism, abuse of privilege, corruption, exclusiveness, supporting rulers and turning its back on the oppressed, and otherworldliness, or ignoring the secular world. There have been so many mistakes that we blush and are ashamed.

But the love of Our Lord and the light of His revelation inspired the brilliant statement of the Second Vatican Assembly and the recent work of the World Council of Churches. I believe that in all church history, Our Lord's holy spirit has never been more clearly expressed than in today's church. I rejoice with unspeakable joy when I see the proud image of the church today.

Dear Our Lord!

It was July 3, 1957, when I was baptized and accepted in Our Lord's embrace. I had the great honor of receiving special education in the doctrine from Father Y'un Hyŏngjun. Dr. Chang Myŏn was my godfather under Father Kim Ch'ŏlgyu's guidance, and I was baptized in Archbishop No Kinam's office in his presence.

Since then, however, I have not always been faithful or enthusiastically dedicated, and I have been guilty of many sins. It was when I was abroad after Yushin that I began to truly seek Our Lord and sincerely cling to Him. At that time, I was cut off from my country and my family, and my days were spent in loneliness and solitude, wondering if I would ever see my home again. In the midst of this unhappiness and despair, I instinctively sought Our Lord and constantly turned to Him in prayer. Since returning home a year later, I have not enjoyed a single day of security or peace for these last 9 years and 4 months. Prison life alone accounts for 5 years and 5 months. I have also had to face death several times.

Ah! If Our Lord had not been with me, how could I have borne it? In a dark prison cell, a fearful courtroom, everywhere, Our Lord has always been with me as my mentor and friend who taught me, encouraged me, and sometimes shared my sorrow.

Our Lord lovingly shared with me my heavy load. When I think about it, I do not believe anyone has ever been more graced by Our Lord than I have been. When I was imprisoned by the Communists during the Korean Conflict, Our Lord helped me to escape and survive, while 140 of the 220 in prison were murdered.

When I was campaigning nationwide in 1971 in support of National Assembly candidates, Our Lord prevented an assassination plot just in the nick of time, and the van I was riding in was almost hit by a huge 14-ton truck.

When I was abducted for five days between August 8 and 13, 1973, Our Lord was with me from beginning to end and saved my life. Finally, Our Lord saved me from the death sentence last year.

Ah! How great and profound is the grace of Our Lord! What am I that Our Lord shows me such great grace? How great were the efforts and power of many individuals, at home and abroad, and especially in Our Lord's churches? Our Lord has appeared before me three times. The first was at the time of my abduction. He was standing beside me when I was tightly roped and was about to be thrown overboard into the ocean. That was the moment at which my life was saved.

The second time was two years ago when I was

being investigated. He appeared and I heard His voice saying, "Do not fear; keep the faith," just as He said to Jairus, chief rabbi at a synagogue.

The third time was when He appeared in a dream right after I arrived in this prison. I was taken to a field outside the city, naked, in severe cold. I was driven in a cart and was to be dumped into a death valley. Two rays of light came down from heaven, warming me and the men who were escorting me, and I was taken back to a safe place.

I believe that all this love Our Lord has given me is because he wants me to serve our neighbors and society. Therefore, I am determined to dedicate myself completely, with all my heart and effort, to doing Our Lord's work, which is to save this world by making freedom, justice, and peace a reality and to save the souls of all men and women through our faith.

Our Lord! I am powerless and weak and lack wisdom. Please help me and guide me rightly.

Thinking back to when I spent last Christmas all by myself in this prison cell, I remember how I thought about Our Lord, my family, and friends, and sincerely prayed for Our Lord's blessing for the coming year. Indeed, Our Lord's grace has been richly given to me this last year. There was joy for my family. Everyone was healthy and courageous in the faith; in the family of the eldest son, Hong-il, the daughter-in-law and granddaughters were all baptized and are keeping a harmonious and happy home.

The second son, Hong-up, has not yet gotten permission to leave the country, but Our Lord's church in America has sent him an invitation to come and study, with a financial affidavit whose terms are very favorable.

Our Lord's grace to the last son gave our family the greatest joy: Hong-gul was admitted to the French Department at Korea University, which was his first choice.

I have received both tangible and intangible support from citizens and groups, both at home and abroad, and I was awarded a prize by an Austrian human rights group.[1]

My wife also received an award from her alma mater in America and is continually consoled and encouraged by prayers at home and abroad.[2]

More than these tangible things is the joy of having our faith strengthened and learning more about Our Lord from our studies this year. During my two prison terms, I have read scores of Korean and foreign books on theology. Among them, the works that influenced and inspired me most are the report of the Vatican Assembly, *One Faith*, coauthored by European scholars of Catholicism and Protestantism; the writings of Father Teilhard de Chardin, a true servant of Our Lord, which represent the summit of twentieth-century theology; and works by Korean writers in Minjung theology. I am grateful to God's providence that made it possible for me to read this precious literature. Please give me wisdom and the ability to understand these works correctly and do Our Lord's will properly.

Finally, I want to offer a prayer for this world and the people of our country. Our Lord! Please make everything come true, with your benevolence and power. Please lead our church and believers to understand and act rightly. And please cause everyone living in this era to awaken and join in Our Lord's mission.

To begin with, I pray for the whole world. Please help the church to become truly the witness of Our Lord and the light and salt of this age by rejecting its mistaken and contrary teaching that is centered on otherworldly and individual salvation. Inspire the church

1. This was established in honor of the Austrian prime minister Bruno Kreitsky. The award was given in November 1981, but was not actually received until 1982.

2. The award was given in recognition of outstanding service by Scarrit College in Nashville, Tennessee. It was actually received after the Kims arrived in the United States.

to take up the cause of freedom, justice, and peace for the oppressed and troubled.

Second, please help this world become one world, free from self-centered nationalism, since it already has become one world in such areas as communication and transportation. Let the church reflect critically, repent, and love, so that this can be one world.

Third, mankind today is faced with the threat of communism, which would herd us into slavery and subject us to a personality cult under the pretext of economic equality. Please help us all to understand this threat correctly and realize that the way to save the world from this crisis is for the leading nations of the free world to take enough bold measures to correct the sharp economic differences between south and north. The leaders of all non-Communist countries must recognize that popular freedom and economic and social justice are the means to overcome the Communist threat. Please help us do our best in putting these into action.

Fourth, human society is behaving irrationally, stockpiling nuclear weapons that can destroy the world thirty times over. One famous twentieth-century historian said that of the four greatest sins in the history of mankind, slavery, racial discrimination, exploitation, and war, the first three have already been eliminated or rejected by human conscience, which is largely attributable to Christian civilization (not the church). That is Our Lord's providence at work.

Wars, however, are becoming larger and larger and more and more destructive. Eliminating the three sins mentioned above is still a great challenge for humankind, but the threat of instantaneously destroying all of mankind is urgent and dreadful. Only the reawakening of human conscience through Our Lord's providence and the denunciation of those who dream about wars involving the entire human race can prevent it in time.

Our Lord, please save mankind from the threat and catastrophe of war.

Now, I would like to pray for our country and people.

First, democracy is the founding principle of our country, but we have not achieved it today, nearly forty years after the liberation. Democracy alone is the road to freedom, the road to economic equality, and the road to social welfare. Democracy alone is the road for the people of the Republic of Korea to feel purposeful and proud. It is the road to promote the desire to fight against the Communists. Our Lord! Please grant that democracy can take root firmly in this country, so the happiness of the people and stability of the nation can be achieved.

Second, the people are the master of the country and the principal force of history. The masses, however, have always been left out and their rights ignored. The restoration of the rights of the masses can be accomplished only by their awakening, efforts, and sacrifice. This is the only right way. Our Lord, please awaken our people and cause them to stand up against violence and destruction, according to Our Lord's will, so they may fully enjoy their divine rights given by Our Lord.

Third, no country has suffered more than Korea in the bitter history of division and fratricide. The threat of communism has not abated. Please help our leaders and the people to reflect critically on how to bring freedom, justice, and prosperity to the peninsula so that we can build a strong bulwark against communism. Please make the Communists abandon the idea of forceful unification and make them ready for peaceful coexistence and unification.

Fourth, please help those who are in key positions, such as politicians, businessmen, journalists, and officers of the court, to determine the fate of our country by judging and acting in the interests of the country and the people, recognizing the transitoriness of personal fame and wealth. Please awaken their conscience and bolster their courage.

Fifth, please help all those in this land who are longing to become masters of their own fate and destiny. Please bless those who are in adversity because of their beliefs and shower them and their families with Our Lord's benediction and grace and have them witness and sing Our Lord's glory and victory.

Amen

Philosophers and Political Views

Last month I discussed Plato, Aristotle, and Rousseau but could not finish writing about Nietzsche. I will do it here. (This is always the trouble. No matter how small I write, I cannot write all that I want to. More than that, once written it is difficult to correct. Even though I am not satisfied, I have to let it go at that, feeling very frustrated. At any rate, I am grateful that I am holding up and especially that my eyes are enduring this difficult work.)

Nietzsche (1844–1900)

His life and his writings Nietzsche was born the son of a minister. His father died when Nietzsche was five years old, and he was brought up by his grandparents, with whom he stayed until he entered the university. He was surrounded by women: his mother, his sister, and two aunts.

Nietzsche majored in literature at Leipzig University and became a full professor at the age of twenty-four at Basel University, thanks to his outstanding ability. He was greatly influenced by Schopenhauer's works, which he discovered by accident, and he declared himself heir to Schopenhauer's philosophy of life. In reality, Nietzsche was far superior to him, and he should be regarded as the founder of the philosophy of life. He steeped himself in Wagner's music and at one time was an enthusiastic admirer. Later, he parted ways with Wagner and published many writings strongly criticizing him.

In 1878 at the age of thirty-three, he resigned from the university because of a chronic eye ailment, headaches, and other ailments. He traveled widely in search of medical care. He no longer wrote after January 1889, when he became mentally ill.

His works include *The Birth of Tragedy*, *Thus Spake Zarathustra*, and *Between Good and Evil*. They do not have any distinguishing characteristics epistemologically, but he had a great influence on ethics and on criticism of religion.

Nietzsche's philosophy of life originated in Schopenhauer's work, but he opposed the latter's nihilistic philosophy. He praised the power of life, faith in life, joy in life, and stressed the will to power. That is, he emphasized the will to live and the will to express and control oneself. He spoke of the eternal cycle of life, which is inevitable. After death we are reborn, thus pain is inescapable, so there is no choice but to love fate. This may be why he is linked to existentialism.

Nietzsche emphasized the need to become superman, charged with the will to power—a Dionysian strong man who overcomes the pain of life and strides toward dynamism, vigor, and creation.

Although he was critical of romanticism, his thought was formed under the influence of the two pillars of late romanticism in Germany, Schopenhauer and Wagner. Specialists consider him to have been strongly influenced by romanticism, as shown in his adulation of the romantic poet, Byron.

Nietzsche's argument on political ethics Nietzsche's arguments were based on the fundamental idea of a superman with the will to power, the Dionysian man, the eternal cycle of life and love of fate. For the sake of creating one great man, the pain of ordinary beings did not matter. The majority of people are only tools for a few outstanding individuals, and the majority has no right to demand happiness. The misfortune of an entire race cannot equal the pain of one strong man. The French Revolution was justified by the birth of Napoleon; all the hope of our century depends solely on Napoleon.

What is good according to traditional Christian morals is evil, and what is evil, good. True morals are not meant for all men but only for a few aristocrats. Both good and evil belong to a few nobles. They are not matters of concern for the rest of the masses. A noble person should turn his back on the masses and oppose democracy. Democracy means that vulgar groups conspire to become their own masters.

Sympathy is a moral of the weak. Sympathy or love is a machination of the weak to avoid being injured by the strong.

The German spirit should be established, and the sick era can be cured by it. (He made the emergence of charismatic leaders possible with this sort of argument, but he was not a nationalist. He was a passionate individualist and a hero-worshiper.)

Nietzsche's view of women Nietzsche was always awkward with women. He courted twice in his life—not directly but through letters delivered by someone else—only to be rejected both times. According to one version, he was infatuated with a very intelligent woman who was a member of the Russian aristocracy. He supposedly attempted suicide when he was spurned by her. He could never maintain smooth relationships with women for any length of time, not even with his mother or sister, Elizabeth. His sister was very cunning and caused Nietzsche a great deal of discomfort. She schemed to separate him from the Russian woman of whom he was so fond.

Nietzsche's complaints go on and on.

Friendship cannot be shared with women. Men should be trained for war, and women for their recreation. Are you going to see a woman? Make sure you bring a whip. We have to treat women as possessions, the way Orientals do. (His arguments about women are self-explanatory and have no basis in theory or in his personal experiences.)

Nietzsche and Christianity Nietzsche was a son of a renowned Christian family. His grandfather was supervisor of a local parish and his father was a minister. He was a devout Catholic until he entered the university. His anti-Christian transformation was a result of inner changes and does not appear to have had any outside cause. He argued as follows.

Christian ethics are the morality of weak men and slaves. The church about which an ordinary anti-Christian talks is said to be an ally of autocratic despotism and an enemy of democracy. This is not consistent. The French Revolution and socialism are fundamentally Christian.

Buddhism and Christianity are nihilistic religions because they deny the ultimate difference of values among human beings. Christianity is corrupt and full of rotten excrement. The New Testament is a gospel for the most abject of people.

Christianity deserves to be damned because it denies arrogance, discriminatory feelings, great responsibility, vigorous spirit, unique stoicism, stimulus for struggle and conquest, emotions, vengeance, and anger, debauchery, adventures, and sanctification of knowledge.

Instead of Christian saints, we want noble persons, that is, domineering nobility. (Nietzsche believed he was the son of Polish nobility. This was not true and was said to have been a story made up by his grandparents.)

Several opinions on Nietzsche How do we evaluate Nietzsche's philosophy, which, at first glance, seems absurd? What usefulness does it have? What is its value? Is it a mere delusion of an insane person? In the final analysis, the influence of his arguments was greater on literary, artistic, and cultural figures than on philosophers, but many of his prophecies, for example, the outbreak of great wars, were accurate.

Nietzsche specialists argue that when the pre-Nazi history is written, his idea of superman, the will to power, and aristocratism will always be remembered. Several specialists share the opinion that Nietzsche's idea of superman, his contempt for women, and his denial of Christian ethics are probably the result of fear. Bertrand Russell, who wrote on Western philosophy, Karl Jaspers, who wrote a study of Nietzsche, and even his own biographer all point to the incredible fear Nietzsche suffered all his life.

First, his contempt for women is like keeping women at arm's length and criticizing them. This is what men who are afraid of women might do to bolster their pride. We often meet such people.

Second, his criticisms of Christianity can be seen as a product of his fear of Christian love, considering that he felt nothing but fear toward his neighbors. It is pointed out that he never understood that there were saints who sympathized and served others not out of fear but out of spontaneous and compelling love.

Third, his idea of superman is, after all, the product of fear of neighbors. One who does not fear others has no need to become a despot. Nietzsche admired Frederick the Great, Napoleon, and other military men. This too could be interpreted as a reaction to his fear.

Nietzsche pretends to be a strong person. His idea of

superman is a sort of waking nightmare, and his lofty thought can be criticized as brutal, cold, cunning, and savage and the thinking of someone obsessed with his own power and without regard for others (as exemplified by Hitler).

There are some who trace Nietzsche's peculiar philosophy to the condition of his health, especially the influence of the latent period of his mental illness. It would be a great mistake, however, to view Nietzsche's basic arguments as those of one who is mentally ill, for they had consistent logic and unusual insight.

Thought Fragments

⋆ The theologian Boltman has said that the characteristics of a Christian life are not psychological phenomena but are defined by attitude toward faith. This serves as a useful warning against a recent tendency in some Korean churches to treat self-loss, in which one claims to have been blessed by the Holy Spirit or babbles away in a trance, as evidence of being a true Christian. In the church of Corinth, Saint Paul warned against such a commotion over holy spirit. (Corinth. 14:26)

⋆ Through Faust, Goethe said that this is the highest wisdom and only those who conquer it anew every day will obtain life and freedom. We have to be reborn every day and make fresh progress every day. The object of our conquest is ourselves. We have to fight and conquer the self that is complacent, the self that tries to escape, the self that is arrogant, and the self that is carried away by a single moment of success.

⋆ There are brotherly competitions and hostile competitions. In the former, one cooperates with the competitor and competes in helping others survive or in order to help others. In the latter, competition is a lonely struggle to destroy others.

⋆ God is not a strong being in the physical sense. He is weak in power but strong in love. The life of Jesus testifies to the fact that this is the nature of God.

⋆ History records that the Great Wall was built by Shih Huang in the Qin dynasty, Sokkuram Grotto by Kim Taesŏng, and Kyŏngbok Palace by the Taewŏn'gun. No one doubts this, but on reflection it turns out to be absurd fallacy. They were not the real builders; nameless masons, carpenters, painters, and ordinary people did the building. When we realize this fact, we can renew our respect for the nameless people and our awareness of who is the true master of history.

⋆ Today's humanity, which tries to attain happiness by maximizing consumption and possessions, will only taste defeat and alienation. Our genuine happiness comes from developing our ability and by loving and serving neighbors.

⋆ The real purpose of politics is to guarantee the rights and life of the oppressed and the poor and help them to become the principals in politics. In this process, however, even those who used to oppress and those who used to take things by force must be freed from their sins and allowed to participate. Then politics will become art.

⋆ When we choose our occupation or position we have to make the decision not on the basis of temporary income or status but on the basis of whether we can feel the value of life through the work. It is only through such a decision that we can expect to make contributions to society and display our abilities. Furthermore, from a long-range perspective, such a choice often brings improvement in earnings and status.

⋆ When we relate to others we have to open our minds and accept them. And we have to give generously. It is with our whole being that we have to give and take and must become one with others. This is not meant to suggest that we have to be blind to their shortcomings or errors. Observing such things, we should still relate to others and give and take with our whole beings.

Designer: Randall Goodall
Compositor: Wilsted & Taylor
Text: 11/13 Bembo
Display: Bembo
Printer: Murray Printing Company
Binder: Murray Printing Company